Dance AND THE SPECIFIC IMAGE

SPECIFIC IMAGE

Improvisation

DANIEL NAGRIN

University of Pittsburgh Press

PITTSBURGH AND LONDON

Published by the University of Pittsburgh Press, Pittsburgh, Pa. 15260
Copyright © 1994, Daniel Nagrin Theatre, Film and Dance Foundation, Inc.
Manufactured in the United States of America
Printed on acid-free paper

Library of Congress Cataloging-in-Publication Data

Nagrin, Daniel.
    Dance and the specific image : improvisation / Daniel Nagrin.
        p.   cm.
    Includes indexes.
    ISBN 0-8229-3776-X (alk. paper). —ISBN 0-8229-5520-2 (pbk. :
alk. paper)
    1. Workgroup (Dance group)—History.   2. Improvisation in dance.
    I. Title.
    GV1786.W67N34   1993
    792.8—dc20   93-27793
                                                               CIP

A CIP catalogue record for this book is available from the British Library.

Eurospan, London

*This volume on improvisation and the history of the Workgroup
is dedicated to*

Lee Connor

1947–1987

*He was in the company from beginning to end.
Of all of us, he was the most silent,
except when he danced.*

Contents

Introduction

For many if not most dancers, and certainly for myself, improvisation has always been there from the very beginning, but never as a central focus. It was a delight, a diversion and a tool for choreography. In the late sixties, my career took an unexpected turn. A brief contact with the Open Theatre opened my eyes to a breathtakingly different way of working in the theatre and in art. Improvisation was the source from which all else flowed. The pursuit of this new way led to the formation of a dance company, the Workgroup.

The seeds of the Workgroup were sown in 1969. It had an experimental start in 1970, and it began its existence as a performing company in 1971. It lasted until 1974. Its central focus was to explore the possibilities of interactive improvisation and to develop the forms and skills to perform improvisation for the concert-going audience. A mimeographed sheet, mailed in November 1969, invited dancers and others to join the work:

> Dance now is in a beautiful state of flux and indeterminacy. Just as audiences are learning to expect anything as they enter today's dance theater, so do the choreographers approach each new work with less predetermination and certainty than at other periods. Ironically, those least prepared for the new directions and demands are often the skilled dancer performers who have been trained in the romantic tradition.
>
> There is still another phenomenon to be reckoned with: The Open Theatre, The Living Theatre, The Polish Lab Theatre and other acting groups are moving away from literature and the domination of the word toward movement unleashed to a degree never seen in Western drama. The actors are dancing, and, despite their technical limitations, in profoundly moving and personal ways. By contrast, most professional dance works take on the gloss of elegant body control and clean movement designed to bury under good manners and romantic aesthetics what is really there.
>
> Another challenge comes from the young people who are dancing on their Saturday nights with freedom, invention and personal expressiveness that make most theatrical jazz forms look stilted and mannered.

Introduction

....

Going out into the streets and onto the campuses across the country, the political demonstrations take on theatrical and choreographic forms that challenge the very vitality and relevance that has defined American modern dance.

The plan of the Workgroup is no plan. It takes its shape from those dancers who participate in the exploration of the new challenges. The Workgroup is open to choreographers, intermediate and advanced dancers. Also, musicians, composers, film-makers, playwrights are invited to participate.

When the group started to tour, the following statement always appeared in the program:

The way of the Workgroup moves in a shifting balance between the poles of improvisation and structure. Therefore, the results are the product of the creative energies of all. For us, in improvisation, the director usually plays the major role in setting the structures and problems of each piece. The dancers have the creative responsibility of working out the problem. Why do we divide the responsibilities? Since each of us has only a partial vision, in order to make a bit of sense out of a common experience, we have to see/hear everyone.

Why the uncertainty of improvisation? If one of the many definitions/ uses of art is a rehearsal for the life one fears, hopes, expects to live, and if one believes we are living in a swiftly changing environment, then the art form of improvisation becomes an exercise in attuning to an uncertain existence for the improvisor and for the audience that accepts this vision of contemporary living.

If one is to do more than simply recognize the existence/ache of alienation, then improvisation with its strongest focus on the other is one of the ways to develop the capacity to learn/guess a little about each other. If we look at/probe/dance off each other, you who look at us sensing each other may learn as we may learn. If this task is deeply futile, it is a mystery before which it is worth risking failure—again and again.

These two statements contain the philosophy and attitudes that shaped the work we did and the results that you will find in this book. It is not only a collection of improvisations but also a telling of what we found and did in the way we improvised. This account could not come at a better time. When we launched the Workgroup, postmodern formalistic work in dance prevailed. We were clearly working against the current of that time. Now, at this writing, many of those same formalists are looking about uneasily and talking of "the referential nature of movement," "dance and social change" and being at long last overwhelmed by the intensity and awareness of existences beyond dance itself. What we did then in the Workgroup is about now.

About This Book

The most direct way to present this material would have been to organize the many improvisation exercises, games and structures in some coherent order and simply describe them. A more complex way is not only to describe them but to tell how they came to be. Thus, we would have the improvisations embedded in a history that takes in the aesthetic and philosophical premises that shaped them. A history it shall be. The reasoning? The first procedure—a bare-bones description—would suggest that this is *the way* improvisation should be, but I have spent my life going up against dogmatism and all neat, schematic floor plans for life. Relating the evolving forms of improvisation as they happened lets the reader realize it could have been otherwise. It opens the door for all to use, twist, change, develop or ignore what they find in these pages. What is here is *a* way, the way of the Workgroup, not *the* way. If it serves, fine, if not, fine. Readers will find their own way, using what is here, or not, and more power to all of us.

On "He" and "She"   There seems to be no way to lay out the structure of an improvisation without frequently using the third person singular. Ever since the earliest days of the Workgroup, 1969, I could not bring myself to say "he" when I meant "anyone," man or woman. I quickly took to saying "heshe" alternating with "shehe," and saying them both as one word. When I came to write How to Dance Forever (1988), that was how I wrote the third person singular. The publisher and the editor would have none of my innovation!

In the last few years, many solutions have been put forth. In this book I use one of my own devising, a period between the two words: "he.she," "she.he," "him.her," "her.him," "his.her" and "her.his." The use of the period has no logic to it at all, except for the fact that upon being read the intent is immediately apparent. Further, the use of "she.he" and "he.she" will alternate from context to context.

On "The Object" and "The Other"   Two phrases will appear and reappear in this book, "the object" and "the other." Though they are common and ordinary, we invested them with meanings that were at the center of our work. It is best to be clear with key words, particularly when critical concepts are being developed: For "object," read "purpose," "aim" or "goal" as in "the object of the game." "To dance" is one of ten thousand possible objects in the performance of our art, whether it be choreographed or improvised. Most dancers narrow the object of their performance to one thing, "to dance." For us in the Workgroup, whatever object was possible for any human to want or do was an option for the work of our imagination. The glorious act of dancing was one among all those options—or objects.

"The other" is both an obvious and an elusive something. Elsewhere, I once jotted down: "Too often we really look at the other only twice: once upon first meeting, and the second time when we know we will never see that face again." It could be said that the chief thirst of our work was to become fully alive to the mysterious "other," the one with whom we were working. The space problem that preoccupied us was the space between us and the "other." We further believed that if that hunt for the reality of the "other" is pursued with the greatest rigor possible, *with a minimal focus upon self*, one gains an unexpected gift, a deep insight into our own mysterious selves.

On the Specific Images Used in the Text

In order to make points clear and vivid throughout the text, there will be specific images which we used in our work. If the image given heats you up, by all means use it or bend it to your taste and your needs. If it clarifies but does not get your imagination going—find your own. It matters not whether the kicker is borrowed, stolen, or your own personal creation, it's what you do with it that makes it yours. Art historians will seize upon a work of art and assiduously follow every antecedent when the vital issue is, What has the artist done with the antecedent? Francoise Gillot, in *My Life with Picasso*, speaks of the terror of some painters in Paris when Picasso expressed great interest in going to their studios to see their work. And why not? If he saw anything of interest, he would hurry back to his studio and use it, giving it a twist that made it his own.

A Note for Actors and Musicians

Almost everything in this book can be used by actors. This should not be surprising since the ideas that spawned the entire concept of the Workgroup came from actors. Actually anyone who steps out onstage is at heart an actor. Most obviously, an actor-actor usually makes extensive use of speech. A singer carries speech into the poetry of sound in order to act. A dancer forgoes speech and uses the poetry of motion to act. Actors, teachers of actors and theatre directors, you will feel at home with this book.

Musicians have their own chapter (13) for I believe that, "with few exceptions, the mass of the material presented in this book can be brought to a rich life by musicians without a dancer in sight." This thought is developed in detail with a theoretical rationale and a practical succession of exercises, games and structures for any musicians game enough to venture into an unfamiliar arena. But be warned, this chapter will make little or no sense unless the whole book is read first.

A Note for Dance Therapists

In recent years one of the most successful modes of mental and emotional healing has been dance therapy. It is a burgeoning field with significant promise. It is no surprise that most of the practitioners of dance therapy are or were dancers. Though this book has been written for dancers, with ingenuity and imagination much of what will be found in it can be turned to the use of therapy.

A Note for All Readers

All readers, whether they be professionals or students in the dance field, professionals in the other arts or general readers, are going to find a few of the improvisations complicated and difficult to follow. Except for those who are actively engaged in doing them, little will be lost by some judicious skimming. The history and the theoretical points are all embedded in the text and should raise no such problem.

Copyright

If any material in this book is used in rehearsals, classes and/or workshops, it would be an act of courtesy and accuracy to inform the dancers and students of the source, giving credit to the book and its author. This is common to all good teaching in any sphere. If any games, structures or exercises are used in performance for the public, permission must first be obtained from The Daniel Nagrin Theatre, Film and Dance Foundation, Inc., 208 East 14 Street, Tempe, Arizona 85281.

Acknowledgments

An Individual Fellowship for 1991 and 1992 granted by the National Endowment for the Arts eased the way for the final writing of *Dance and the Specific Image: Improvisation.* As becomes a history, in the course of unfolding this life of the Workgroup, I have written of the artists who were involved in and responsible for many aspects of its creative development. They are recalled with gratitude. There are three more to whom I am indebted: Dr. Elizabeth Lessard, the Chair of Dance at Arizona State University, whose faith gave me a stable base from which to do this writing; my editor, Catherine Marshall, who gave me support and preserved an ideal balance of editorial control and receptiveness to my verbal idiosyncrasies; and finally, my wife, Phyllis Steele Nagrin, who was the critical audience for all stages of the book and generously shared the labors of proofing every word and comma.

PART I History and Theory

1 Before the Workgroup

Prior to the time of the Workgroup, everything I performed was choreographed,[1] but almost everything choreographed was pursued and found through improvisation. Improvisation was always there as a tool. When choreographing, I would improvise until something "felt right" and then try to remember and pin down what that was.

My earliest introduction to dance was by way of improvisation. As a high school student, sitting still for the hours spent doing homework was near impossible. Among my restless diversions was practicing a poorly learned box step for the foxtrot. Social dancing was the passport to meeting girls, and though I never solved the box step at the time, I gradually slipped into the sheer pleasure of rolling, running and jumping to whatever music I found on the radio. A couple of years later, when I started to take dance classes, all improvisation stopped while I attempted to take command of the complexities my dance teachers threw at me. Well, almost. Actually, I was a slow learner. All new material was a threat and my failures at picking up movement given in classes filled me with fury. In time, I discovered a solution. I would find time and space outside of class to digest what I could not learn in class. That solitary time became the arena in which I really danced. I probably looked awful in most technique classes because I approached them uptight and expected the worst. Alone, I could slow down and really learn the new stuff, and then I would have fun bouncing around—or, more seriously, try to be creative.

If you were a modern dancer in those days (I began the study of dance while in college in 1936), you possessed real dignity only if you were "creative." I had studied for less than three months and already I was in the

---

1. Well, almost everything. Many of my solos had brief passages that were deliberately left loose because they would have suffered had they been set too precisely. After the Workgroup, when I returned to the solo form, several dances were complete improvisations, though specifically focused and highly structured.

studio alone, trying to make up dances! Much of what I did then could best be described as floundering improvisations and not well focused. I drew what I could from the music in the stack of records that always accompanied me.

During this period, I took my first acting classes with Miriam Goldina, who had studied acting in Moscow with Vakhtangov, one of Stanislavski's best directors. I loved this way of working. A central part of the technique was improvisation. Students would be given a situation parallel to the characters and situations in the scene they were studying. Generally, the improvised scene would be set in a time, place and set of conditions close to the students' lives. All we had to work with were the characters and the conditions at the beginning of the encounter; no dialogue was given. Everything had to be improvised on the spot, and we were judged on how truthfully we responded to whatever occurred.

Though my technique was still raw, by the time I began to work with Helen Tamiris,[2] I had acquired a double facility: I could improvise dance not only with freedom but with delight, and I had a modest grasp on the skill of acting. I liked the game of becoming someone else. It was Tamiris who helped me knock down the wall that separated the two and make the act of dancing and the work of acting, one. Creatively, improvisation was the weld that joined them. Tamiris would tell me, "You are so-and-so and you are doing such-and-such." I would go off to a corner of the studio and become so-and-so and doing such-and-such. After a while, I'd be back showing what I had come up with and Tamiris would then shape it this way and that to mesh with her concept and choreography.

I never had the illusion that it was my choreography. Tamiris, though encouraging the creativeness of her dancers, could at any moment come up with reams of rich movement out of her own body, but she knew that when the dancers have personal input, they perform with a much deeper involvement. An awesome example of this took place one evening in our loft on lower Fifth Avenue. While choreographing *Memoir*, Helen needed a large group of slum children, playing in the streets of New York's Lower East Side, to dance the horror of the events they witnessed in their daily lives. The work had already been choreographed and performed twice: once at the Perry-Mansfield School in Steamboat Springs, Colorado, and once in New London, Connecticut, at the American Dance Festival. For the New York premier, she had drawn on a talented group of students from the High School of Performing Arts. Their ages ranged from fifteen to eighteen. She said to them, "There is a part of you which you have always hated. You can rid yourself of it through movement. In the next sixteen measures get rid of that hateful part." A fury, a turmoil and an anguish filled the space as those adolescents dealt with a pain known too well by the wounded vanity most of us carry within. It was excit-

2. A brief biography of Helen Tamiris appears as Appendix A.

ing, true to the piece and utterly different from the previous two versions. After the music stopped she said, "Now calmly and objectively recapture what you were doing and how you danced it. Later when you know it well, you can allow the inner action to release the emotion you will need to perform the truth of the moment." It's too far in the past to be certain, but my memory says she barely touched what they had done except to control the spacing, leaving them to shape what had poured from their bodies during those sixteen measures.

In giving a sequence in technique classes, she would often tell us to regard the end of it as the beginning of an improvisation, that is, taking the impulses, textures and feelings of the exercise as a springboard for a new, unpremeditated movement flow.

In her choreography classes, Tamiris had two exercises that often had a profound effect upon her students. One had no name, but for this writing I will give it the name **Stillness**. (Note that all exercises will be set off from the rest of the text and most of them written as if a teacher/director was addressing a working dance company or a group of students.)

Stillness **1.1**

On my signal, with no more focus than the impulse of the moment, begin to move without premeditation or planning until you hear me say, "Find stillness," at which time you should pause where you are and be still and only move when you must. As you are being still, your focus is precisely that, stillness, which is not moving, for stillness is a form of motion. Since you are focused on stillness, to plan or anticipate what you will do when you begin to move again should be impossible. Resist the first few impulses to move. Only move when you must, not knowing what you will do next and continue until you again hear, "Find stillness."

Another she called **Body Contact.**

Body Contact **1.2**

Two by two face each other, hands raised shoulder height and palms touching. Sooner or later one of you will begin to move one or both hands in the same or different directions. All movement should be slow in this exercise. Whoever starts the moving has a commitment: once started in a specific direction there can be no wavering, curving or change of direction. Continue the motion until it is not possible to move any further. Whoever is being moved has an equally important but more subtle commitment: the pressure of the mover must be answered by pressure from the moved one, that is, the moved one maintains an answer life all through the slow thrust of the mover but never with the intention of stopping or hindering that thrust at any point. When the mover has reached the full length of his.her thrust and is not able to go any further, the moved one becomes the mover and initiates with the pressure of hands the next thrust, which similarly is unwavering in a straight line until no further progress is possible. Your feet never move until they must. Little convenient shifts of weight by foot movements are out. Remember, no sudden movements; all is slow.

When anyone tears away from these ground rules, it becomes immediately apparent as a betrayal of the commitment. When both stay with it and, in the oft-repeated cry of Tamiris, they "follow through," the experience of doing and of viewing it touches deep places. Body Contact is not easy to pull off at first, but after some practice, exquisite and astonishing events can occur. Tamiris and I taught actors extensively, and this was a particularly fertile exercise for them. They would slide into pelvic falls that would otherwise take months to learn.

Body Contact has many variations:

- Do it with three, four or many. (In *Dance for Walt Whitman*, Tamiris choreographed a whole chain of linked dancers using Body Contact).
- Do it with the palms of the hands close to each other but not touching.
- Give secret and sometimes contradictory inner actions to each of the dancers. This is best with three or four dancers.

   Examples: "Keep your distance from the others." "Be protective and shelter the others." "Tower above the others."

   Note: In these examples, one can express one's will only when one's turn comes up. Each person must "give in," even though unwillingly, while the will of the other is being expressed through pressure of the hands.

When I began to work with actors, giving them movement training, the first and most rewarding approach circled the matter of rhythm. I became aware that one of the critical elements that defines our individuality is our rhythm. I would give one of the actors some chewing gum, a newspaper and a chair in the center of the studio, telling her.him to look through the paper for an advertisement for binoculars. The students observing the actor were to beat silently with one hand the rhythm they could see in the gum chewing and with other hand, the rhythm of the page turning. Almost invariably they were closely linked: the animal rhythm of chewing and the learned rhythm of page turning. The students were asked to pin down what they had observed, then to rise, find a space and let those rhythms take possession of their bodies. The revelation of doing this exercise was how different it made them feel. The rhythm of the other made them feel like someone else. This led to the actor's exercise called **Inner Rhythm.**

Inner Rhythm 1.3

In your mind's eye, bring to life the character you are working on now in your scene-study class. Continue to observe him.her until you can sense/feel/see the inner rhythm of the character. When and if it is experienced and assumes a concrete form let that rhythm take over your entire body. Let it move you as it will.

If you find the inner rhythm of the character, good. If you don't, that too is good. You were there, inside the character for a time. In my instructions I emphasized that if they pretended to sense/feel/see the rhythm of the character when nothing of the kind had happened, that was self-betrayal and a loss of learning time. The worst ploy of all is for students to bend and shape class work into what they think a teacher wants and expects. The act of learning should never be a performance for the teacher. Once a problem is given, the students' only commitment is to their understanding and response to the problem and not to the teacher.

The follow-up to this exercise was to ask actors who were working together on a scene to spend preparation time doing the rhythmic dance of the character just before playing the scene in their rehearsals and also before presenting the scene in class. It worked for many of them.

The reasoning behind this exercise is that no matter how thoroughly one researches the facts and probes the imagination about the details of the character's existence, there is just so much we can know about anyone—real, imagined, or even ourselves. Performing the inner rhythm of the character stirs up the animality that lurks in the shadows of everyone. Each of us is different, and each contains a unique physical-emotional motor that drives us through our lives in ways we hardly suspect and rarely notice. Dancing the inner rhythm of the character stirs up deep elements that cannot easily be reached by reason or analysis.

What does this exercise mean for dancers? Everything, if you consciously—or unconsciously—relate in your work to a *specific image* and to a particular identity. Some performers and choreographers profess to deal only in abstractions—generalized feelings or pure movement—but I suspect that the ones who have vibrant life in their work have something quite specific in focus, even if it is unnamed, but then, that is my prejudice and preference. I think the most generalized abstraction contains a specific seed at its core whether the performer is aware of it or not. "The moment a dancer enters the stage arena, she.he has assumed a role and the performance of a specific act, *whether the choreography is abstract or dramatic in nature.*"[3]

Everything is shaped by rhythm, and I think of rhythm as central to the creative act. Rhythm is the pulse of the irrational center. If one finds the rhythm of the person or the thing one is supposed to be onstage, one has begun to penetrate the truth of what is being danced.

In the summer of 1965, Paul Draper asked me to teach two weeks for him at the American Dance Festival. One of the classes was "Rhythm for Dancers." Paul, a great tap dancer, is, by that token, an outstanding musician. Not for one second was I going to try to follow in his footsteps. I explained this to the class and projected instead a two-week focus on "Sources of

---

3. Quoted from a course outline for my class, "Acting Technique for Dancers."

Rhythm Other Than Music." The sequence of exercises I presented on my first day with this class had a curious outcome.

The Music Comes In Here and Goes Out There 1.4

The Music Comes In Here and Goes Out There.[4] The pianist will improvise at different tempos and in different styles. Walking in time with the music, sense whether the music seems to penetrate your body at a specific place. When you hear, "Let it out!" let the music come pouring out of your body. Take note of what part of your body is most affected. When there is a radical change in the music, return to the simple walking in the beat and again sense where it is that the music enters your body. Wait until you hear, "Let it out!" noting what part of the body needs to dance that music.

Ambient Sound 1.5

Ambient Sound. Sit erect and listen. Take whatever you hear and become that sound; let that sound take over your entire body.

I introduced the next exercise, a radical variation of what I had used with actors by saying, "In order to give you the scope of these two weeks, the next exercise jumps to the end of the book, so to speak." This turned out to be a major mistake.

Inner Rhythm for Dancers 1.6

Inner Rhythm for Dancers. Sit erect with your legs crossed and clear your head. We each of us have an inner rhythm. When you are ready, try to become aware of your inner rhythm. When you sense it, study it. When you know it, become it. Let your whole body enter into that rhythm.

Interesting? What happened was even more interesting and taught me a teaching lesson. After about five minutes, I became aware that very few people were dancing, some were stretched out as if sleeping, and one group was talking. Aloud, I said, "Talking at this time is evading the problem at hand." After about ten minutes, one man came to show me what he had done. He seemed nervous as he sat down cross-legged before me, covering his left hand with his right hand. Though I could hardly see that hand, I could tell that in time it began to quiver with a furious intensity. He had come to *not* show me his inner rhythm! A very few dancers followed, showing tense and awkward versions of what they thought I wanted to see. The next day, out of the forty-odd students, a bit more than half showed up. The rest stayed away for the two weeks, but those who stayed became loyal and fanatical devotees of the search for "Sources of Rhythm Other Than Music."

What did I learn from that wholesale desertion? When you ask people to look inside, some will resist. Why? Are they frightened? Uninterested? Do they believe motion is the only proper area of dance and this internal stuff is intrusive, intellectualizing, or on the way to sentimentality and self-

---

4. "The Music Goes Down and Around and It Comes Out Here" was the title of a 1935 song (lyrics by "Red" Hodgson and music by Farley and Riley).

indulgence? I can guess, but I wouldn't presume to know what motivates them. All I am certain of is that some either do not need or cannot handle any deep internal focus; and equally, that for some, when that source of power is opened to them, their dancing gains qualities and strengths they never knew they possessed.

The second lesson? Never jump to the "end of the book, so to speak." When you're unveiling a new way, one step at a time is as fast as you dare go. New ways may be exciting but they are also threatening.

In the ensuing two weeks, more exercises emerged:

Conduct a Picture 1.7

Conduct a Picture. Bring in an art book with an illustration of a painting that is particularly meaningful to you. You will work with a partner. One of you will act as Music Stand for the other, kneeling and holding the book open so that the Conductor can view the painting. Conductor, you will study the painting until you can feel an underlying beat that pervades the entire work. When that rhythm becomes strong in you, let it be carried by your feet as an *ostinato*—a repeated phrase. When it is established and rolling, let your eye gradually travel from one part of the painting to another, and as you pause at each part, use your arms to give expression to its rhythm. All the while you are maintaining the same basic beat of the entire painting with your feet. When you have finished, the Music Stand becomes the Conductor.

As we went on, I had the students take rhythms from each other walking, from animals, leaves in the wind, the grain of the hardwood maple dance floor, rain and whatever moved and excited them individually. The intensity of the work with the "survivors" was gratifying. Each day felt like a voyage of discovery. Except for Inner Rhythm, all that we did was new to me as well.

When Helen Tamiris and I worked as directors of the Tamiris-Nagrin Dance Company from 1960 to 1964, improvisation was not the order of the day. Creative problems were usually choreographic, with an assignment given and students finding their own space and way in which to work. Some did find their movements through improvising and some through the deliberate and thoughtful placing of one movement upon another. That aspect was not supervised or directed—only the result. There was Body Contact, and for the moment that is all I recall.

I made up **Tandem Solo** in a workshop in Sedgewick, Maine, in 1960. It became the favorite at our occasional parties. I would pick some strong music with a powerful momentum, and start it off with a good improvisor.

Tandem Solo 1.8

One of you will go to the center of a circle of dancers. As you listen to the opening strains of the music, catch an idea out of what you hear and then take off. After a while, I will call out the name of another dancer who will replace the first one in the center of the circle. The challenge for that second dancer will be to realize what he.she reads as the intent of the first dancer. After a while, I will call out a third dancer who tries to continue what the second dancer had been doing, and so on, until near the end of the music, I will call out "Everyone finish it."

Years later (1973), Tandem Solo developed into Relay Solo (7.7), which was a part of *Sea Anemone* (see chap. 8). Actually, the richest improvisation experiences for Helen and me were at parties. We would start with whatever the music asked for—a foxtrot, rhumba or the Lindy—but sooner or later we would break apart from that man-pushing-the-woman-around style and, anticipating the free style to come in a few years, begin dancing off each other. Not only did we attract a circle of attention, but we loved doing it. We were even a success in a Greek restaurant that featured dancing by the patrons. In a quiet moment when the marvelous gentlemen customers paused for a rest from their dancing, I placed a few bills on the bandstand, led Helen onto the floor, and we both showed off, had fun and generous applause when we finished. The dance floor is the birthplace of much of what we dancers do. On it, we can encounter some parts of what we really are, unexpected truths, joy and a profound reservoir of what makes dance. Many dancers make a habit of this experience. Too many do not.

It was, I believe, in 1963 that an ironic moment occurred. Anneliese Widman had been for a brief time, a member of the Tamiris-Nagrin Dance Company. She was a forceful dancer who could realize the kind of power and intensity that Tamiris demanded of dancers generally and that her role in *Memoir* needed.

After her season with us, she invited us to a concert of her own work with a small group of women in her loft on West Seventy-fourth Street. My memory says the program clearly indicated that what we were going to see performed was improvisation. Undoubtedly, that set off negative ripples in my mind and Helen's. Improvisation performed? We knew it would smack of a lack of discipline. Some part of our deeply ingrained work ethic probably snorted in the background, "Improvisation! What an easy way out of doing the hard and exacting work of choreography!" I wouldn't venture for a moment to "evaluate" what she did—I was too prejudiced against what I was looking at. But eight years later I was going to be directing a dance company that performed improvisation.

2 The Open Theatre, 1969

In the unplanned events that change our lives, a theatre director, Jacques Levy, moved into my loft building on Bleecker Street. At the time, he was co-directing the Open Theatre with its founder, Joseph Chaikin. This was one of the most adventurous theatre companies in New York City, and an invitation in 1969 from Levy to give them some movement classes excited me. What happened proved seminal. It was while teaching members of the Open Theatre that I experienced a few improvisation exercises that made unexpected demands upon me as a performer. In time, I came to realize that aesthetically and ethically what was involved here were some of the most interesting challenges I had encountered in all of my experience in theatre and in dance.

I had just given the actors of the Open Theatre a movement class in a huge chaotic loft in Soho. I recall Joe Chaikin thanking me, and then,

Solo Singer
2.1

by some signal I didn't notice, one of the actors stepped into the center of the room and proceeded to let loose a river of sounds which seemed to ride on his impulses of the moment. The other actors moved into a circle about him and silently began to live in and off those sounds. By "live," I do mean dance. Everyone's motion in that circle took a slightly different adjustment to what she.he was hearing. Some followed the rise and fall of his voice. Some were negative about what they heard. Some supported the turbulent energy of the singer with a subtle, steady rhythm, but however they danced, it was about what they heard this man do. (This came to be known as **Solo Singer**.)

Solo Dancer
2.2

I can't recall how or why it stopped, but then once again, someone came to the center of the circle. I think it was a man again. He began to move and strut and thrust about, dancing with the clumsy, wildly imaginative and startling way of some actors who are not trained in dance. The ring broke into a cacophony of sound, that is, it sounded like a cacophony until I realized that each person's voice was living (singing, shouting, grunting, barking) off the motions of this actor. Some were supporting, following, encouraging the dancer, and others seemed downright hostile, mocking, challenging vocally, tripping up with their voices the strutting, flailing actor. Again I can't recall how long the sequence lasted, but I stood on the perimeter of the circle just observing and somewhat astonished. No one had explained the ground rules to me but they were apparent. (This came to be known as **Solo Dancer**.)

The Chord
2.3

When the second exercise ended, I was suddenly grasped about the shoulder by a sweaty arm which drew me into the center of the room, whereupon another arm from the other side wrapped around my neck and I found myself in a huddled ring of about seven. After all the noise that had filled the room, the quiet was thick. All that was audible was the breathing of those closest to me. It took some time to realize that the breaths of the circling people were weaving in and out of each other. It was as if each breath was like a surfer riding on the other breaths. Suddenly a sigh brushed ever so close to a vocalization. Then, in the most subtle transition, others shifted gears from breath to a tentative vocalization that seemed to wrap around the first vocalization. This slowly grew to a rich chord of gentle singing. Hearing those to the immediate left and right of me pouring out soft singing, I rather timidly allowed a sound to come out of my throat.

I say "timidly," because due to an unfortunate introduction to music as a child, I have long had a tension about doing any kind of singing, passionately wishing to produce a beautiful tone with accurate pitch and always fearing that I wouldn't. In that huddle, I can recall trying to produce a "good" tone in a pitch that blended and would sound good and I was so afraid that I wouldn't. Gradually, the intensity and volume of sound coming from the many throats increased and was quite beautiful.

As I tried to keep pace with what they were doing, I struck a wall, as it were, turned and beheld what I was really doing. I was awful. At the center of all my good intentions, my noble wish to blend in with everyone's effort, was the overweening consciousness of my own voice and the sound that I was producing. I barely heard what they were doing. I was working very hard to produce a beautiful tone for the ears of my neighbors. I wasn't surfing through, over and under the particular voices that were pouring in from my left and from my right and from across the circle. I needed to sound "good."

Again, no one had explained to me the ground rules of this exercise, but in that moment of self-vision without any cogitation I clicked into a radically different mind-set. I let the thread of my voice float on the voice nearest me. Listening very closely to those nearest me, I tried to lay down a track of sound that fit into all the curves of my neighbor's sounds. (The Open Theatre called this **The Chord.**)

12

For a little while, my only thought was to be as intimate as I could with those other voices. Needless to say, the consciousness of my own vocal production finally obtruded. An old game and a new game; an old consciousness and a new consciousness were contending with each other. The form that The Chord followed after this crescendo was to slowly diminish in volume until there was silence. I think that for the Open Theatre, The Chord was a symbolic ritual of who they were, how they worked and how they related to each other.

These exercises were used regularly by the Open Theatre, and I followed the same form when I first began to give them in workshops. But very quickly, I became uneasy with any improvisation whose shape could be anticipated. That seemed a contradiction in terms. An improvisation to me was any structure whose shape was to be discovered, not shaped or directed. In time, the ground rules for The Chord as practiced in my workshops and by the Workgroup were these:

The Chord 2.3a

Any group, up to eight, come close together—sitting, standing or lying down. Initiate nothing. If you hear anything from anyone, make a sound that adds the thinnest coat of more to it. Create nothing. If the sound gets too much for you, then do a hair less. If you're tired, stop.

Sometimes a rich musical chord would well up; other times, a cleared throat would grow into a pack of angry panthers, or a giggle would become a hysteria of laughter. They all ultimately wore themselves into silence. Initiating nothing, creating nothing became the hardest discipline to learn yet in the end it was most rewarding because people began to really listen to each other.

I continued to work with the Open Theatre for another month or two, but no theoretical clarity emerged. I simply admired their adventurousness and deep involvement. Then, when I went on tour, giving concerts and dance workshops, I began to set up improvisation sessions using these three structures and also devising new exercises and games. *They were all about what the other person was doing.*

One of these I learned about through a phone conversation. A friend who was taking a workshop with Joe Chaikin and the Open Theatre mentioned something called **The Mirror.**

The Mirror 2.4

As described by this woman, it consisted of two people facing each other sitting cross-legged like a pair of buddhas, their knees about two or three inches apart. The task was little short of outrageous. You were to initiate nothing. *You had to become the other person.* You not only had to pick up, as a true mirror does, every movement, gesture and breath of the person you were observing, but your body was to assume the other person's posture, energy of lift, weight of body, inner impulses, and so on. There is a marvelous irony to this. You are imitating someone who is imitating you imitating him.her imitating you, . . . into infinity. A mirror facing a mirror. It is nowhere the simple exercise it appears to be and doing it can give one unexpected insights. Most important of all, you couldn't initiate anything, you only followed/became what you observed.

My friend told me that one day she had done the exercise with another woman, whom she did not know, and they had both found themselves weeping. I felt that I had to try this exercise at the first opportunity.

I attended a workshop led by Joe Chaikin in which there was an exercise called **The Conductor.**

The Conductor 2.5

In groups of three, one person, out of an immediate impulse, sets up a rhythmic flow of motion that can cover space or not. The motions of the other two live off, are a function of, are about what the Conductor is doing. Doing the same motion as the Conductor is only one of ten thousand possibilities. They never lose sight of the Conductor. At intervals, Joe would call out, "Change," and another of the three assumed the role of Conductor. Then the third person was called to lead by, "Change!" Finally, the call was for all to follow all with no conductor. I don't recall how he ended it. When I give The Conductor, I say, "You will come to a moment when you all know it has been done and bring it to a close."

Note that the word flow in this context is a perfect example of language that can create a specific result, in this case, flowing motion. A better phrasing would be: "In groups of three, one person, out of an immediate impulse, sets up rhythmic motion that can cover space or not."

At the American Dance Festival in 1992, I gave The Conductor, and then, after I had called out "All" and the dancers had pursued that for a while, I called out—on an impulse—"All, all the entire room." The room swelled with activity and interactions that went on for at least an hour if not more.

There are some engineers who are inadvertently artists. These are the road builders who pick out those lookout points on mountain roads that catch you by the throat and make it hard to breath for the excitement they have created. There are some artists who carve out lookout points that give all who pause there a view that goes on and on. Joe Chaikin and the Open Theatre did this for me.

3 On the Road, 1969–1970

Although the impact of the Open Theatre was considerable, I did not spend much time with them. I had premiered *The Peloponnesian War*, an evening-length work, in December 1968, and many bookings were coming in. Engagements and tours took me out of New York so frequently that for a while I lost my connection with the group. However, in three engagements on the road, I managed to pause long enough to play a bit with the five Open Theatre exercises—EGAS—described in chapter 2: Solo Singer, Solo Dancer, The Chord, The Mirror, and The Conductor.[1] To my amazement, they were seeds sprouting unexpected forms that surprised, delighted and a few times, even frightened me.

The actual dates were: July 28–August 1, 1969, in Grand Rapids, Minnesota—a summer workshop for the University of Minnesota in the lake country; September 29–October 10, 1969, in Austin, Texas—a two-week workshop for dancers and actors in the Department of Drama and Dance at the University of Texas; and September 18–December 19, 1969, in College Park, Maryland—a semester long, two-days-a-week teaching stint at the University of Maryland.

Grand Rapids, Minnesota

In the sunny recreation hall of a Minnesota resort hotel called Sugar Hill, about twenty eager, almost dancers (summer vacationers) and two exquisitely trained dancers, one wiry and one muscular, were subjected to my first efforts to set up these improvisations. For two days there was nothing but brave attempts at uninhibited and free motion hampered by self-consciousness and

---

1. Throughout this book, I will be at a loss as to how to call these things—exercises, games or structures. An "exercise" is supposed to develop a component of technique. A "game" is improvised play governed by a set of rules. When they are good, they have "structure." The words lap over each other. The solution? An acronym, EGAS, which will mean in this book, "exercises, games and structures."

doubt. The hotshots, no less than the limited dancers were dancing with questions: What is this all about? What am I supposed to do? This is dancing? Everything looked awful, slow and guarded.

The third day, during Solo Dancer, I pitched in, joining the circle, shouting, singing and stamping. Aware of me, they became less aware of themselves and the day took off with some concentrated work. That afternoon, I assigned a choreography problem involving couples to make the burden of creativeness lighter and less self-aware.

Late in the afternoon of the fourth day, I asked to see the composition studies. Almost all had an unpretentious simplicity which pleased me, one being a hilarious pantomime of an inept learning to ride a bicycle. The two "pros," one of whom was my assistant, were last. They did not do a choreographed study but rather an improvisation; one that swept all of us into that question which is at the heart of the theatre: What is going to happen? I have given it as an exercise many times since, naming it **The Minnesota Duet**.

The Minnesota Duet 3.1

I tell two dancers: Face each other from opposite corners of the space, arms at your sides. Contemplate each other, asking, "What is there in that person across the room that I want very much to possess for myself?" List all those qualities and wait until one shines out more than all the others. When you know for certain what that one quality is, give the signal by clasping your hands or crossing your arms. When the second dancer makes the deciding gesture, both of you approach each other to possess that quality which you are determined to absorb into yourself. Become what you desire. You can use proximity to get what you want but no body contact, no touching, no pointing and no illustrating with the hands.

When they did it that first time, it had all the tension and design of a Western showdown. I used The Minnesota Duet often in the early workshop days of the Workgroup. It was the first step, teaching the people involved not only to act on the basis of observing each other but to anchor that observation in a personal commitment, that is, they were dancing for something they wanted—for themselves.

Possessing the quality of someone else seems like a crazy idea at first but it is the paramount activity of adolescents as they "try on" personalities for size, a perennial activity of some highly impressionable personalities, the professional task of all performers in the theatre—but alas, a terrifying prospect for rigid people desperate to keep intact the image they have of themselves. More of this later.

There is an ironic twist to all of this. Years later, in another workshop in Philadelphia, the muscular one of the original pair told me that their inner life and raison was not at all what I supposed it to be. Disconcerted at first, I realized that because they had shared a powerful specific image, it could fire the imagination of viewers, including myself, who in turn made a very good exercise out of it.

It took me a bit of reflection to understand the connection between their study and my five little exercises. The three days of improvisation had cleared a new space for those two. Whatever they did was about the other—the other person. Further, it was an improvisation, not the set study for which I had asked, but because they were so secure with the inner premises of their piece, they could perform it with the same assurance as if it had been choreographed. They probably thought of it as choreographed, and on the fifth day, when we had an impromptu performance of the studies, their performance, though somewhat different, had the same core and was every bit as powerful as the first time. It is not the easiest exercise to pull off but is worth the gamble, because of the fierce attention and imagination it demands of the pair.

Austin, Texas

In the fall of 1969 I was to give a two-week workshop for the Department of Drama and Dance at the University of Texas in Austin. It was a large department—300 students and over 20 faculty—and it included dance. During the day, I taught technique classes for the dancers and special movement classes for the actors. The evening improvisation workshop was open to everyone—including faculty. At that time, teaching at Austin was anything but experimental. Traditional theatre concepts predominated. But I was hoping to really explore the implications of those apparently simple Open Theatre exercises. Taken together they implied an unsettling and nontraditional credo. It was a series of negatives that added up to a challenging new discipline for performers:

- It didn't matter what you looked like.
- You were not to be concerned with your success with the audience.
- You were not to try to be interesting, creative, inventive or original.
- You were not to try to show either your personal beauty or your personal skill.
- To sum it up, you failed if you tried to be successful.
- Success was not the object.
- The task was the object. The point of all the work and all the exercises was to concentrate on the specific object (task) at hand.

During the two weeks, as my pattern of experiment and uncertainty became apparent, some fell away and others became almost religious about the work. There were an equal number of dance and acting students plus a sprinkling of faculty. The latter were consistent, and in the preparation for this book they were very helpful in recalling details and generous in their praise of how they were subsequently affected by the work. The actors who stayed "went all the way." By and large, the dancers entered into the work, but most kept a distance, rarely getting deeply involved. It taught me that to fully involve dancers one had to move slowly, not skipping any transitions.

I started with The Mirror (2.4). What better way of making the point than focusing on another? A failure. It created exactly the opposite effect. After a short period of tight silence, laughter began to ripple through the room. And why not? Looking into the face of another human being is no light matter, and just as weighty is being looked at. Most people, being asked to stare into another's face for more than three-and-a-half seconds will be embarrassed or dissolve into uncontrollable giggling. I had to find some way of clearing the minds of the dancers so that they would be open to each other without this embarrassing self-consciousness. Perhaps because of the Buddha-like position in which they faced each other, I hit upon a meditation I later called **The Mind-Wash**.

The Mind-Wash 3.2

Start seated, cross-legged and facing a partner with your knees two or three inches apart. Close your eyes and clean out your head. Whenever you are ready, open your eyes to look at the tip of your nose. Unlike the classic yogis who spent a lifetime doing that only, whenever you've had enough of looking at the tip of your nose, let your gaze drop to high on your chest and gradually allow your eyes to travel down your body, across the floor, across the ankles, across the floor between you and your partner, across your partner's ankles, a little bit of floor, and then travel up the body of your partner, across the face, over her.his head, to the wall beyond, the eyes climbing in a path as wide as your eyes, up the wall until they find the ceiling. Then traveling across the ceiling and finally as far back and behind as you can, without falling over backward. Take as much or as little time as you need for this visual journey. When this maneuver is complete, return to look upon the face of your partner, and when your partner meets your gaze begin The Mirror, becoming what you see before you.

The Mind-Wash worked. It solved the problem of giggling and embarrassment. Someplace along the way, self-consciousness got lost. The beauty of a maple wood pattern, a tear in a dance shoe, the unshaven chin of the partner, the trivia of wall cracks, stains on the ceiling—all seemed to acquire an importance equal to anything else in the world. The tool of attention had been sharpened and best of all, focused on things other than self. Finally, at the end of the journey was the other, the other person, and she.he was no longer a laughing matter.

As a preparation for the mirror exercise, it was perfect. In the first part of the eye-journey, the dancer lets the eyes travel over his.her partner's face as slowly or as quickly as wished. By the time the journey is completed, for most people, the mind achieves a waterlike clarity and a certain emptiness. (Any number of dancers have told me that this exercise has served them as a meditation technique. I have used it myself innumerable times when my head was too turbulent to move on to the next step.) I named this sequence—The Mind-Wash followed by The Mirror—**Yoga Mirror** (3.3).

It was a beginning, but there was still the monumentally aggressive push of the young actors and the ever-present self-conscious decorativeness of the dancers to deal with.

The Obstacle 3.4

The Obstacle. The second evening, I slid a folding chair out into the center of the room and deliberately pointed to an attractive, skillful and elegantly decorative dancer and said, "I have a challenge for you. Can you pass under that chair without moving it?" It looked to be an impossible task and yet, with careful manouvering and much concentration she emerged on the other side of the chair, disheveled, panting a bit and somewhat confused.

I asked, "While you were trying to achieve what you thought was a somewhat impossible task, were you aware of how you looked?" Wide-eyed, she shook her head. "Were you trying to look good while you were doing it?" "No," she said, still somewhat confused by this weird assignment in a dance workshop.

Having given this task many times since, on rare occasions I will get just the answer I don't want: yes, they were aware how they looked, or they were trying to look good.[2] More often than not, the answer has been no, and the experience becomes a revelation. For some, it is perhaps the first time they just do something without trying to look good doing it. The object, to pass under the chair without moving it, was not muddied with a focus on appearance or style. (For variations, see 3.13 and 3.14 below.)

What am I trying to say? Almost every minute and detail of every dance class we have ever taken is an arrow pointed at the ideal of looking good, looking beautiful. Why should anyone do anything if not try to be successful? That's what the whole thing is about, isn't it? What's wrong with trying to get an audience to like you? To think you look beautiful?

Well, there was something about these exercises—Solo Singer, Solo Dancer, The Chord, The Mirror and The Conductor—that raised radically new questions. Is it possible that one can achieve a beauty, a self-realization, yes, even a virtuosity, through a new discipline that calls for loss of self? Can one lose focus on one's own person and throw all one's attention to the object? The Open Theatre actors danced to what they heard in the flight of the singer. The voices of the circle watching the solo dancers were defined by their feeling response, understanding and perception of his motions. The breathers and the singers in the circle wove a delicate, complex rope of sound

---

2. We teachers are a sneaky lot. We ask subtle, ostensibly open-ended questions, all the while searching for only one answer.

around what they heard. The Mirror asked one to turn observation into becoming what one observed.

What is being projected here is indeed an aesthetic and an implied ethic. It speaks in a manner and substance not unlike the ancient Chinese Taoists. The search is for the revelation of what is, not with what is made. Beauty is identified with light, with vision, with insight, not with ordering. Highly significant thinkers in art have said that art is the bringing of order to the chaos of life. The Taoists of ancient China saw differently. They sensed that there is an order in life and not chaos and that understanding, insight, science and art are engaged in *finding* the order that is there. How to do this? For the Taoists, it lies in being open to The Way, The Tao, to what is there.[3] This means paying attention and being receptive on all levels without preconceptions. It means that focus on the self muddies vision of the object. It attempts to dispense with history—to see as a child sees. For adult humans, this is difficult and well nigh impossible on a pure and absolute level. How to even approach this way, this mind set? The first step is to forgo the deadly demand for the "pure and the absolute." The second is to look past the self and seek the object, the task, the other.

In projecting this aesthetic, I use two examples. One is that of a surfer who can't afford to generalize; who succeeds only in the depth of her.his absorption in and attention to the vagaries of the wave she.he is riding at that moment. You can't surf the last wave or the next wave, only this wave.

The other example is possibly more helpful. I will pick a dancer who is wearing a leotard, asking him or her to stand, and point to the garment saying, "This piece of clothing will fit perfectly at least one eighth of the adult women of the world, or men, as the case may be. Centuries upon centuries of tailors and dressmakers have tried to make a garment really fit the body. This amazing fabric respectfully follows every swell and fall of the body of this person. How wonderful it would be if the motions that poured out of your body in any one of these exercises were to embrace the object of your attention as truthfully as this cloth embraces your body." The point of the work was attention. What was done was based on what someone else was doing.

The work in Austin for the first couple of days proceeded unevenly. The improvisation sessions were scheduled for two hours every evening, and they always ran over to three. It was here that I learned that to make improvisation really work, one needs time—lots of it. Three hours are good, four are much better. It is late in the sessions that the flow starts; people stop watching themselves and begin to watch each other, responding with speed and directness. On the whole, there was high energy and interest but we were

---

3. The name of the Open Theatre came from being "open-minded" and being "open to change," words that are, deliberately or not, close to Taoist thinking.

still feeling each other out and we had yet to really get under way. I was reluctant to give The Conductor because I had done it only once in New York and felt unfree doing it. I needed a game that ran on rhythm to take its place. As noted earlier, whenever I want dancers or actors to reach animality, to enter the irrational and the sweating reality of the moment, I turn to the use of rhythm. On the third day, I hit upon **Rhythm Circle** and the place erupted. It was the first exercise I added to the original five.

Rhythm Circle 3.5

Five to seven dancers sit (or stand) in a circle. One person starts by beating out, on impulse, any rhythm that rises up out of the moment, clapping, beating on the floor or the body or snapping fingers. Use all the time you need to settle into a rhythm until you can repeat it over and over again with confidence. When that rhythm is under control, look at the person to your left and nod. That's the sign for the next person to learn what the first person has just found. The second person in the circle will try to duplicate the rhythm. The giver must stay with the learner until the rhythm is done accurately. If the learner is missing some part of it, the teacher can make a special emphasis to clarify.

Thus we have a Teacher-Learner relationship. When the Teacher thinks the Learner has it, she.he can stop, but comes right back in if an error crops up when the learner is doing it alone. When the Teacher is certain that the Learner has it, she.he nods in assent. The Learner then takes a time to "show off," as it were, his.her ability to go it alone. After this "graduation ceremony," the Learner gradually modulates this rhythm, with no abrupt changes, to a new and personal rhythm. When that rhythm settles into a repeatable groove, the process is repeated. The new Teacher will then look to the person on the left and nod, indicating that the rhythm is ready to be learned and the third person in the circle becomes a rhythm Learner, absorbing the second person's phrase to finally getting the "go ahead" from the Teacher. This third person continues the pattern until the whole circle has learned and taught a rhythm. If anyone finds a rhythm too difficult, you have the option of saying "I pass," to the Teacher, upon which the Teacher shifts her.his attention to the next person over who becomes the Learner. All the others in the circle can also learn each new rhythm but must beat it out soundlessly so as not to interfere with the Teacher-Learner work.

Vocalizations were never used. I don't know why but that seemed right, then and now. When I first worked with these improvisations, they always got going hot and furious, but I never knew how to end them. In time, I found a finish to Rhythm Circle.

When the last person in the circle begins to evolve his.her own rhythm, he.she turns to the one who started it all, teaching it to the first Teacher. When that one, now a Learner, masters it, she.he nods to the rest of the circle and all learn to do that same last rhythm. Rhythm Circle ends when the first Teacher ends it.

This usually makes for a rousing finish. The exercise allows for an enormous amount of aggression from people who are strong rhythmically, and yet in order to do the work well, they must be both good learners and good teachers. This can be achieved only with close attention to the other.

I still can't explain what happened in Austin except to note that there were five participants who were rhythmic virtuosos—two actors and three dancers. They took to this game with a ferocity I've never seen equaled. One would crack out four of the trickiest bars, followed by a wild four-bar variation, and then meticulously repeat the entire eight-bar sequence over and over again. The next, with a deadpan expression, would coolly absorb the complexity and come up with an even more hair-raising phrase. They were like great hoofers challenging each other. The intensity and speed was so great, a few found blood blisters on their palms.

The best of the rhythm whizzes was something of a leader. He was bright and outspoken, but in every improvisation he would get caught in one characterization: a stiff military figure with mannequinlike elegance. Getting locked into one mannerism is a dead end. It is a gambit to avoid doing anything that is unexpected or revealing. To get him to come loose, I devised a variation combining elements from Solo Dancer (2.2) and Rhythm Circle (3.5) and made it **Go 1-2-3**.

Go 1-2-3
3.6

Make a circle of anywhere from six to a dozen or even twenty people. One person goes to the center. When I call out "Go!" that person begins to dance off the impulses of the moment. The focus of the people making up the circle is to sense, feel and finally determine the inner rhythm that is driving the dancer. Finding the underlying, basic, repetitive rhythm that supports the improvisation of the soloist is an individual and silent activity. If it helps, you can, without making any sound, pat out the rhythm you perceive on your thighs. After a period of time I will shout "Go 2!" whereupon everyone in the circle will beat out with hands, feet and/or voice the rhythm you found individually. Try to be heard by the soloist despite the chaotic sounds of the others and hang on stubbornly to what you believe is the best rhythm to support the soloist—yours.

After a while, I will call out, "Go 3!" Now, as you are supporting the soloist listen closely to your neighbors and, retaining the character of your rhythm, musically blend it with what you hear. Once you are meshing with your neighbors, shift your focus to the soloist. There are many choices open to you at this point. While keeping a musical relationship with your neighbors, your sounds can either challenge the soloist, support the soloist, mock the soloist, or whatever. Your attitude toward the soloist and what he.she is doing will shape the music/rhythms you and the others are creating.

I asked my oh-so-bright young rhythm whiz to take the center space. He started, as always, with his toy general posturing, but the circle wasn't buying what he was doing and they began a combination of a heavy rock beat and a pounding African rhythm. They were seeing what he apparently wasn't doing. He stubbornly ignored their orchestrated sound in favor of his prim, jerky style. His endurance was less than theirs, and to catch his breath, he slouched to his knees; but they would have none of it and increased the volume and intensity of their rhythms. A bit more of this and he rolled over on his back. Mocking them, he began to shake his shoulders, and before he knew it, he was swept into a wild thrashing about that resembled a tantrum. Again, driven to exhaustion, he stopped and, in the simplest way, rose to his feet, the circle going with him and relaxing, went a quiet, kooky shuffle—totally unlike anything he had ever done before. Finally, I said, "OK," everybody fell back, aware that something had really happened.

As noted, at that time I didn't know how to end most of my exercises, except by saying, "OK," but the peculiar value of this EGAS was that the longer it went, the deeper it reached. He got so tired he could barely go on, and it didn't seem to matter what he did. The toy general disappeared and a latent fury flared for a bit, followed by a slightly embarrassed self-mockery. I have never done this EGAS with more than twenty people, but I imagine it could succeed with more than that. To stack the deck, I would pick a hot and responsive improvisor.

This was the first breakthrough. Something had loomed up that was different from what I had seen with the Open Theatre or anywhere else. Returning to Go 1-2-3 again and again, there in Austin and later, I would witness dancers start the exercise mannered and controlled and then, in that sea of sound and past the point of exhaustion, with a new flush of energy, strike out in forms, gestures and dance that were not only startlingly beautiful, but almost always a retrospective surprise to the soloist, the dancer. Turning the corner of being too tired to care, movement would pour out that seemed to come from deep, lovely, and sometimes dark places, though after Austin, I never saw anything quite as violent.

Because Rhythm Circle and Go 1-2-3 focused on only one individual at a time, I hit upon a structure that would involve everyone. I had an old rock record, so badly worn that at about its third minute it would invariably get stuck in a maddening repetition. Early in one of the sessions I said to the entire group:

Lose Your Head **3.7**	Find a turning movement that meshes with what you hear. Your inner action is to lose your head, whatever that means to you. Call it **Lose Your Head**.

I let this go for a long time, hoping the dancers would get to a place that wasn't constantly checked and controlled by the narcissistic self-conscious attempts of most dancers, actors and people to *look* like something rather

23

than to *be* something. It "worked," but I only gave this a couple of times because the group was large and my observational skills were as yet untrained. I wasn't sure of what I was seeing. The very "success" of the exercise produced enough wild movement to create a risk factor I thought best to avoid.

Toward the end of the workshop we were invited to give a showing before the entire theatre department. In the first couple of exercises, my workshop people were acting as if they were caught doing something naughty, and the audience seemed to agree with them. Something had to be done. I gathered them together and told them to run as fast as they could in a circle filling the entire stage, and every time they reached downstage center they were to shout as loudly as they could whatever they thought of the audience. A few mild obscenities and some intellectual putdowns hurtled toward the startled viewers who now warmed to my workshoppers.

I then set up a Go 1-2-3 and gave center space to my best dancer who, of course, started off with classroom modern dance technique and many lovely attitude turns. Again the circle would have none of it, and they set up a rocking, insinuating body of rhythms. Soon she began to dance a laughing, lazy Salome. It was a most witty and sexy dance and afterward she muttered over and over, ". . . but, I never did anything like that."

In subsequent workshops, I rarely have found groups as rhythmically skilled or musically cohesive as this one. To solve this, I occasionally use a variation of Go 1-2-3.

Go 1-2-3
Variation
3.6a

During the phase of Go 2, which can become a fierce cacophony, the soloist carries the improvisation around the perimeter of the circle listening for the "musician" who seems to understand and support him.her best. When the soloist makes a decision, he.she calls out, "Go 3!" in front of the chosen one. All the others in the circle now move as close as they can to this music leader and begin to blend their rhythm with the one chosen.

This eliminates the need for a leader to call the changes and it makes for better music, but because the soloist chooses, the confrontational possibilities are diminished. Without confrontation what happens to theatre and art?

The mix of actors and dancers in the Austin workshop was working: one group challenging the others with its easy access to emotions and the other flaunting its physical freedom. A few people in each group were musically trained, and because word had spread that something was happening, some musicians began to come to the sessions. Trying to draw in all these talents, I came up with a strange structure, Tell a Dream. The story of how it evolved is typical of the way most of the Workgroup structures achieved their forms. The fifth evening I gave this setup:

Those who wish to be musicians, be it singing, beating out percussion, or playing an instrument, line the back wall. All the others but one spread out on the floor, standing, sitting or lying down. One person will offer to tell us a brief recurring dream. The task of all others—musicians, dancers and actors—is to respond physically and/or vocally to whatever comes from the Teller: individual words, intonation, general story line, or what you see. The Teller is free to move or not.

The first time I gave this, there were flashes of enormous excitement and unexpected development, but too much was happening at once, with no depth. The second time, I asked the same Teller to repeat the dream, but to say only one word or brief phrase at a time, allowing a large chunk of silence in between. This excruciatingly slow-paced method produced results that were startling and sometimes a little frightening. This was true of a number of the exercises I gave in Austin. Was there something in the peculiar nature of that group? Could it be Texas? It is sloppy thinking to generalize about people and places. Suffice to say, the violence of some of the images and interactions that occurred there both excited and repelled me. I never encountered anything quite like it again. What follows is a fairly detailed description of how **Tell a Dream** finally achieved a well-worked out form:

Tell a Dream 3.8

I will ask whether anyone has a short recurring dream and is willing to tell it to us. The volunteer sits in the middle of the room with a loud percussion instrument, like a pair of claves. Two loud raps precede each time of speaking; it is the signal for everyone to quiet down.

The Teller reveals the dream in single words and/or short phrases, saying each word or phrase twice and then allowing twenty to thirty seconds to elapse before speaking again. Example: Teller raps twice, "I . . . I . . ." Pause of about twenty to thirty seconds. Teller raps twice, "am standing . . . am standing . . ." pause . . . raps, "in front . . . in front . . ." pause . . . raps, "of a door . . . of a door . . ." and so on. After listening, the others allow each word to set off a chain of associations and responses—in movement or vocalization—with as little "taste" as possible, that is, no matter how obvious, arcane, literal, surreal or abstractly kinesthetic the association and its concomitant responses are. Make no attempt to screen them. Words—verbalizations—are out. Why? Words are too often and easily a tactic to evade deep feelings. The Teller is exposing a potentially vulnerable part of her.himself. Negative sounds and motions may be disturbing to the Teller, but words can really break bones.

Everything we experience can be said to move/send energy in two directions. A stone dropped into water sends waves out along the surface but also descends into the depths. Just so, anything we experience spreads out, making connections to this and that and simultaneously slides down through our layers of consciousness, ultimately touching and provoking matters of which we are dimly or not at all aware.

Allow what you receive to shoot out into the open with the most literal and obvious connection responses and also allow it to penetrate into obscure corners of your minds, experiencing what the Teller says without any qualifications of logic. You may or may not interact with each other. Interaction with the Teller is possible, but never to the extent of interfering with the telling. The double percussion raps are the signal to all the listeners to stop making any sound or movement until the Teller speaks. The Teller must speak loudly and clearly. (If it is a very large group and in a large space, a P.A. system should be used for audibility.) When the Teller raps *three* times, that is the signal that the next word or expression will be the end of the dream. From then on, everyone, Teller and listeners, can leave the floor when you feel you have dealt with what the material evoked in you. Interaction between the Teller and the others is an option.

As in so many of these structures, it is critical that the listeners recognize that slow responses are devices for distancing oneself from the given material. Responding like light reflecting from water gives no time to reflect, plan or evade the unexpected or a deep but uncomfortable reaction. Also, there is the trap of listeners getting into a "shtick" rather than responding specifically to each new word or phrase.[4] After a while, the listeners have the interesting problem of responding not only to the individual words but to the emerging sense of the dream and finally, of course, to its totality.

Tell a Dream was a part of almost every workshop until 1970 when the percursor Workgroup got under way. I never quite got over my tensions about it, for though it brought out strong and surprising work from many, it brought out the worst in others. Perhaps the memory of those exciting but hair-raising sessions in Texas kept hovering in the background. In later years, so many new, rich forms were coming up every day that Tell a Dream sank below the horizon, though I have never forgotten how it helped open the door to a new and powerful way of dancing. I think it was and is potentially a very productive line of work, though I never pursued or developed it.

As I write this, I am wondering why I never evolved an obvious and probably fruitful variation, **Tell a Poem**. To make amends, here it is.

Tell a Poem
3.9

A week before, the dancers are given the assignment of finding a short poem which quickens them: a Haiku or a short Indian poem.[5] Better still, ask them to write their own two-sentence poems. Follow the same structure as for Tell a Dream.

---

4. A schtick is literally a vaudeville bit. Colloquially, it is a piece of theatre business that pleases, tickles, gives confidence to the doer and tends to become a mannerism, i.e., an automatic response which more often than not is inappropriate.

5. See pp. 94–95 below.

As a part of the scheme of the Austin workshop, I would open up some of the time to the students, saying, "By now, you see the direction in which we are heading. Would any of you like to contribute a game or exercise, or some new ideas based on this material?" This being 1969—encounter time, touching time, "authentic experience" time, etc.—some of the students brought forth garbled versions of Esalen exercises. I'm not putting these down. It's simply that they were often not relevant to the focus of the workshop and a few were manipulative like the blunt command, "Love the person next to you!" However, one student gave a structure that proved to have value, and another one made a suggestion that in time evolved into the central structure of the Workgroup. The first was right off the Monterey Peninsula and the Living Theatre. Later, I dubbed it **The Big Oh!**

The Big Oh!
3.10

A circle of five to eight surrounds a dancer. With eyes closed, the dancer falls in any direction with arms at the side, feet together and a body that doesn't bend. The task of those in the circle is to catch the falling/tilting figure and gently push him.her into balance. The dancer is constantly falling from one side to the other. Gentleness is the order of the day. It takes some people a long time not to bend the body to avoid a "blind" fall into limbo. Learning to fall with a straight body and closed eyes asks for a faith in the other dancers. Most people who do this exercise learn it quickly and enjoy the feel of it.

After a while—three, four, five minutes—the circle senses the end of this phase, and the dancer is tilted backward into the supporting arms of the others to be suspended horizontally. Carefully and slowly, the dancer is lifted overhead and when everyone's arms are outstretched, the group slowly rotates about three times. Then, gently lowering the dancer, they cradle and rock him.her forward and back. After a while, the "cradlers" will know that the sequence for that dancer is finished and they will gently tip the dancer back up on his.her feet.

The usual reaction of the dancer upon standing and opening the eyes starts with a bit of dizziness, then a childish smile, a bewilderment, and the oft-expressed wish that it had gone on longer. In setting this up, the leader must, of course, first assess the strength of the group and the weight of the person being lifted.

A couple of years later, for the Workgroup, I suggested that if any of the company came in hurting, lonely, upset, whatever, that person would have the privilege of announcing, "I need attention," and we would all be beholden to perform The Big Oh! for her.him. Weird, no one ever did. In subsequent years of workshops I learned that it is a useful sequence for a group that is uptight, having problems with the contact and close proximity of other dancers. They learn that the support and touching of others can be nonthreatening and actually liberating.

The Big Oh! also sheds light on another aspect of improvisation, how a group finishes an activity and/or commences another by "common consent." At first, beginnings and endings were set verbally by me as the leader. When the Workgroup began to take shape with me as one of the dancers, confusion arose. How to finish what had not been choreographed without a leader/director? Working an improvisation alone, one senses with little equivocation, "Aha! The end is here!" But how do you get two, four, six, or even eight people to stop without a messy, staggered series of uncertain terminations? The loveliest surprise of all: after working with each other for a while, we developed a sensibility that could recognize when we had accomplished our task and made our point. In time, the moment to stop became as palpable as a bell ringing. We just knew, but it took time to get there. It's too much to expect people new to improvisation and new to each other to be skilled at this. However, if from the beginning they are told that they can stop when they sense they are finished, they will, in time, develop that skill and sensitivity internally and in concert with others.

During a lull in the second week of the Austin workshop, I again asked whether anyone had a form along the lines of the work we were doing. My best dancer spoke up: "Back home in Connecticut, I have a big basement in which my friend and I would practice whenever we could. One of the things we loved to do best was to put on a piece of music we both liked and then dance looking at each other. It was as if I was dancing about her and she was dancing about me. I don't mean "about" as "around." I mean that she and what she was doing was the subject of my dance and vice versa. We could do this all afternoon."

It sounded good, but not sensational. I said, "Fine," and asked her to explain once again to everyone what they were to do. People paired off and I put on my then favorite piece of music for an extended improvisation, Stravinsky's *Sacre du Printemps*. It turned out quite well. Not only did the energy flow right through its entire length but the actors and the dancers appeared to lose self-consciousness and become fully absorbed in each other. They were playful, teasing and serious in turn. I immediately saw that this was a useful form. It involved everyone, built up a good dance heat and, best of all, it asked for and seemed to produce exactly the frame of mind I had discovered with the Open Theatre and had been trying to create at this workshop: a loss of focus upon self, replaced by focus on the task at hand and/or the other—the other person. To repeat her description of **A Duet**.

A Duet
3.11

Everyone pairs off. (If there is an odd number, three can form a trio or someone can drop out to observe.) When the music starts, you dance looking at your partner and dancing about your partner, *about* his.her hair, clothing, personality traits, eyes—anything that gets your attention.

From the seed of this simple structure there sprouted the spine of the Workgroup. Out of it came almost a dozen EGAS that made for wonderful dancing and profound experiences not only for us but for our audiences. Too bad, I no longer know the name of that young dancer. At the time, I had no inkling where this little exercise would lead us. Perhaps she will read this and know that I thank her and, while I'm at it, the rest of that group of young actors and dancers who took every challenge I threw at them and carried them further than I expected. They opened doors for me. In Austin, Texas, at times all hell broke loose but that's where the Workgroup idea was born— even though I didn't know it at the time.

College Park, Maryland

During the 1969 fall semester, except for the two weeks in Texas, I took the train from New York to Washington, D.C. every Thursday morning and returned to New York late on Friday. I taught several technique classes and on Thursday evenings conducted an improvisation workshop—for dancers only. Here the atmosphere was radically different: cautious, uncertain, a bit defensive and never far from being concerned about how they looked, but with all that, very curious, intelligent and trying hard to get at what I was putting before them.

I spun them through all of it, but little took fire except for two games which evolved there. Go 1-2-3 was a lead balloon. Desperate for them to learn to sense the inner rhythm of another person, I came up with a new one, **Rhythm Portrait**.

Rhythm Portrait 3.12

Prowl around each other, observing everyone covertly: never let anyone catch you looking at them. You are looking for the person in the group who interests you the most, positively or negatively. You are looking for the one who gets to you the most. Once you have made your decision, concentrate your powers of observation on that person only, learning all you can by the simple act of looking—still never allowing that person to know it is he.she in whom you are interested. Ultimately what you are trying to sense is his.her internal rhythm in the form of a repeated phrase.

When I call out, "the rhythm," start to physically beat out, with your hands or your mouth, the rhythm you have unearthed—but do it silently. When I call out, "Now!" make the rhythm audible and as loud as is true of the character you have been observing. Allow what motions are needed to support the rhythm.

Second stage: One by one, take the center of the space and beat out for all to hear the rhythm you have discovered, moving and covering space at the same time. All the others learn the rhythm and follow the motion of the dancer in the center.

Third stage: When everyone has had their turn in the center, I ask each to find a private place in the studio. Once there I ask, "Which one of the rhythms you learned felt good? Made you feel strong? Made you want to dance? Try to recapture that rhythm. Once you have a handle on it improvise with that rhythm as the center of your focus."

When they finished I asked each dancer to go back to the beginning and once again do the Rhythm Portrait of the person that interested them originally and then, one by one, announce aloud her.his name. My hope was that in the second stage each person would be attracted to what another had observed as their "own" rhythm. This happened in only a few cases. All that really worked was the initial step, the creation of the Rhythm Portrait. It seemed that if one looked deeply into another, one could glean a powerful piece of music, a rhythm that was arresting without being arbitrarily inventive. That was exciting to the group and to me. They did not try to *make* rhythms; they *found* them. I've hardly ever done this again. I suspect that it can work with a group that is not only rhythmically sophisticiated but has developed the skill to plunge into an awareness of others.

The next one never acquired a neat name. I called it **Passing Through a Physical Object.**

Passing Through a Physical Object 3.13

Form a big circle. When I tap any one of you on the shoulder, go to the center of the circle and on the impulse of the moment take any position—standing, sitting or lying down. The next person in the circle does the same, only some part of his.her body must touch the first person's body. Person after person, going around the circle, adds her.his body to the structure of bodies until one person is left. This one positions him.herself at the point where the diameter of the group is the greatest and must now walk, wend, crawl, wriggle his.her way through—never around—the group without disturbing or forcing anyone to change her.his position. Coming out on the other side, he.she taps a body who rises, permitting the first person to take her.his place, and now this second person performs the same task of passing through the widest part of the conglomerate of bodies without disturbing or changing anyone's position. If one of you is tapped and has already made the "journey," convey that fact by not responding to the tap, which tells the person to try another.

After everyone has traversed the structure, I will call out, "Find a private area for yourself." Now alone, do what you did working your way through the others. Do exactly what you did with only the *memory* of the other bodies to guide you. Do it once alone, then find a partner and do it for him.her to critique, and then observe your partner critically, thus both helping each other learn to make the imaginary tangible.

This exercise is valuable for several reasons. First, it opens up the possibility of body contact, without which improvisation is impoverished. Second, the task is so demanding, like the challenge of crawling under a folding chair without moving it, that self-preoccupation and self-decorativeness are improbable (The Obstacle, 3.4). Finally, Passing Through a Physical Object is an ideal exercise in sense memory for dancers because it uses the whole body. The familiar actor's exercises, like sewing on a button or putting on a garment, place the strongest emphasis on the hands—which already are the smartest part of the body, physically. Sense-memory exercises are a staple of the actor's training and a skill that no dancer can afford to neglect. It means what it says: having a vivid, sensual memory of actions with real objects. In the exercise, or in performance, the real object is imagined/remembered/sensed—whatever—so that the motion of the performer is determined by truth of the remembering.[6]

Another less personal and more athletic version of Passing Through a Physical Object is **Slalom**, which is exactly what it sounds like.

Slalom
3.14

Everyone picks an observation-partner. All the observers stand aside—to observe! The others, one by one, form a single line, about one to two yards apart. This line can be arrow straight or chaotically crooked, it matters not. When the last person is in place, I will shout "Go!" and the person who started it all will run full tilt down the line, slalom style, and take a position at the other end. When she.he arrives, the next person in line does the same.

When the last person has performed the run, all gather around the point where the line started. One by one, run from where you started, duplicating the slalom run as if all those dancers were still standing there. When the running group has done this, find your observer-partner and learn how vividly and accurately you repeated your run. The critique concluded, the second group repeats the ritual. Finally, repeat the entire sequence a second time, the running and the critiques.[7]

As Picasso was so fond of iterating, "Art is a lie." There is so little onstage that is real, that without a rich and continuous infusion of imagination, the whole edifice of credibility collapses. Passing Through a Physical Object and Slalom, two highly physical sense-memory exercises, are essentially exercises in imagination. The muscles of imagination always need exercising.

Earlier, I noted that a few at the University of Maryland were defensive. One was an athletic and strong dancer. After what I think was the fifth session, just before a class was about to start, he came over to talk to me. He was worried. He felt that we were doing dangerous work, that one could get into a fantasy world and not be able to get out. At the time, I was not only shocked by this fear but I did not have a good answer except to say, "Don't do

6. Tamiris had an exercise in which she had actors going through, over and under furniture to a rhythmical beat. Heightened sense memory was not the target of this but rather the cultivation of agility and physical daring. See the discussion of Backs (6.11) below.

7. In an Asian dance or theatre school this EGAS would be repeated many times until the illusion of the line would be as vivid as the runner.

anything you don't want to, and if you don't want to do the work at all, don't come to class. Write up what we've done to date. Don't worry about the grade. You can have an *A* either way."[8]

I've heard this fear expressed only once again in over twenty years of doing this work. It may have been present and not articulated more often than I realized, so I would like to confront it here. It baffles me. I myself am delighted at every opportunity to enter an imaginery world, to become someone else, be it a happy figure or one caught in a tragedy. It's a game I love. Ergo, I am a performer. Those who fear the game of losing self in the imaginary world are not performers at heart. Moreover, they may have been living with an anxiety of stepping off and not being able to get back long before they came in contact with these improvisations.

One occasionally runs across the myth that actors can go mad, unable to free themselves of a role. The closest this comes to reality, in my experience, is that some film actors say they became depressed when working for several months on a grim character; but most indicate that when the shooting is over, they emerge from it. I've never heard of any person of the theatre getting irretrievably lost in a character other than their own—except for people with a history of mental imbalance, and they were not in the profession.

My guess? That young man got to a place he didn't like, he didn't want to deal with it, and wouldn't risk going there again. That's his prerogative; mine has always been if it's there, I want to know about it, no matter how hair- raising. For me, the fantasy world clarifies the "real" world. Experiences in the world of imagination help me live in the "real" world. The last two sentences could very well serve to delineate the function of art. I should add that I use quotes around "real" because in art it is an ambiguous word when juxtaposed to "fantasy." If there is a fantasy, it exists, and if it exists, it has a reality that may need defining—but it does exist. Thus, a "fantasy" in this sense is as much a part of reality as what we are prone to call "real." If this were not so, actors, dancers, musicians and poets would be out of work.

After this encounter, whenever I sensed the slightest reluctance from an individual or a group, I would say, "You don't have to do anything you don't want to do, and if all of this is too much for you, drop the course (or the workshop)." For improvisation, I think that's a good ground rule. Knowing that one can back out makes it easier to try things. The first thing a cat does on coming into a strange area is to see whether there is a way out. Smart cats.

8. Being only a visitor to the academic establishment at that time, I could afford to make broad gestures. When I taught as a faculty member at Arizona State University from 1982 to 1992, be assured, no one got a free lunch.

The semester at the University of Maryland finished, I, a soloist by profession, was ready to work with others on this new and provocative stuff that had sprouted out of a few simple Open Theatre exercises. Back in New York, I mailed out an invitation to the dancers I thought/hoped would be ready for this leap. (Part of the text is quoted above, in the Introduction.) The call was for Saturday, December 13, 1969. My appointment book for that day reads:

2:00 P.M.   Workgroup

This is the first time that the name "Workgroup" appears in any of my notes. On the facing page were some notes that I used to address the twenty-odd dancers who attended:

no judgment
not care what anyone thinks.
the right to fail
working thru the cliché
Chaikin's for whom?
Dancer = actor = dancer
u don't have to do anything
u don't know what it looks like
u don't try to be interesting
u don't try to be effective.
Positive—You act—you do
Knee pads
There is no system
———
20 Cent Art   Formalism?
———
Romanticism   Existentialism
———
For a while no notes
———
freedom sought here is
direct response to the object
———
Our movement facility

Though some of these notations are a bit obscure to me today, this list contains what developed into the guiding principles of all that followed. Katie Fraser, a dancer and my secretary, took notes at that first meeting:

We came together and chose a premise that we can apply to the Workgroup: The essence of the experience cannot come from any individual. It must come from those around him. . . . One oustanding fact is that physicality tends to become such an overwhelming force that dancers become slaves to body control and perfection. . . . Can we use the control and concentration to kick deeper and deeper *into* rather than form a protective layer *over* the essence of whatever is going on inside?

4 The Workgroup Workshop, 1969

The first step had been taken with the meeting on December 13; the next was a workshop open to all who wished to attend—the Workgroup Workshop. It would meet every Saturday for an hour-and-a-half technique class, lunch (I always leave time for lunch), and three to four hours of improvisation. One dollar charge per week for expenses. We met in a cavernous Soho loft on Broadway which I rented from Meredith Monk. It was L-shaped, over one hundred feet long, a ceiling at least twenty feet high and badly lit. There was something about the too much space, the bare harshness of the place, the impoverished lighting, no place to dress, a toilet miles away in a neighbor's loft, that was alienating. I never felt at home there, though the large areas of darkness were peculiarly appropriate to the fruitful hunt that went on during the long Saturday afternoons.

Very quickly, the work fell into a pattern that was built around four exercises: The Mind-Wash (3.2). The Mirror (2.4), collectively called Yoga Mirror, A Duet (3.11), and the yet to be described Circles (4.1). Though they were not yet held together by a single specific theme or action, there was a subtle thread that accounted for their sequence. People were asked to pick partners, to sit facing each other cross-legged, and to start with Yoga Mirror: The Mind-Wash followed by The Mirror. There was no decisive way to end Yoga Mirror except for me to announce "OK," based on sensing as best I could that all had "done it."

"Done it." What did that mean? I felt that deep within this not so simple act of looking at the other and "becoming the other" by passively mirroring whatever the other did, every dancer in the room had the rare chance to gain an insight into the human with whom their dance would flow, not to dance with *a* dancer but with *this* dancer. If we didn't know at least a bit of who and what the other was, who and what would we respond to once we moved into the world of art and artifice—the world of imagined and created beings?

Following Yoga Mirror, I would wait until I felt the room saturated with connections between people. Then, I would introduce **Circles**.

Circles
4.1

With your eyes closed, listen to the sequence of the next exercise. You will hear better with your eyes closed. First, you will hear music.[1] After a while, I will say, "Someone or something is doing something," choosing any verb; flying, loving, hunting, planting, destroying, shielding, ad infinitum. Suppose I say, "Someone or something is *running* to or from someone or something." The "someone or something" must come from you. It can come from any part of your mind: books you have read, films, history, TV, friends, your own life. When you know who or what that someone or something is, with your eyes still closed, stand. Be certain that the someone or something is a specific. Is the runner a woman? a lion? a bird? a raindrop running down a window pane? If it is a woman, what is the color of her hair? Does she have a name? Do you know her? In other words, you must find in your mind a specific running man or woman or bird or lion or whatever and never, ever, the general idea of a man, a woman or a bird. When everyone is standing, we will go on to the next step. While you are standing, waiting for the others, use your time to learn all you can about X, the someone or something known only to you. Look at X from all sides, from close up and far away. Can you smell X? The more specifics you learn about X, the richer and more personal will be the movement that emerges from this work.

The images you select may range from the literal, like the time you broke your nasty neighbor's window and fled the scene, to the metaphoric, like the memory of a raindrop running down a window pane last week. You might recall Atalanta from the myths of long ago Greece, the princess who would marry only the man who could beat her in a foot race. If he lost, he also lost his head. A crafty suitor, Hippomenes, hid three golden apples in his tunic, throwing them in her path one by one. She paused to pick them up, and thus Hippomenes won the race—and the princess. You may choose anything—yourself: fleeing, a raindrop, Atalanta or Hippomenes—so long as it is a specific image and not a generalization or an abstraction.

When everyone is standing, I will stop the music and rewind the tape to the beginning. As I am doing this, each of you should sit, stand, kneel or lie down—whichever is an appropriate place from which to become X. Above all, know that it is you who are doing this and not X. Do not for a moment try at this stage to "become" or look like your X. To do so will shape all you do into a chain of clichés.

When you hear the music, something that may appear strange will

---

1. The favorite at the time was a thirty-minute tape of superb and varied African drumming, ending with fusion of smokey jazz and North African drumming. The high, ecstatic energy seemed to lubricate their imaginations and their bodies. Originally, the scores I used were rich with varied texts, like Stravinski's *Sacre du Printemps*. In time, I learned that in most cases, the best scores for improvisation were those, unlike *Sacre*, that had a long sustained line that did not change frequently.

happen: your scalp, your ears, your brows, your eyes will become X running. Do not question the logic or the feasibility of brows running. At the center of what we do as dancers is the use of the body and its parts as metaphors for the whole world. Is there any gesture as giving and baring of oneself as the arabesque? If running is the action of X, then run with your scalp, your ears, your brows and your eyes. If it is appropriate to X that your eyes remain closed, fine. If open is true to this moment for X, then open let them be.

After a while, I will say, "Whenever you are ready, become X running with your jaw, your nose, your lips, your tongue." If you are still deeply involved with the first action, finish it before going on to the mouth. When you do go on, *do not lose what you have done.* That continues.

In time, I will continue, saying, "Whenever you are ready, with your neck, become X running."[2]

Then ". . . with your chest become X running."

Then ". . . with your shoulders become X running."

Then ". . . with your elbows become X running."

Then ". . . with your hands become X running."

As you go on, lose nothing of what you have been doing. You are constantly accumulating, though at each stage your action is being led by that new part of the body.

Then ". . . with your waist, belly, voice become X running."

Then ". . . with your pelvis become X running."

Then ". . . with your thighs and knees become X running."

Then " . . . with your feet become X running."

Then "Whenever you are ready with all of you, with your totality become X running."

In this last stage, a time will come when you will have "become" X. When you sense that transformation, celebrate it and then leave the floor.

Two negatives: First, this is not an exercise in isolations; rather, the entire body supports the action of the individual parts. Second, this is not an exercise in exploring the range of movement that is possible, say, of your mouth or your hands or whatever. The motions are governed strictly by the image and action being fulfilled. Sticking to the specific action of a specific someone or something will create rich movement. Isolations or variation games will convert the entire exercise into an academic excursion irrelevant to our work and intention.

I would then give a quick review of Circles and then open the space to questions before actually starting. I created it as part of our ritual because I believed it would accomplish two things. It was the simplest way to intro-

---

2. Timing the intervals between calling out the parts of the body is a delicate matter ideally done by feel and not by the clock. A section can be one minute, two or three. The conductor of the exercise needs only to pay close attention to the flow of energy in the group.

duce, in a way that dancers would understand, a source of creative movement that I had learned in the Stanislavski technique of acting and from Helen Tamiris. In Circles, one never asks for an emotion or a mood. That is the direct highway to banality. One always asks for an *action* on the assumption that the specific "who" doing a specific action in a specific context will arrive at a truthful emotion or mood. To ask each part of your body to become in turn a fine-boned, young, red, female fox fleeing the hounds in a driving rain would in time produce a gut emotion of unquestioned intensity, a genuine feeling in the body of the dancer and some fascinating movement.

The second value of Circles is that it becomes a profound lesson in the metaphoric possibilities of the various parts of the body. Without this awareness, which opens the door to a mastery of poetic dance metaphors, the entire way of working that is presented here would degenerate into one continuous flow of literal movement which is the last thing one wants from dancers. In dance, a strategic moment of the literal has been the strongest part of some of our best works and the key to some ostensibly abstract dances. But as a primary mode of expression, the literal becomes acting and negates the meaning and point of the dance art.

One both unexpected and yet obvious note: During the various stages of Circles, the dancer will probably come across one part of the body which translates into a literal action. Say the image is of Hippomemes in the Greek myth racing to keep his head from being cut off and to gain Princess Atalanta for his wife. At the moment when the leader calls out, "With your feet become X running," the dancer may find him.herself dashing through the studio. Here, the literal may prove to be the most exhilarating of all the segments. Moreover, if most of what had gone before was retained, the running may be like no running that had ever been done, since this literal movement is an island within a circle of metaphors for the same action.

You never know anything until it happens. It is very important in all improvisation not to look ahead, not to anticipate. Anticipation and, even worse, planning cut out the heart and meaning of improvisation. Improvisation starts out with a set of givens, rules and wishes, and from then on, one deals with the immediate present never knowing what will happen until it does happen.

Circles as a concept was derived from my reading of *Character Analysis* by the psychiatric thinker and writer, Wilhelm Reich. He believed that the body had specific bands of energy that radiated out from the spine: from the skull, the neck, the chest, the waist, the pelvis, and so on. His thought was that a healthy, well-integrated human being has freedom of motion through the entire length of the body. "Motility" was the lovely word he used. He further believed and taught that the lack of motility in a particular horizontal circle of the body indicated a specific emotional disturbance, and he described this immobility and rigidity as "armoring." I felt that using this schematic division of the body would be a way of freeing it imaginatively—and it did.

The improvisations were full of surprises both to me the viewer and, more importantly, to the dancers in the workshop. In the little talks we would have after a break in the work, time and again, a dancer would say, "I never did anything like that." "I never moved like that." "I was completely into that." "I forgot the studio—all the others." "I didn't know I was dancing."

I am not carrying the flag for Wilhelm Reich and his theories, but I did draw another good structure from his idea of counterpointing "motility" and "armoring," **Hot to Cold to Hot.**

Hot to Cold to Hot 4.2

When the group finished Circles, I would sometimes ask, "Was there some part of the body that felt remarkably free? Was there some part of the body that felt frozen, almost incapable of moving? I will play the music again. Take all the time you need to get back into X. When you are there, let that part of the body that was freest take the lead. When it is flowing and hot and whenever you are ready, shift to that frozen part as the lead *while thinking, feeling, sensing the fluidity of the free part.* Keep shifting back and forth to thaw out what resists the action.

Thus, one part of the body can lead the more timid part into a freer and more expressive mode of moving.

Returning to the notes of this period kept by Katie Fraser:

December 20, 1969 (Our first session.) Circles: Starting with the top of the head, then the mouth and jaw, neck, shoulders, chest, arms, elbows, hands, belly, pelvis, legs, feet, each to lead the energy, then the whole thing. Then back to your partner for the duet. You start from wherever you both ended up. And you take your movement off your partner.

A Duet (3.11) was done just as described earlier: they danced to their partners, only now each had had the experience of going through The Mind-Wash (3.2) and Yoga Mirror (3.3) with the same person, separating to do Circles (4.1), and then coming together again loaded with the richness of Circles and the impact of the earlier contact. The sequence had an obvious logic and a surprising result. The duets now were not merely two dancers dancing to each other and the music; instead, complex and intense relationships seemed to appear from nowhere. Some pairs seemed mutually privy to a scenario created spontaneously without a word being exchanged: a wild animal and a tamer exchanging roles, a manipulating seducer and a fearful quarry, a struggler enveloped by a mothering figure, a prophet of old circumventing a gyrating Salome.

More than ever, I knew I was on to something fertile, and over the weeks, as dancers came and went, gradually a Workgroup nucleus began to form. They too sensed that something important was happening in that monster cave of a loft. In the ensuing weeks, I introduced some vocal exercises and later, for a few visits, this work was graced by the fine teaching of Joe Chaikin and Paul Zimet, one of the Open Theatre's finest actors. My logic was simple: the actors found times when they needed dance to speak their poem. Might not we the dancers find the time when we needed speech to fill out our dance? If the tool of the voice had to be available, should we require it, it had better be a good strong voice—as strong and expressive as our bodies. It was a very good idea, but it never really unfolded in the life of the Workgroup.

Tamiris's Body Contact (1.2) was given several times, and it became a vivid litmus test for us of our sensitivity and responsiveness. Grouping a pair of pairs, one to do and the other to observe, showed how transparent was a false, inattentive move and the beauty, yes, the visual beauty of a well done Body Contact.

What stands out in my memory of A Duet at this stage: It was strongest when people went deeply into the preparations involved in The Mind-Wash, Yoga Mirror, and particularly Circles. Secondly, it kept its vitality when each dancer fiercely and intently observed and truly danced off the other person. Thirdly, given these circumstances, these duets went on, full tilt, for twenty and thirty minutes. Endurance did not seem to be a problem. A few would start at wild levels of energy but tire quickly and stop—quit! I came to recognize these people as artistic onanists. Their passionate focus never really went beyond the wall of their own skin and the preoccupation with the ecstasy of their own energy. Oppositely, when dancers became thoroughly engrossed in each other, they seemed to have the energy to go on forever and continually arrive at movements, concepts, images, events that not only surprised and delighted me watching them, but the dancers themselves.

I always left time after each duet for partners to rest, think over what had happened and then talk with each other about the shared experience. I could tell by the level of animation of the discussions how deep and rewarding some of these duets had been. I kept my distance from the discussions because I felt there would be more spontaneous and open exchanges without the evaluations of "Herr Direktor." Finally, I would assemble the entire group to share information and questions. Throughout the history of the Workgroup and even now in workshops, this time of talk was/is my barometer, telling me what was working, was was not, and what needed to be done to move forward. Occasionally what happened was so strong, so moving and so right, we savored it silently and after a while went on with something else.

Tell a Dream (3.8) and The Chord (2.3), were soon introduced to this group. Dream proved to be provocative and evocative while The Chord was elusive. The rule that no one was to initiate produced interminable stretches of silence, or an inadvertent cough might set off the sound effect for a tuberculosis sanitarium. Long afterward I came to believe—or realize—that for the Open Theatre, The Chord was a ritual, meaning they knew what would happen and what it would sound like, and it was a ritual that served their communal spirit. I was then in my purist stage, and planning, anticipation or rituals were all anathema.

Whatever Happens, Happens 4.3

As we gathered for the fifth session of improvisation, someone said, "Wherever you are, you are. Whatever happens, happens."[3] There was a large group present, including several very good musicians. Two hours later we wound down and stopped to rest silently, knowing we had all been swept along by a complexity of events: a jungle of animals, childhood prayers, a Christ figure, statues and politicos on chairs, a mess of independent small-group scenarios, a mock birthday party, Clyde Morgan taking off in a wild solo to drums and then drumming himself only to return to a long lyric solo in which we were his audience and musical supporters. Over a dozen structures and games had emerged spontaneously in one continuous two-hour flow.

An open-ended improvisation such as **Whatever Happens, Happens**, is done occasionally and ideally with people who have had the experience of working together and have arrived at some understanding of their mutual direction. Without these conditions the way is open to self-indulgence, too few insights of value and, worst of all, physical danger. In some dance communities, there are weekly sessions wherein any number of dancers and too many would-be dancers assemble to improvise—simply improvise. Having witnessed but a couple of them, I can only speculate upon their value. To my eye, there were a few moments when "something was happening," when people were communicating and sharing a strong experience. To my eye, the wasted time, the floundering, the self-indulgences and the sheer danger of undirected, unsupervised work with strangers outweighed any perceived advantages. Improvisation, to be a fruitful experience, demands a precise framework and a set of ground rules which are understood and accepted by all who participate. A good improvisation structure is exactly like a game of tennis, basketball, or chess. They are all primarily improvisations, each of which is defined by a precise set of rules, as precise as the lines painted on a tennis court. What happens within those lines and within those rules in unpredictable, as improvisation should be. Ideally, at all times, there should be someone watching to catch moments of value and to call a halt to forestall a bad turn of events. An observer with some authority is required for the rare times when people get rough and take wild risks with themselves or others.

Improvisation can become enormously frustrating when a serious and well-intentioned dancer struggles with the burden of a weak command of English, the only language in which the ground rules have been stated. Let there be one dancer on the floor who has misunderstood the given improvisation structure or who, wilfully disregards the ground rules, and all will begin to flounder and wish the damn thing stopped.

Following that first time we did Whatever Happens, Happens, we dis-

---

3. There are three versions of who said it: Katie Fraser writes it was Charles Hayward (a dancer) or Michael Sahl (a musician), I think I said it.

cussed the intensity of the experience, and questions arose: What about rage? What about erotic moments? If real emotions flooded the room could "real" acts be performed? This was no idle question. This was 1969, the very middle of a period that had just discovered the Lost Continent of Feelings. Feelings were sacrosanct, whether they were tender or dangerous, creative or stupid. By some, they were not to be inhibited by evaluation, only sought, particularly by a few acting teachers. They allowed and even encouraged actual hitting, they frightened classes by setting up an invasion of "criminals" or "police," or they themselves might force an erotic gesture upon a timid young woman so that she would for once in her life *feel something!* Little of this invaded the dance field, but then it was in the air and not a few dancers studied acting.

The point I made then and the point I make today is that you can do *anything* in dance as long as you are doing a metaphor for it. Metaphors are what we dancers do for a living. It is unthinkable to physically hurt or actually eroticize another in the course of our work. It would be equally unfortunate were we to impoverish the depth of our artistic life by not dealing with these impulses, and any other impulses, poetically.

During that same fifth session the opposite question was raised. "What do you do if you're out of it? Cold. Watching yourself. Disconnected." No easy answer here. Many possible answers. Keep going, but slow down. Don't force any emotion into the empty space. Pause. Look around. Find a specific focus—the simpler, the better. Find a specific task in relation to that something or someone. Take all the time needed to perform the task, constantly brushing away all self-evaluation and self-criticism as if they were mosquitos. Stay with the task. Don't look ahead. Don't look back. Stay with the task. There is no guarantee that this will deliver and get you "into it," but at least you will be doing something honest and there is a good chance of finding the heat again, particularly if you don't look for it.

More notes from Katie Fraser:

March 28, 1970

No Daniel:
Yoga Mirror first. Agreed to do Circles in a new way. Begin from the inside core and proceed to other areas of the body at your own pace, in any order and linger where you will. When you're done, you're done.

Intermittently, during the time of the Workgroup, I would take off on solo engagements performing *The Peloponnesian War*. As anyone who paints knows, add a color and everything changes. Take a color out and everything changes. Let a director go out on tour—"No Daniel"—and things change. I do not attract dependent people. "No Daniel" never stopped anything and in fact, left to their own devices, the Workshop dancers and later the Workgroup company members working on their own continually came up with new developments that were incorporated in the work.

This new variation on Circles was one of our most important develop-ments. It became **Each Alone**. From then on to any group new to the work, I would give the ground rules for Circles, adding, "This exercise will be given only once. The next time you do the ritual of becoming someone or some-thing doing something, you will be on your own, and that will be called Each Alone." The ground rules for Each Alone start out exactly like Circles. Because this is one of the key EGAS to so much of the work, I am includ-ing the entire description, although some of it repeats the instructions for Circles.

Each Alone
4.4

Each Alone. With your eyes closed, listen. First, you will hear music. After a while, I will say, "Someone or something is doing something." The "someone or something" can come from any part of your mind: books you have read, films, history, TV, friends, your own life. When you know who or what that someone or something is, with your eyes still closed, stand. Be certain that the someone or something is a specific. When everyone is standing, we will go on to the next step. While you are standing, waiting for the others, use your time to learn all you can about X, the someone or something known only to you. Look at X from all sides, from close up and far away. The more specifics you learn about X, the better.

When everyone is standing, I will stop the music and rewind the tape to the beginning. As I am doing this, each of you should sit, stand, kneel or lie down; whichever is an appropriate place from which to become X. Above all, know that it is you who are doing this and not X. Do not for a moment try at this stage to "become" or look like your X. Doing this will create a banality.

When the music starts up again, call up the vision of X doing what X does. Immediately, without plan, allow some *one* part of your body to per-form that act, as X. In time, you will feel as if you "have done" that part— that it has become X doing what X does and you will be ready to move on. Without planning or thinking, another part will be ready to do this. Tak-ing all the time that is needed, you will move on in whatever sequence your body tells you. As you move on, try to retain what you have done. Symmetry is possible but not necessary: the focus of activity might be the shoulders or only the right shoulder. Discard the rigorous logic of Circles and follow instead the dictates of your body and your feelings. Sequence and timing are yours to control. You may never get to body parts men-tioned in Circles and you may become absorbed in an area untouched by Circles. There will come a moment when all the pieces come together and you will be X doing what X does. Celebrate that becoming and then leave the floor.

Without the constant intrusion and interruptions from me, and with the concentration of permitting the action of X to flow through the body undirected, the dancers were able to go much more deeply into the life of X, discovering surprising movement metaphors and, best of all, moving in an imagined context with conviction and freedom. If anything could describe the goal of all performance, "moving in an imagined context with conviction and freedom" certainly touches the center. Each Alone became the key to the powerful rituals that developed out of A Duet. One had to become another in order to be, think, act and dance as another.

These Are Perilous Times was done only once. For some time afterward, the title became a Workshop joke, and it served as an ironic commentary on the life around us.

These Are Perilous Times 4.5

A pair of "weapons" are fashioned by rolling up and taping together about four sheets of newspaper. Set up a "bridge" fifteen to twenty feet long, a narrow corridor shaped by masking tape, benches or chairs that barely permits the passage of two people moving in opposite directions.

Close your eyes and listen. These are perilous times. It is wise and even necessary to go about armed. You are in a lonely place. You are about to cross a bridge when you see at the opposite side a stranger also about to cross. The stranger is armed, just as you are. I will choose two of you to make the crossing, conducting each of you with your eyes closed to opposite ends of the bridge and give you a weapon which you should hold in one hand at your side. When I say, "Open your eyes," everyone, the travelers and the observers, will do so.

The travelers will contemplate each other and on the basis of that long-distance observation arrive at several decisions: Who am I and what are my intentions? Am I an innocent traveler or am I a robber? Who is this person on the other side of the bridge, and what do I think her.his intentions are? Will this person attack me or let me pass? Being what I am and what I have surmised, what is my strategy with an equally armed person?

When each comes to a decision, he.she grasps the "weapon" in both hands. When both have made this move, they begin to cross the bridge, at their own pace, taking whatever action they choose. Whoever strikes the other first "wins." Whoever crosses the bridge safely "wins." Both can pass without attacking. Both can win. Both can be "wounded."

In those days and today, I do not push a structure when I sense resistance. Forcing what is not going down well will probably arrive at forced-flowing improvisation, the exact opposite of what we are seeking. The mockery that a few attached to These Are Perilous Times was enough for me not to return to it; yet it implies, for me, a premise I have long held about people, a premise that lies very close to the heart of the reason for doing the kind of interactive improvisation which is being presented here. I believe that we are all transparent. I believe that we are constantly sending signals—visible signals of what we are thinking, what we fear, what we love, what we hate, what we think of ourselves, what we think of the person before us and *what we are about* to do. Reading these signals is a barely understood skill. Some appear to their fellows to be uncanny in their ability to "read" other people. Some are, as it were, "illiterate" as they gaze upon and interact with other humans.

How to cultivate this talent? Before anything, there must be the *need to know others*, not as they seem, not as they present themselves, but as they are. Knowing others is no light matter, for if we did, we might become responsible for the needs and the pain of the other. Much of our behavior consists of subtle devices to avoid precisely such a burden. We say we feel fine when we don't. We hear a co-worker say she.he feels fine, but if we really listened and looked, we could hear a cry for help, a threat or a declaration of love. I don't believe anyone can lie to you if you want to know the truth. A successful lie needs the cooperation of the listener.

And what does all of this have to do with interactive improvisation? These Are Perilous Times was for me the first expression of a growing belief that our form of dancing—with, to and for another—was a schooling; we were working to develop an acute sensitivity to that subtle and continuous flow of signals we never stop broadcasting to each other, even if we aim for concealment. Our motions, postures, clothing, sounds, choices of space and distance, gestures and words all add up—if only we pay attention to each other, and yes, to ourselves. We spend more energy at cloaking our real intentions from ourselves than from anyone else. If we weren't so good at self-deception, all the counselors and therapists would starve.

As the forms of the exercises, games and structures continued to develop in the next few years, the hunch became a strong belief: that this work could teach its participants the rudiments of "reading the other." These Are Perilous Times might even have worked if the name had been less vulnerable to jesting. Try calling it Crossing the Bridge. Better still, try it. You may get better results than I did.

On March 7 and the session that followed, I got the first hint of how vulnerable people were when they improvised. Woody Vasulka, a pioneer of independent videography who had taped my *Peloponnesian War*, invited the entire Workgroup Workshop to a video studio where he had a job. "Come and do one of your sessions. I'll tape it and you all can look at it." Between fifteen and twenty of us accepted his offer. The session was hair-raising because everyone went overboard with their own predilections. The integrity angels were never so pure and focused, the aggressive ones climbed into the camera lens and the onanists thrashed about, legs quivering and pointed to the ceiling. All stayed to see what they had wrought, giggled a bit, hooted a lot and the next week all of four dancers showed up at Meredith's loft.

This was the beginning of my education regarding improvisation observed, whether by video, still photography, an audience (even in the studio) or, worst of all, by critics. Nothing less than a massive amount of work, a lot of self-evaluation, a very gradual process of inviting a few friends, informal audiences and out-of-town performances can build up the confidence and concentration necessary to the gamble called improvisation.

In the notes, I find **Dawn Chorus Rite**, which memory says was easy to do, exciting, liberating, done a few times and mysteriously, never done again.

Dawn Chorus Rite 4.6

A leader dances a brief phrase while chanting in a language foreign to him.her (impulsive made-up words). The group, including the musicians, repeat his motions and chant twice. The leader utters and dances another brief phrase, and the group repeats it twice and so on. How did we end it? Can't recall. Did the leader stop or did he.she sit or bow before one of the group who became the new leader? You decide.

The relationship to the musicians in this Workgroup Workshop was wonderful. At one time or another some fine ones joined the sessions: Eric Salzman, Mike Sahl, Rhys Chatham, Charlemagne Palestine, Richard Steinberg and several exquisite singers from a preclassic group called West Wind. All had come from a tradition of improvising in many styles of music, including jazz. In dance, improvisation was as yet little explored. They were as fascinated as we were with its possibilities in movement and its relation to music. They gave richly and freely of their ideas and sounds and, most venturesome of all, they were willing to enter into any and all of the exercises, accepting the same roles and tasks as the dancers. Sometimes they even laid their instruments aside to participate as movers!

In Katie Fraser's notes of March 21 she records this:

> We took then, a first shot at a big problem: HOW DO YOU DO IT AGAIN? (If indeed you can repeat) We must develop a technique to repeat improvisatory movement. Our first attempt utilized the following method. (1) With an observer at hand, begin a duet. (2) At a signal A from the observer, know that from that point A to second signal B, you will try later to repeat whatever happened between. At B, stop and begin to repeat A.
> It was very awkward for both musicians and dancers. It was claimed that something which reaches a high intensity level for an individual could be repeated by that person. This may be the place to start, although eventually it should be that you could repeat what it was that a director liked. Either we must solve or abandon the problem.

Her last sentence summed it all up, recognizing the probability that the improvisation, by its very nature, resisted repetition. It took me another year to realize that accepting this was not "giving up," but moving forward to the recognition that the last thing we should attempt is to repeat an improvisation, no matter how wonderful it was, and that improvised dance could be a valid and exciting theatre form. Before this time that started with the Open Theatre, improvisation, when it wasn't done for the sheer delight of letting go, was an invaluable tool for choreography, not performance. Though I did not realize it then, what all of these games, structures and exercises were pointed toward was not to make choreography but to improvise. Elsewhere, I will point out the paradox to this statement, that is, how all of these EGAS *can* be used to choreograph dances. Without being conscious of it, in the way our sessions developed, in the people we attracted to our workshops and in the things that happened, we were headed toward a performance form and every attempt to repeat a great improvisation failed.

During this Workgroup Workshop, I became aware of the power and usefulness of a repetitive phrase of motion. At one session, there happened to be an unusually large number of musicians present, perhaps as many as there were dancers. I thought this would be the ideal time to set up a Go 1-2-3. I asked Clyde Morgan, who attended many of these first sessions and was at the time a member of the José Limon Company, to be "it," the solo figure. Clyde, a big man and a powerful, zestful dancer, almost immediately found a rather long and somewhat complex phrase of movement which to my surprise and irritation, he began to repeat over and over again. In all the time I had given Go 1-2-3, everyone who had taken the central role found a style and pattern of movement but no one had slipped into repeating a single phrase. From that first improvisation which I had witnessed at the Open Theatre, where a solo dance figure worked to a vocal accompaniment of the other actors, to all of the versions of Go 1-2-3, dancers chose a constantly evolving series of motions. Here for the first time, Clyde Morgan broke that pattern and kept doing the same thing over and over again for a very long time. He constantly varied the emphasis, phrasing, and timing of the phrase, but he never lost the sequence of the phrase. When I called out "Go 2," there was the usual cacophony, and I was certain that now Clyde would begin to develop the material, but no, each repetition became more intense and twice as involved. By Go 3, the room was shaking. The musicians were as wild and involved as Clyde, and a concerted piece of music emerged. The longer Clyde hammered at that repetition, the more excited the music makers became. After dancing it forever, he, sweat pouring down, in a most deliberate manner slowed to a quiet stop. The emotional exhaustion that filled the room was accompanied by the awareness that something important had happened. And it had. That repetition opened the door to a whole series of setups to arrive at rich and complex states of being. It was implicit in that early structure I had given at the American Dance Festival, Inner Rhythm (1.3), but at the time I had no idea of its potential.

With me and while I was away on tours, the Workgroup Workshop met every Saturday until the end of April 1969. In May, I netted a three-week workshop that earned me enough to actually take a summer vacation, just like when I was a kid. I spent two months in a quiet valley north of Taos,

New Mexico. Looking over the notes of that time, I did not seem to be aware of where I was actually heading—the creation of a dance company. There were many notes for solos. I built a gigantic man-sized whirligig as an experiment for a work which would involve building something onstage. Six years later, in *Ruminations*, I did just that, except that I built a small bench. As for the Workgroup, there was only this:

> July 14, '70
> If the Workgroup is to develop its creativeness in improvisation and its performing skill, it will have to go back in history and borrow from jazz a strict time structure like the blues, using the twelve bar structure with a theme stated twice within the first eight bars and a variation on that for the last four bars. One way to build such a structure is to start incorporating it into the dance phrases of technique.

On the same page were these notes:

> July 1 '70
> Unison dance for all but each in their own style and phrasing. The piece with ad lib sections

> July 2, '70
>   a. A man's dance
>   b. A woman's dance
>   c. The men do the women's
>   d. The women do the men's dance
>   e. All do a mix. All are nude on top
>   f. Style same as unison dance.

> Political Prisoner dance

> Undated
> If art is rehearsal for life—what should we rehearse? If that is the general rule for life, it would seem that a major skill essential to survival is improvisation.

Everything noted was prophetic, and nothing worked out as I expected.

5 The Precursor Workgroup, 1969

Came the fall of 1970, it was apparent that a weekly workshop open to all who wished to participate was no longer to the point. The work ahead needed a group of first-rate dancers who could build a solid body of experience in improvisation by working together several times a week. We held auditions. Who were we? A rare group, not a single woman but rather four men: Lee Connor, Charles Hayward, Clyde Morgan and I. During the spring of 1970, they had been consistent in attendance, inspired in improvisation and solid dancers. Lee was the rawest, but he was acquiring a technique as quickly as a dolphin swallows fish. We held a few crowded auditions and in the end chose four women who did not really audition. They had heard of what we had been at, showed up and declared their interest. When dancers of the quality of Margaret Beals, Ze'eva Cohen, Libby Nye and Carla Maxwell expressed the wish to join us, hesitation would have been stupidity.

Before we started work, I had two out-of-town engagements. The first was a workshop on Labor Day weekend on Lake Champlain for the patients of Dr. Robert Akeret, a psychiatrist. Each day, I gave a simple dance technique class followed by improvisations drawn from the repertoire of the Workgroup structures. In the technique class, one of the best pupils was a powerful one-legged man, who did pliés without his crutch and could jump over a chair with that one leg. In the improvisation work, I never tried to introduce any element of therapy, not being a therapist. I used what material any group of amateur adults could find rewarding. However, I am convinced now, and I was then, that many of the structures we uncovered in the Workgroup can be bent by a skilled dance therapist to serve mental and emotional therapy. Here are the ground rules I laid down for the participants. I leave it to therapists to determine whether what follows would be useful in their work.

- You do only what you want to do. Don't force your strength or your endurance or your ego.
- Everything that happens can be used: silence—the unplanned—the unexpected—even the blocks—things you don't like—i.e., getting angry.

- Don't drown in the anger but use it rather than walking away from it.
- The object, not the self. To find the self, find the object—not the self.
- Perform the action in relation to the object. Resist all considerations of what you look like or what others might think of you, of trying to be beautiful or interesting.
- Transposing an action from one part of the body to another is one of the chief ways of finding dance movement.
- Rechanneling a force often increases its energy and its reverberations. Dam up a river and the overflow sent through a turbine will create electricity.
- Extensive talking during the session destroys its rhythm. Brief questions are OK; more than that, save for later.
- The voice is a legitimate part of the work. Sounds are more evocative than words.

The sessions on Lake Champlain were good, but nothing new emerged. My second engagement that fall was an intensive, fifteen-hour workshop at San Diego State College with thirty-five of the better dance majors. The difficulty was that I would have only three sessions with them; the good was that each session was five hours long. By this time, I had learned that the best way to do our work was in four- and five-hour sessions, but it would be challenging to get to the kind of depth I was aiming for in only three meetings. Recognizing this, I developed a few new structures.

First off, I felt the need of dealing with the mountain of excess baggage dancers always seemed to bring into the studio. They came loaded with their self-defenses, their vanities, their expectations, their desire to please, their hostilities and what not, and still do. I needed something to help them shed the clutter of what they dragged in and to bring them quickly into flesh contact with the moment at hand. I wanted what was present to be paramount in their minds. I hit upon **Goldfish Bowl**.

Goldfish Bowl 5.1

Make circles of about eight and sit. Close your eyes and clean out your head with your breath. In a while I will say, "OK, go." You will then open your eyes, rise and whenever you are ready, you will walk to the center of your circle. The moment your body comes in contact with another body, you will close your eyes and you will become a goldfish in a very small bowl. You love to slither and slide among your fellows, and above all you like finding yourself in the middle of all the others. However, you are gentle by nature, and you would never force your way in. You only hope and wait for the opportunity to slip-slide into the center. Slithering and sliding is easier with the arms extended overhead, but that can be tiring.

Blind Journey 5.2

After a while, I will say, "Go on a **Blind Journey** of curiosity." Leaving your goldfish bowl, you will pause, taking a moment to decide what it is in this space among the people and the objects you would never really experience with your eyes open. When you know what that is, embark on this blind journey of curiosity. Of course, move cautiously. A swift or violent move could injure you or another.

After a while, I will say, "Return to your goldfish bowl." With your eyes still closed, you will attempt to locate the others with whom you shared a small space and resume what you love to do, slithering, and sliding deep in the midst of the others. Is it important that you return to your original bowl? You decide that.

After a time at this, you will hear me say, "Go find a private place." When you get there, be sure to remain standing with your eyes still closed. When everyone has found their private place, I will give the next sequence.

Invariably, when I give a sequence for the first time, I follow it with an abbreviated recap and then ask for questions. When the group includes anyone who does not fully understand English, I take particular care that they are encouraged to ask for any ambiguity to be clarified. Usually, the first time a group does Goldfish Bowl, at least one person will introduce an aggressive or rough energy that confuses and disturbs the others. Almost always, when the dancers return to the Goldfish Bowl, they are much more gentle and sensitive to each other, having learned tentativeness in Blind Journey.

When Goldfish Bowl is finished and the group is standing waiting, each in their own separate area, I say, "With your eyes still closed clear out your head with your breath." After a bit, I introduce **Breath Rhythm**, the first of the rhythm EGAS:

Breath Rhythm 5.3

I am going to ask you to observe something that is delicate, hyper-responsive, and easily altered. Odds are the act of observing it will change it. Make an effort to observe without changing. Observe your breath. Note its duration, rhythm, depth, texture, intensity. Note everything about your breath. When you are convinced that you have it, become your breath. Let your breath take full possession of your body. Let your body become the metaphor for your breath. Neither think nor imagine what your body will look like as you do this. Only do it. Become your breath. If what you become needs to cover space, open your eyes. Otherwise, all through this work keep your eyes closed.

There is no way to indicate precisely the duration of a particular exercise. My principles are: I give the dancers all the time they need to get into the problem, all the time they need to get fully wet with it and *time enough so that something happens*. Whenever possible, I respect the timing of the "slowest" person in the group. A few times I am pushed beyond my limit by the rare ones who seem to have dialed Eternity. All these principles are continually shattered by workshops and classes hemmed in by unreal, tight schedules.

When I sense that the group has "done" Breath Rhythm, I will say,

Continue what you are doing. Without losing any part of your rhythm, neither its intensity nor its intent, continuously narrow the range of your movement. Every move will be smaller than the previous movement. A time may come when you will appear to be still—but you will know that you are still moving.

When the group comes to an apparent halt, I continue:

Pulse Rhythm 5.4

Let that go and now observe another rhythm in your body. This one is more subtle and harder to detect. Sometimes when you are very quiet, you can actually become aware of your pulse at the base of your neck, or the tip of your nose, or your fingers. Try that. If it doesn't work, try the usual technique of pressing the finger tips to the artery above the big bone in your wrist. Study your pulse: its tempo, rhythm, force, texture, intensity, intent. When you think you have it, study it a bit more because unlike the Breath Rhythm, once you begin to move, you will not be able to keep observing your pulse. You will have to keep it alive in your memory. As with Breath Rhythm, become your **Pulse Rhythm.** Let it take possession of your body. Let your body become a metaphor for your pulse.

When the dancers have "done" Pulse Rhythm, sometimes, rather than suggesting diminishing the range of movements I will simply say,

Taking all the time you need, let your Pulse Rhythm wind down.

When there is stillness, I continue:

Internal Rhythm 5.5

You contain still another rhythm. Go into the space within you and in that silence, feel, sense, hear what you can. You may find a rhythm. You may sense the rhythm that drives, that governs your eating, walking, talking, your doing. Your internal motor has similarities with what it was when you were ten, and it is in some way different than it was ten minutes ago. Seek out your **Internal Rhythm.**[1] If you don't find it, do not make one up. You will find a value in listening to the silence. Sometimes, just shifting your position may help you feel it.

When you find the internal rhythm, study it. When you feel saturated with what you have found, let it take possession of your body. Let your body become that rhythm. If it is complex, fine. Do it. If it is simple, fine. Do it. If it isn't interesting, fine. Do it, without trying to make it "interesting."

But what if it is too much, frightening or dangerous; a rhythm so violent, you might hurt yourself attempting to realize it? Here, you have no choice. You cannot walk away from it. If you can't deal with all of it, deal

---

1. This is a sophisticated development of what I did more than ten years earlier with actors and later with dancers at the American Dance Festival. See Inner Rhythm (1.3) and Inner Rhythm for Dancers (1.6).

with a part of it. Do its echo. Do its reverberation. Do what it feels like to observe it, but don't walk away from it. Make nothing up. Only deal with what you find and with what you can.

It is possible that the reader has become aware that in the above sequence from Goldfish Bowl through the entire rhythm series, the dancers are being asked to keep their eyes closed for a very long time—an unusual experience the first time. When did we begin to work with eyes closed? I remember a talk with Charles Hayward. It was a spring day, just before we were to start the 1971 summer's work. We were alone in the 550 Broadway studio and were reviewing the work to date. He began to talk about his wandering around a studio with his eyes shut and then demonstrated it. There was nothing sensational or even interesting to look at, but I immediately sensed that this was a *fertile* process, our word for anything in the work that opened the door to new possibilities and to revelatory dance. I had danced with my eyes shut in many circumstances without taking note of it. In my own technical warmup-workout of the time, almost all the floor work was done with the eyes shut, affording a penetration and sensitivity to what was being done. In my concert work, some passages were always performed with the eyes closed: the opening of the slow section of *A Gratitude*, for one.

With our eyes open, we are *en garde*, more deliberate and more aware of how we appear to other people, even if their eyes are closed. Eyes open tend to be inhibiting. Eyes closed, we enter a space where the odd, the unexpected and the hidden that live inside us have the courage to venture forth. Most of us become less self-conscious and freer—creatively. A wider range of possibilities and images becomes accessible. Moving about with eyes closed intensifies all the neglected senses and elicits a sense of danger and adventure. The usual protective self-focus is diluted by the sheer necessity of finding others and touching the environment. Bodies bumping, as in Goldfish Bowl, set up an intimacy and sense of community with the other dancers without the *en garde* mentality that haunts most human relations. I'm sure there are occasional faint erotic flurries which are, in the context of the studio, just that and nothing more. The Blind Journey raises the awareness of every motion and passage through space to a heightened level. Taking nothing for granted is not only a ground rule for a blind journey but for art. Not seeing, all the sensitivities are honed. "Eyes closed" and "working blind" will be used often throughout the exercises, games and structures described in this book.

The ritual opening of an improvisation session was now Goldfish Bowl, Blind Journey, Goldfish Bowl again and finally, Internal Rhythm. Each of these played a role in opening up doors of awareness and self, essential to improvisors who are alive to others and the life within. (See below, chapter 6.)

Some people have difficulty finding an internal rhythm. They may feel shamed because they seem to lack an essential talent or become hostile to the whole "stupid" idea. It is vital that in setting up the exercise the leader state, "If you don't find it do not make one up. You will find a value in listening to the silence. Perhaps the silence has a rhythm. Sometimes, just shifting your position may help you feel it." Almost always, these unhappy ones come out of the second or third session with shining faces, "I found it!"

Most groups being given Internal Rhythm for the first time approach it with uncertainty and a few, with apprehension. Of late, when giving the exercise to a group new to it, I have adopted a devious ploy. Instead of asking them to find their own rhythm, I take a side road.

> Is there is someone with whom you are now dealing who rouses conflicting feelings in you? Is there a person who has many qualities you admire, while at the same time she.he ticks you off in an unpleasant way? You admire and dislike this person. If there is such a one let's call her.him X. Now see X in your mind's eye. Take a good look from the distance. Then come as close as you dare and study X carefully. Walk all around X, observing thoroughly. Now, look deep into X, sense what it going on inside and try to feel the rhythm in her.his body. What is the sound of X's internal motor? What is the rhythm that dominates her.his walking, talking, eating?
>
> When you find X's internal rhythm, study it. When you feel saturated with what you have found, let it take possession of your body. Let your body become that rhythm. If it is complex, fine. Do it. If it is simple, fine. Do it. If it isn't interesting, fine. Do it, without trying to make it "interesting."

Amazing. Giving this exercise first almost invariably elicits quick and strong involvement, not infrequently tinged with caricature. The movement pours out freely. Having done this, it becomes a much easier leap to "do themselves." Asking for their own internal rhythm does not appear so strange as it would if that were asked for first. There doesn't seem to be any question that another person has a rhythm that dominates his.her every move, and so it follows that each dancer also has a unique rhythm.

These structures helped get the work going on a deeper level, but there was one more area where I suspected that too many shallow and impersonal choices were being made. This occurred whenever I would throw out the "Someone, something is running . . . or flying . . . or celebrating" or whatever. I began to wonder how banal, clichéd, obvious or, worst of all, evasive were the choices. Finally, I hit upon two meditations or mind trips that have since served to open up the most unexpected doors to most of those who have participated in this work, including myself. The first one starts with a useful convention.

Backdoor
5.6

> With your breath, empty your head. (Pause.) In a little while I am going to say a word or short phrase. The moment you hear this word or short phrase, allow an image to appear in your mind. Allow a picture to appear on the screen of your mind." (Now, in order not to direct the minds of the

dancers visually, I say, "The moment your hear the word or phrase allow a smell, a sound, an image, a word, anything, to appear in the center of your mind.") With the next breath—or sooner—whatever is in the focus of your mind must change to something else. This process is continuous: a change in your mind with every breath, or sooner. Continuous change is the only control you are to exert on the process. Above all, don't try to impose any overall conception of how one thing should follow the other. You don't try to make a logical flow or, conversely, try to make surrealist or strange connections. You simply observe passively whatever will emerge, logically or illogically. There is only one compulsion: whatever occupies your mind must change with every breath or sooner.

Now, reader of this book, may I suggest that you yourself do this exercise, right now? Try closing your eyes and do what I asked those students to do, namely, do some deep breathing with your eyes closed to clear some space in your head. Once you have done this, open your eyes briefly and look at the word printed upside down at the bottom of this page. The moment you read that word, close your eyes again, and start the process just described. Generally speaking I let the students do this for four or five minutes. Then I say, "OK, wind it down, and as soon as you are ready, open your eyes." So, this is your moment to try this exercise in your own timing.

After plus or minus four minutes, I ask people to let it wind down, and when it has, to open their eyes. When everyone's eyes are open, I ask: "Is there anything remarkable, special, unusual, confusing, or interesting about what took place? I am not asking about your specific sensations and images, which I am sure are interesting. I am really curious about what, if anything, you found interesting in the process of what you have just done." Sooner or later, the following pattern emerges in any group of ten or more people: a large number have a recurring image. Of these, some find that image logical, and others find it rather unexpected and surprising. For some, the image is rather attractive and interesting; for others, it keeps recurring even though they don't like it. Not a few experience a strong image they had never seen before. Almost everyone answers affirmatively upon being asked, "Is there some image that even now stands out beyond all the others? Is there some image that seems to be in color, and the others are black and white?"

Immediately upon giving, doing and discussing **Backdoor** another exercise is given:

Hub
Meditation
5.7

Close your eyes and clean your head out with your breath. In a little while I will say, "Someone or something is *doing something*." It will be a simple verb. Picking one as an example: "Someone or something is rising and

BACKDOOR

falling." From that point on, let your mind roam and search for everything in your experience of rising and falling. Rising and falling in nature, in history, in films, TV, the people you know, your own life. A piece of bleached driftwood in the surf, a child on a pogo stick, a red autumn leaf in a cold wind, a close relation's struggle with an addiction, a graph of a sine wave, the breast of the woman who has just been crowned Miss America, a white line of paint running across a Jackson Pollock painting, the sound of the waves one evening when you were in Maui. The list can and should feel endless. Each of these will be for a moment in the center of your mind, at the very hub of your consciousness.

After a while, you may discover that even though you continue to raise up new images, the hub of your mind is occupied with one thing. There you are on that frightened horse being bounced up and down in the saddle as he galloped off the road into the desert away from the blaring horn of that monster white trailer truck.

Please note in this example that everything was *specific*. Don't reach for anything as general and grandiose as the rise and fall of the Roman Empire. Avoid unspecific feelings like going from gaiety to sadness to gaiety. These will land you neck-deep in cliché and banality.

When you realize that the hub of your mind is occupied by one image regardless of whatever other images come up, accept that and move in to get a close look at what is there. Then open your eyes. You will have just done a **Hub Meditation.**

Reader, if you wish to try this, pause to close your eyes, clean your head out with your breath, then read the phrase at the bottom of the page. Close your eyes to do a Hub Meditation. When the hub of your mind is persistently occupied by one specific image, examine it closely, then open your eyes.

It is at this point that I state what I feel is a ground rule for all the work described in this book. "The worst idea for a dance is a 'good' idea. The best idea for a dance is one that won't go away, whether you like it or not. The best idea for a dance is like a nettle that sticks to your garments." I accept with a passion the statement by Ben Shahn, in a book which I feel is of great value to anyone interested in the arts and the creative process, *The Shape of Content*. He says, "Whatever crosses the human mind may be fit content for art—in the right hands . . . it is the fullness of feeling with which the artist addresses himself to his theme that will determine, finally, its stature or its seriousness."[2]

The most disturbing thing that Doris Humphrey wrote in her book, The *Art of Making Dances*, was that some things cannot be danced. I am waiting

2. Ben Shahn, *The Shape of Content* (Cambridge, Mass.: Harvard University Press, 1957), p. 72.

SOMEONE OR SOMETHING IS SEARCHING FOR SOMEONE OR SOMETHING

with impatience for some young choreographer to read those pages and be inspired to create a strong and beautiful work based on one of those ideas which she said are impossible and unsuitable for dance. Understand that though I disagree in this respect with Doris Humphrey, I nonetheless have the profoundest respect for her as an artist, teacher, and human being.

The revelation that Backdoor and Hub Meditation bring is that given enough time in a focused meditation, the mind will find itself occupied with an image that dominates all others. Whenever a "someone, something" is given as the seed of an exercise, each person is to let her.his mind roam over the given area of interest until one specific image asserts itself. It matters not whether the image is attractive or repulsive, whether the image is fascinating or on its surface quite dull, that is the image to work on. Not to do this is not to pursue the essence of this work.

A relevant story: I had a talented and devoted student who took a number of workshops in choreography with me. She always produced work that was personal, strong and unexpected, but in the improvisation exercises involving imaging which I use to snowball choreography, she would lose concentration, resort to literal pantomime and fall into dead-end repetitions. Finally I spoke up, "What gives, Sarah? Every time we do a Duet you mess up."

"Well, every time you give us a Hub Meditation, I see Archie Bunker."

"So, did you ever do Archie Bunker?"

"No! Of course not!" Too bad. She missed out on something that was more important to her than she was willing to realize. For her values and conscious mind, Archie Bunker was not material worthy of dance or art. She should have read Ben Shahn. What defeats any number of young artists and too many mature artists is a self-reflective snobbery. They keep under covers a passionate connection to something that they fear is not "good" enough for ART—in favor of what? Better to spell art with small letters and learn to respect one's deepest feelings as the source and focus of the work.

The last thing one should do is to hunt for a "good image," a "creative image," an "exciting image"; worst of all is to try to find an image that the student thinks will interest, excite or please the teacher. The basic dictum to the work says: if it isn't personal, it isn't worth working on and it has nothing to do with art. What else dare we bring to the audience? Good intentions, generalities, noble ideas, unusual ideas, fishing for ideas that nobody else has thought of are all vulgar, opportunistic uses of art *if they are not personally and deeply felt*. There is an astonishing passage in *Ten Rungs: Hasidic Sayings* by Martin Buber: "When a man embarks on something great, in the spirit of truth, he need not be afraid that another may imitate him. But if he does not do so in the spirit of truth, but plans to act in a way that no one else can imitate, then he drags the great down to the lowest level—and everyone can do the same."[3]

---

3. Martin Buber, *The Ten Rungs* (New York: Schocken Books, 1947), p. 50.

Ideally, when the creative process is flowing out of a deep internal necessity, it matters not to the artist whether the manner of expression is traditional or innovative. One work may demand a radically new way and another an ancient mode.

The San Diego workshop had an unexpected perk. Three musicians—a soprano sax, a piano and a percussionist with bongo drums—were part of the group. When I gave the setup for Circles (4.1) and was ready to give the "Go," the pianist, aware that this was not quite like anything he had previously witnessed, spoke up. "What about us? What do you want us to do?" On the wing, I pulled them all close to me. What ensued was **The Tight Trio.**

The Tight Trio 5.8

To the pianist I said: "Find a dancer in the room who catches your interest. Draw your music out of what he.she is and does." To the sax player I said: "You have only one focus, the pianist and what he plays. Whatever you play is a response to what you hear from him." To the percussionist: "You have only one focus, the saxophone player and what he plays. Whatever you play is a response to what you hear from him."

What followed was a sensitive, winding stream of music that might have pleased the ears of Debussy. Another time, to the same three musicians:

I asked the percussionist to look at the sax player as he held his instrument and to draw what music he could out of that vision. Then I asked the pianist to observe and listen to the percussionist to feed his music and the sax player to focus only on the pianist.

This was a self-contained trio and it too consistently produced coherent well-structured music. This was the prototype of two games that evolved in the next two years: Wind II (6.13), a quartet, and Quiet Dance (7.4), a trio. Both used as a foundation this structure wherein one person focuses on only one person who in turn focuses on one person, and so on, back to the first person. The one-way circling river of attention in the hands of sensitive musicians or dancers creates, a believable interaction and an often beautiful design within the gamble of improvisation.

Returning to New York early in November 1970, we assembled: Margaret Beals, Ze'eva Cohen, Lee Connor, Charles Hayward, Carla Maxwell, Clyde Morgan, Libby Nye and myself. Beginnings are so charged with ambitious plans. We would invite the Open Theatre gurus to give us work in voice production (we did and they did); Maggie (Margaret) would teach us yoga (one or two sessions); ballet classes from Libby (a few); we would share our personal approaches to dance technique (we didn't); we were going to solve the problem of crystallizing an improvisation, that is, develop the skill of repeating an improvisation (we tried but we didn't); work with film-makers (no), musicians (yes), composers (yes), singers (yes), poets (no), playwrights (no), painters (no), scene designers (no); and central to our work, we were

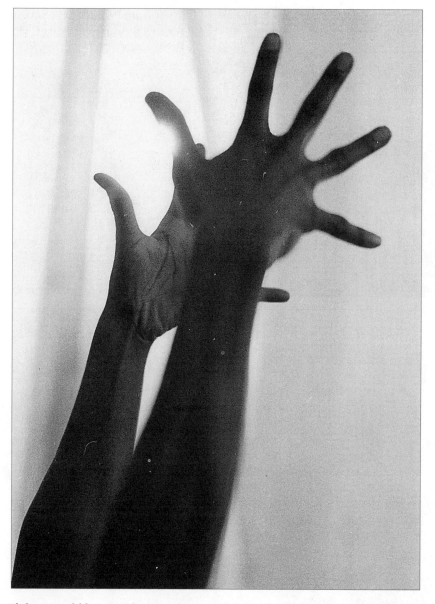

If there could be a single metaphoric image for the Workgroup it would be these hands reaching. That was the sum of what we did. Whose hands? Clyde's? No. Ours.

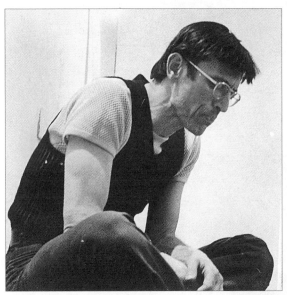

What comes next? Every new step in our work pointed forward, but where? Here I am, puzzling it out.

Lee Connor and Libby Nye in Body Contact (1.2).

Ze'eva Cohen and Clyde Morgan. The wonder of the work was how often the dancers would slip into a place where the imagined world they created became their real world.

Carla Maxwell and Margaret Beals.

Clyde Morgan and Daniel Nagrin. The surprise and delight of every well-constructed improvisation is how the discrete dancers mesh into rich stage designs without conscious manipulation.

Musicians would get carried away as easily as the dancers. This is William Zukof, a countertenor with a New York choral group, Western Wind.

going to explore all the EGAS that had already evolved with a view to developing our own new forms (we did).

We literally ran through the repertoire of improvisations, starting with that first Open Theatre Solo Singer (2.1) up to Internal Rhythm (5.5). Along the way, new exercises and games kept budding. Some of these came from Paul Zimet of the Open Theatre. In the generous spirit of the sixties and seventies, he came and reciprocated my teaching of them, gratis. The first he called Sound-Motion. I later renamed it **Master-Disciple** because that title clearly established the active relationship embedded in it.

Master-Disciple 5.9

Make a circle of six to nine with one person in the center who becomes the Master. The Master will, on impulse, let out any sound and a simultaneous motion. The word "impulse" is used advisedly. Deliberately "making" a sound and a motion will be perceived as precisely that and thus destroy any sense of spontaneity and rob the exercise of its vitality. The sound-motion should erupt out of the moment *ahead* of any thinking or planning.

Taking as long as necessary, the sound-motion is repeated, allowed to evolve and change until it crystallizes. When it does, without stopping the repetition, the Master then chooses one person to focus upon. That person becomes the Disciple who joins the Master in the center and whose task it is to learn the appearance *and the inner impulse* of the sound-motion performed by the Master. The Master continues repeating the sound-motion until he.she feels the Disciple has mastered it. The Master stops, allowing the Disciple to perform the sound-motion alone, without any coaching. If the Master is not satisfied, he.she resumes the repetition of the sound-motion until the Disciple is judged to have mastered it—externally and internally. If satisfied that his.her demonstration is no longer needed, the Master joins the circle, leaving the center arena to the Disciple to celebrate her.his ability to do the sound-motion alone.

After demonstrating her.his ability to go it alone, the Disciple evolves, develops, modulates the Master's sound-motion to her.his own sound-motion impulse. *This is not an abrupt change. It is a gradual shift from what was given by the Master to the impulse sound-motion of the Disciple, who by this act becomes the new Master.* As before, when the sound-motion finds a repeatable form that satisfies the new Master, she.he turns her.his attention to a new Disciple who joins the Master in the center to learn the sound-motion both in its appearance and its inner impulse. The same process is followed of repeating until believing that the Disciple can do it, allowing the Disciple to do it alone, and only if satisfied, stopping altogether and stepping back into the circle. This transference of the role of Master continues through the entire circle.

When the last person in the circle becomes a Master, he.she gives a sound-motion to the first Master, who becomes the last Disciple. When satisfied that this last Disciple can become a Master, he.she joins the others in the circle who now take up and learn this last sound-motion. The final Disciple-turned-Master can modulate to her.his own continuously evolving sound-motion-impulse with the entire circle learning and following every change. When the final Master decides to stop, all stop.

Though I thought this a wonderful exercise and it spawned several other good ones, one aspect disconcerted me: at any one time, only the Master and/or the Disciple were active, until the end. In time, I added this:

Throughout Master-Disciple, everyone in the circle, observing the two in the center, supports what one or both are doing with quiet sounds and subdued motion as if you were an orchestra behind soloists. Doing the same sound-motion as they is only one of ten thousand things you might do.

Sound-motion exercises are used by many directors and teachers to get actors to explore movement. Most actors not only have a skill and freedom vocally, they like to sound off, but moving about terrifies and confuses many of them. Coupling motion with sound peels away their inhibitions.

The effect on dancers is a mirror image of what happens with the actors. For them, injecting sound into motion is disorderly, and by that token it suddenly becomes possible to indulge in disorderly motions, even wild motions, *nothing like the neat, controlled actions which are the spine of their training and their ideal.* Sound-motion for dancers is like being on a holiday or being a bit bad. Sound-motion exercises break down the narrow inhibiting walls of what is permissible. There is nothing wrong for a dancer to pour out neat, controlled actions in an improvisation *just so long as the moment cries out for neat, controlled motions.* To really improvise, the dancer stands ready *to do anything in any style.*

Wind I is what I called a lovely, difficult improvisation taught us by Paul. I have no memory of what he called it.

Wind I
5.10

Six to nine stand in a circle. What is the energy coming off the group as a whole? Let that energy charge your motion.

Later on I added:

Something is happening with every human—all the time. Focus on the people facing you across the circle. Draw your energy from them. Initiate nothing. Only what you see/sense in the others will activate you. How and when to stop? The group, as a whole will know when it is over, when it has been done.

This is not a sure thing. One group of dancers may freeze in uncertainty; another pours out tons of arbitrary and concocted movement. Simple as it appears, and difficult as it was to do well, Wind I had quite a history. A year later, we performed a lovely variation on it, Wind II (6.13), and in the following year, performed *Paul's Wind.*

Dedicate Your Motion, also taught to us by Paul Zimet, was used by the

Open Theatre for a whole phase of their work. Ever since learning it, I have used it in unexpected ways to jolt dancers out of the premise that movement is motion is movement and nothing else. The exercise, as he gave it, is deceptively simple.

Dedicate Your Motion 5.11

Make a phrase of movement which you can repeat, and then continue to do it. (After several minutes of this): Dedicate your motion to someone who is not here.

Rather than to "someone," it can be to "an animal of which you are in awe," or to a "place of great beauty." Many variations are possible. I use this after a group has done Internal Rhythm a few times. Interjecting the suggestion of a dedication, one always witnesses a subtle change, usually in the direction of greater intensity, a sharpening of the movement and sometimes an elaboration of the original phrase. Most striking is to listen to the dancers after they have done this for the first time. There is often a preoccupation and a wonderment in their faces. It may have been the first time they danced with and to someone or something that really mattered to them. Not rarely, that someone/something was a surprise, unexpected and strangely affecting. It becomes one of the first lessons in what it means to fill a motion with action—an action from within. By action, I mean to be *doing* something, to recognize that an arabesque is a metaphor for an action. The reader and I are quite aware that there is a whole school of dance that flatly denies what I have just written. To them, the paramount significance of an arabesque is itself: loading it with meanings and metaphors drags it down into sentimentality or sets it up as a mysterious sign which the bedeviled audience is required to decipher instead of simply exulting at what they are witnessing. To me, to Tamiris who schooled me in my beginning, the sheer elegance and physicality of an arabesque is one of many ways of seeing and experiencing it, not the only way. It can be a metaphor for flight, for offering oneself to another, for baring ones' vulnerability to others or it can be an exquisite and virtuosic configuration. The list will go on and on as long as there is choreography—in spite of the purists.

There was another profound experience set up by Paul. **Seeing Through the Eyes of Another.** How I developed it:

Seeing Through the Eyes of Another 5.12

Any number of dancers sit in a circle. Rotate in any direction and at any speed on your bottom. What you are really doing is observing the others in the circle with a view to pinning down who it is that interests you the most, positively or negatively. When you make this decision, learn all you can about this person while you continue the circling. During all this observation, you never let anyone catch your eye, particularly the one upon whom your full attention finally settles. Your observation remains covert. When you think you have absorbed all you can from this person, stop the rotation at any point, close your eyes and continue to observe and absorb what you see of that person—in your mind. When all stop, I will give the next direction.

(All have stopped rotating.) When I say, "Go," open your eyes, rise and find another place to sit in the circle, but not in the place of the person in your mind.

(They do so.) Now, close your eyes to recapture that person in your mind. When you do, open your eyes and look out at everyone *through the eyes of that person.* Again, begin the rotation on your bottom and through the eyes of that person, observe all the others with a view to pinning down who is the person who that person would find the most interesting, positively or negatively. When that person is found, observe him.her closely and covertly. Repeat the rest of the sequence: ceasing to rotate when the person is absorbed, closing your eyes to continue the study of that person, rising when you hear "Go," sitting in a new place in the circle, closing your eyes to recapture the person, and then opening your eyes to look through the eyes of this person.

The details of this EGAS are complex. In my notes there is a version that summarizes it neatly:

1. Look at someone else. Sense her.him.
2. Go to another place and look at rest of room as she.he would do.
3. Pick out someone else as she.he would do and take that person's place.

When does one call a halt to this process? Two or three times should be sufficient to exercise the powers of observation and the creative possibilities gained by "seeing through the eyes of another." Hidden within this simple and subtle little game is the possibility of a giant moral-ethical leap, but that is something for the reader to pursue in his.her own time, not here in this book.

While recalling this EGAS, it occurred to me that a fascinating way to use this new way of looking at others would be to perform it with a circle of six to eight and, after the second move, let someone, anyone who chooses to, start a Rhythm Circle (3.5). Everyone in the circle would "be" someone other than themselves learning and creating rhythms.

We had some rare and energizing visits from Joe Chaikin. He gave us some relaxation exercises, some vocal exercises and a way of telling a story that bore a distant relation to Tell a Dream (3.8). In his exercise, the others just listened while the Teller followed the impulses, meanings, and intensities that each word ignited within her.him rather than hewing rigidly to the temporal logic of what had happened or to linear grammatical construction.

In terms of our development, the most valuable hint we received from him was something about "working through the cliché." This was a startling challenge. Traditionally, artists of every calling are ever *en garde* against any mannerism or cliché. We are forever checking and being checked by our "best friends and critics" so that we do not repeat habitual gestures, phrases, and solutions. Tamiris, who observed and critiqued my choreography for years, would pounce on any movement or phrase that bore the slightest resemblance to something I had done previously. True, I was challenged to go more deeply into my movement sources, but it took me several years after working with her to free myself of this as a rigid rule. I finally learned that the same movement in a different context is a different movement and not just a lazy solution to a new problem, though that hovered in the background as a possibility.

Anyone in the arts or observing the arts is aware of artists who grow unself-critical and get caught in the ruts of their own clichés. Chaikin's remark, "work through your cliche," made me recognize that the cliche is important! It is a sign, a flag, a metaphor, a door to something that is vital to the artist. His.her task is never to flee from the cliche but to plunge deeply into it in all its ramifications, associations and history, conscious and unconscious. If a prime task of the artist is to make contact with what is deeply vital on a personal level, then the cliche is a door that must be pried open to reveal what is behind it. This observation blossomed into **Cliché Rondo**.

Cliché Rondo 5.13

Ideally, each dancer should be working alone with a piece of music she.he finds irresistible. For a group, the leader should choose some charming, dancey music, for it will be played many times as the EGAS evolves. I found that something short, two to three minutes, was best (my favorite was a Renaissance estampie with a Moorish howl to it). The first go is: "Find all the joy and pleasure you can in this music." (Play the tape. Then, while the tape is rewound):

Pretend that you are not in a room full of other dancers, but rather all alone. Do what you usually do when you're listening to music that makes you dance. Disregard how you look or "how good" the movement is. You are not interested in choreography, interesting moves or virtuosity, only what you always do when dancing for the fun of it and when no one is looking. (The tape is played again. After it is rewound):

This time when the music starts, make a phrase of movement that will resemble a string of beads. In any order, string together two, three or four of the moves and phrases you just did in one phrase of sixteen beats. (The leader should be clear about what is meant by this, pausing to play the music and count out the length of music asked for.) To repeat: we are not interested in choreography, interesting moves or virtuosity, only what you always do when dancing for the fun of it when no one is looking. Link your moves into a sixteen-count phrase. (The same tape is played again.) When you have a sixteen-count phrase that you know well enough to repeat three times without stopping, leave the floor.

With most groups of any size, it will take two or even three playings of the selection before everyone has put together sixteen counts which they remember and can dance. When all have stepped off the floor:

> You are now going to dance a rondo. For those of you who are unfamiliar with that musical form, a theme is stated and then developed, only to return to the same theme and then developed in a different direction and so on. If the theme is A and the developments are B, C, D, E, the structure would be AB AC AD AE, and so on. For our purposes, you will first dance the A theme twice and then take off—ad lib—let happen what may. Whenever you run out of steam, at any time you have the inclination, you can return to A, dancing it once through and then going off in a new direction with the same freedom—and so you go until the music runs out. Our structure is AAB AC AD AE, etc. (Play the music and then rewind.)

> All sit, close your eyes, and clear out your head with your breath. I am going to throw some premises at you. For the time of this exercise, assume they are correct. Afterward, you can reject them all.

> Every move in every dance phrase is a thrust to be somewhere else and to become what you are not. Now, in the dark of your mind, look at the sixteen-count phrase you made. What is its itch? Its longing? Where does it want to go? What does it want to become? When you know, rise. When all are standing, the music will start and you will do the rondo, AAB AC AD AE, etc., only this time you will use all the moves of the theme variations to one purpose—to go where the moves want to go and to become what they are pointing toward.

> Still another line of pursuit can be: use the Cliché Rondo to play with its shapes and rhythms—bending, stretching, elevating, turning, pounding, caressing them to find out all that they contain.

The surprise of all of this was how much gold lay hidden in our despised clichés. Further surprises lay ahead in the next year when Cliché Rondo blossomed into other forms, including performance structures, and finally taught us what the Workgroup was really about.

For me, the most significant lesson of the Precursor Workgroup was that what we were doing challenged, intrigued and fascinated some very good professional dancers. This was a group of serious, busy people and yet we met for three months, mostly four times a week, for three- and four-hour sessions. All the forms I had found and developed were tried. Very few new ones appeared but everything gained greater depth, particularly A Duet (3.11). Some of the duets were utterly astonishing. One was a spontaneous, very long dance of love with a wooing ritual, marriage ceremony, and mating by Clyde Morgan and Ze'eva Cohen. Another, involving Clyde Morgan and Charles Hayward, was of some wild animal and a tamer, with both constantly changing roles. I did one with Margaret Beals in which we made a long, painful, and yet ecstatic tumbling journey across the dance floor, our bodies linked, bound in a complex grip. It could have been the dance of a happy, miserable couple clinging together in love and fear. We later tried to repeat this one and got nowhere. This may have been the beginning of a negative answer to our major question, "How were we to save the gold found in improvisation for choreography? How were we going to pin down the good stuff?"

Of all of us, Margaret Beals had had the most intensive experience with performing improvisation. A few years earlier I had gone to the Improvisation, a nightclub in the Broadway section of New York to see her perform—improvisations! I was impressed by her sheer dance qualities, her beauty and her audacity. The thrust of what she was dancing eluded me at the time.

Why do You
Dance?
5.14

In one of our sessions, I asked Maggie to take the floor—alone. When she was there, standing, waiting, I asked her, "Maggie—no words. Why do you dance?"

Her first response was a bemused expression, and then she plunged. There ensued a long, detailed, complex, improvised solo that never for a moment lost its compelling flow and never for a moment provoked the deadly question, "What does she mean?" Her performance convinced me as never before that when a dancer has a firm grasp on a specific image, reinforced by a strong emotional context with the imagination to find the right movement metaphors, questions of meaning, of intent or content, do not arise in the minds of the viewers. Everyone is engaged and "knows" what they are seeing, constructing a coherent flow of sensations, feelings and conceptions that run parallel and close to what they are witnessing. Ironically, in an audience fortunate to have this experience, everyone, including the dancer, is perceiving differently, though their differences will probably be variations about a single theme.

This is what is really meant when it is said that "the audience was deeply involved in the performance." Audiences asking "What does it mean?" are distanced and bored by a sloppy soup of danced generalizations or puzzled by an obscure, linear, antipoetical scenario better related in a short story. Specific actions poetically juxtaposed can convey the most simple or the most complex artistic insights.

Maggie, standing there, knew the manifold reasons that bound her life to the act of dancing. Her body had the skill to realize the wild poem in her heart-mind. I put the question to her at just the right moment and out flowed a cornucopia of funny, entrancing and gorgeous movement. **Why Do You Dance?** became an intermittent game which I would throw unexpectedly at this group. Never did it with any other group and I can't fathom why.

One of the most interesting directorial hints I picked up from Joe Chaikin came in the form of a question he asked while we were talking over our respective problems: "Daniel, how do you develop new games and exercises?" I said they seemed to flow one into the other, or I would hit on a weakness in the way the group was working. Joe said his arose similarly but that some of the best came from specific blocks that stymied the work of particular members of his group.

One of this percursor company was more disconcerted than stimulated by what we were doing. It wasn't quite what he.she expected. Most dismaying was the untidiness of improvisation compared to choreographed work; in every game he.she tried to control and anticipate the results. Mulling over what to do with this obstacle person, I took the hint from Joe and came up with a duet I called **Pygmalion and Galatea I.**[4]

Pygmalion and Galatea I 5.15

One person stands still and passive. The other looks at and into the quiet one just like Michelangelo studying a raw block of marble to find the figure it contains. This image, vision, conception is what the observer would like to create out of the passive one. When the vision is clear, the active one, the sculptor, manipulates the limbs, torso and head to realize it. Galatea accepts and retains any and all shaping done by Pygmalion. When the statue is completed, the sculptor stands back and says audibly, "Done," and then stands still and passive.

Whoever is playing the statue, the Galatea, now has the challenge to sense who and what she.he has become. The shape fashioned should have a "feel" like someone-something. When the sense of it becomes clear, Galatea comes to life and becomes the sculptor, the new Pygmalion and, retaining this new muscle tone, posture, spinal alignment and this new internal attitude to self and the world, proceeds to fashion a new Galatea.

This game of alternating roles could go on, ad infinitum. At the time, I had no way to finish it. My compulsively tidy one had a great time fashioning, pushing about and controlling other bodies and was fabulous when being shaped, holding every modification precisely and with an uncanny stillness. Years later, Pygmalion and Galatea blossomed into one of the most moving sections of an evening-length work, *Hello Farewell Hello*.

The notes of the period contain a few references which today are mysterious. Did we do them or were they late night notes for maybe-ideas that never saw the light of the studio and the sweat of our bodies?

Double dimension
Deaf Dumb and Blind
Play your vanity to the hilt
Play your shame to the hilt
Faces—the cross
All dance in as close a space as possible

What is clear in the memory is the excitement generated by the precursor

---

4. From the classic tale by Ovid: Pygmalion, a great sculptor, despairs of finding the woman of his ideals and instead fashions a statue of that ideal. Completing the figure, he finds himself hopelessly in love with it. Aphrodite, taking pity on him, brings his creation to life.

Workgroup: These were finally honed bodies, all with professional and solo experience except for Lee Connor, who in the life of the Workgroup achieved artistic maturity at breakneck speed. At one time or another, I saw each member of this group slip into dimensions of power, beauty, audacity and sheer creativeness. They had flashes of dance that equaled anything I ever saw them do later in their careers.

Also among the notes of that time:

what will come of it?
a research lab of personal possibles and insights?
works on the basis of an evolved relationship and technique?

a company?

At a meeting late in December 1970, the answer to the last question was no, and yes. Five wanted "a research lab of personal possibles and insights," but not the company I wanted, a company that would continue meeting four times a week in four- and five-hour sessions with a view to performances in the late spring. All except Lee and Charles were fired up to do their own programs as soloists or as company directors. They did want to continue, but as a place to experiment, meeting one or two times a week. To that plan I could only offer an unequivocal no. I knew this had to be more than a research lab. What was here had to be seen in the shape of a company. On the last page of the notebook of that session was the answer to my question:

1 / 5 / 71

Plan for the new Workgroup.

6 The First Workgroup, 1971–1972

The first act was to find a space—our own space. Luck. A painter advertised an 82-by-36-foot loft, without asking for any key money! He thought he had found the perfect studio for his needs until he learned it was under the thundering heels of Paul Taylor's powerhouse company. He just wanted out of his lease.

The ceiling was twelve and a half feet high but the floor was a horror. This being 1970 and vinyl not the easy solution it is today, we patched and sanded the worn, gouged tongue-and-groove boards, and in a couple of weeks we had a workable studio. "We" meant Charles Hayward, Lee Connor and myself, the survivors of the precursor Workgroup.

We began rebuilding the Workgroup by holding what may be the longest audition ever. After a preliminary screening, we culled about twenty strong dancers, meeting with them every evening for two solid weeks and paying them a small fee. We ran the gamut of most of the work we had done to date. Out of a remarkable group of dancers, we learned that the people who had the freedom to improvise without resorting to clichés or to safe and theatricalized solutions were four women who though fine movers *had little performing experience.* With the others, it was as if several years on the stage had tempered them like steel. Flip a blade this way and that and it whips back to the shape it was fired in.

I needed dancers who could surprise themselves; dancers who would not feel threatened or lost if they found themselves doing what they had never done before—or even becoming another. Ara Fitzgerald, Yung Yung Tsuai, Mary Anne Smith and Saluka were the wildly brave and lovely dancers who joined the three men. Not a single man auditioning was right for us. We now had a company of seven dancers who were quickened and delighted whenever they found themselves in an unfamiliar place. (Throughout this book, I will be giving the names of the people who came to work at 550 Broadway because, by the very nature of improvisation, they all contributed much to whatever will be described here.)

The three who moved on from the Precursor Workgroup to form the first Workgroup: Lee Connor, Daniel Nagrin and Charles Hayward. *Photo: Judith Mann*

This is from the photo session in Judith Mann's studio that almost drove us part: Yung Yung Tsuai, Ara Fitzgerald and Mary Anne Smith. *Photo: Judith Mann*

From left: Ara Fitzgerald, Daniel Nagrin, Mary Anne Smith, Yung Yung Tsuai, Charles Hayward and part of Lee Connor. *Photo: Judith Mann*

Lee Connor and Ara Fitzgerald in their duet (6.8). *Photo: Judith Mann*

Backs (6.11). Saluka, Lee Connor, Mary Anne Smith, Charles Hayward, Ara Fitzgerald, Yung Yung Tsuai and Daniel Nagrin. *Photo: Arthur Alexander*

Lee Connor and Saluka.
Photo: Arthur Alexander

Richard Steinberg was the
only musician to join the
Workgroup. He worked
with us for several months
and accompanied our stu-
dio work on The Male/
Female Dance (6.12).
Photo: Arthur Alexander

The Male/Female Dance (6.12). It is ironic that in this rehearsal shot only Lee Connor and Daniel Nagrin can be indentified. *Photo: Arthur Alexander*

What's next? *Photo: Arthur Alexander*

Daniel Nagrin and Ara Fitzgerald in The Duet (6.5). *Photo: Peter Moore*

One person, a composer, inadvertently helped to finally clarify the question facing us: When and how were we to move from improvisation to choreography—to pin down the wonderful moments that kept lighting up the studio space? It happened during the auditions while I was giving Cliché Rondo (5.13). Because so many were working, I devised a structure that permitted me to observe three at a time.

Rondo
6.1

Rondo. Three dancers, each with an individual movement theme, an A theme, take to the dance space. When the music starts, one dancer dances out his.her theme twice. Observing carefully, the second dancer can tell when the first dancer has completed this and, on beat, this dancer states her.his A theme twice. Similarly, the third dancer. When the third completes his.her theme, all state their themes once again, simultaneously. This means that the third will dance his.her theme three times. Now each one takes off, improvising around and about what the other two are doing. Whenever it feels right, each can return to her.his own A theme and then go into a new improvisation. Thus each dancer is maintaining the rondo form of *AAB AC AD AE AF, but the entire substance of her.his dance is about what the others are doing.* The dance ends when the music ends.

One afternoon, the composer Fred Rzewski came to observe our work. We were sitting on the floor observing trio after trio work their way through the Rondo. My mind was focused on culling dancers. "Who was right for the Workgroup?" was the question at the forefront of my observations. Suddenly, a big sigh came from Rzewski who was sitting behind me and I heard him mutter to himself, "How beautiful!" In surprise, I stopped my head from auditioning and really looked at what they were doing as a group and saw what he saw—an exquisite counterplay of statement and response, the dancers weaving in and out of each other's movement. I hardly paid attention to the shift that took place in my mind at that moment, but it was as decisive as a door closing off one space and opening up another.

What we were doing was what we should be doing: improvise and improvise, finding not only the skill and the freedom to do it beautifully, but finding the forms that freed us to go to strange and lovely places and yes, to familiar and tragic places—wherever. It was strong, challenging work and, best of all, it could and should be performed for the dance audience. At that moment, without my being fully cognizant of it, the Workgroup was on its way to becoming a company that would perform improvisation.

Notes for the first work sessions starting January 1971:

Ground rules for the Workgroup:
- the Workgroup nucleus is building a performing company whose commitment assumes that any significant dent in the schedule will be avoided.
- Schedule: the Workgroup nucleus will start Feb. 1st. and meet thru May 15th or May 22nd, the latest.

- There will be four sessions each week.
- Each session will be four hours.
- There will be one additional session of two hours per week with a teacher from the Open Theatre.
- An extra session of four hours each week as a workshop for dancers outside the Workgroup nucleus.
- There will be some minimal pay. The amount will be determined probably before Feb. 1st, after other costs are clearer.
- Responsibilities for the Workgroup schedule, the studio and ultimately the performances will be spread among all the members.
- The way of the Workgroup allows for and asks for open discussion, suggestions, ideas and criticism.
- As the director, Daniel makes the final decisions.
- Be open and talk———[1]

Once the seven of us began work, we entered an atmosphere of rare freedom. We had made the commitment, there was the time (never enough), but still some time and there was a little pay for the efforts of the company.[2] My notes of the time include utopian plans for a day's work:

Schedule
1/2 hr—yourself	(for a personal meditation)
1 1/2 hrs—technique	(shared or individual)
3 hr—sessions	(the improvisation studies and work)
1 1/2 hrs—special classes	(in acting, vocal production, self-defence—aikido)

This was a six-and-one-half-hour schedule which we rarely achieved but always reached for. In starting, I was aware of two problems: (1) getting the body warm, free and ready for any physical adventure, and (2) getting the heart/mind warm, free and ready for any adventure—intellectual and emotional. Following is a sequence on numbered cards I found among my old notes.

1   massage
2   vocal warmup—Charles
3   personal warmup
4   endurance
5   make music—record it (?)
6   sense memory

1. The alert reader will notice that the word *rehearsal* is never used. *Rehearsing improvisation* is an oxymoron. How can you rehearse what will never happen the same way twice? *Practice* is a better word.

Regarding my leadership of the group: in the second year of the company, among some of the new members there was a sentiment for a collective leadership. Some even resisted public performances. Though I saw nothing terrible about collective artistic production nor about not wishing to perform publicly, neither way interested me.

2. The most significant financial sustenance of the Workgroup came from my earnings on the solo tours of *The Peloponnesian War*. There also was some private funding and support from the New York State Council on the Arts.

> 7   rhythm circle—standing?
> 8   repetition—(playback repetition)
>   where you are
>   vocal into physical
>   or physical into vocal
> 9   cliché rondo
>
> The day's work:
> An observed duet
> tell a story
> The other
> each alone
> duet

These few notes give a very accurate sense of the scope of the work of those first days. Physical readiness took several forms. Most often, each individual would give themselves a "class" followed by my leading them through an endurance sequence I had devised using several of Jimi Hendrix's classic songs. Other times a company member would give us all a class. On rare occasions, we would do the classic **Everybody Warmup** of the sixties and seventies:

Every-
body
Warmup
6.2

All are in a circle and one person starts with an initial exercise which all imitate until that "leader" ceases and indicates that the next person can take over the "leader-teacher" role.

I had mixed feelings about this one. It challenged everyone to be a leader, or one could say a "contributor." It opened the door to a communal spirit. It encouraged a spirit of humor and lightness. Negatively: it tended toward sloppiness in movement; there was always the confusion about moving right or left; and the pervading lightness could easily defeat the serious spine required of all technical dance work. If a group is getting together for the first time, it can thaw the usual tension.

The second problem in starting a day's session, opening the heart/mind for any adventure—intellectual and emotional, was and is much more complicated. The heart/mind is an elusive beast—a hidden garden/or a private hell, depending on what you have hiding there behind your body/face mask. Getting to it is one of the central problems of being an artist or, for that matter, of being human. It was *the* question that haunted Stanislavski and spurred the development of his seminal technique of performing.

A premise of our time, and one that I accept, is that we humans operate with two distinct areas of awareness: one, the intellectual, the cerebral, the mind; and the other, the irrational, the heart, the dream world, the unconscious or the subconscious as identified by Sigmund Freud. I fantasize an ideal way of being: that these two realms coexist, merely separated by a beaded curtain through which one can pass at will and with ease and, while in one maintain a glimpse of the other. "Heart/mind" is the word I like to use, thinking of the slash as that beaded curtain. I am troubled by those who elevate or value one of these more than the other. I tend to define mental and emotional illness as the domination of one or the other; health is when they feed each other.

In creative work, the first releasing techniques I found for myself and others revolved around rhythm. Rhythm sparked my earliest work with actors, with dancers and now with the Workgroup.

Everyone, the "old-timers" and the new company members, had experienced Breath Rhythm (5.3), Pulse Rhythm (5.4), and Internal Rhythm (5.5). The last of these became the focus of a new flow of exercises. It was the key to entering into the work and, in time, it became the ritualistic way to start all our sessions and many of our performances. It fulfilled the function of a meditation—a movement meditation—a way of getting into the body, getting it going, cutting loose from the mess of the outside, relaxing the militant control of the mind, turning the wall between the two realms into a "beaded curtain" and, best of all, connecting with where we were at the moment. If this was our internal rhythm at this moment, then this was part of who we were at this moment. We now renamed it The Repetition.

We found two fruitful ways to do The Repetition. Both begin from a standing position rather than sitting or lying down. This leads to a higher energy rhythm, a clear indication of my preference for high energy.

True Repetition 6.3

True Repetition. Go to the perimeter of the room. There is a place in this space that belongs to you.[3] On the word, "Go," roam the room until you find the spot. When you find it, stand on it, clean out your head with your breath and listen for, sense, find your internal rhythm. If and when you find it, let it take possession of your body. Take all the time you need. It may appear bit by bit like a chick cutting its way out of an eggshell. When you know it is complete, that it is being fully stated by your body, commit yourself to doing that phrase from that point on *and that phrase only, with no changes—for a long time.* Change only if you sense that continuing will cause you physical harm or if you experience a fatigue that is threatening. Otherwise, no changes—at all. Be prepared to go for ten minutes.

Evolving Repetition 6.4

Evolving Repetition. Start off exactly like True Repetition. When the rhythm finally emerges fully in the body, the intent is to do the rhythm as found. If a change happens, allow it to happen. If no change happens, no change is forced on the phrase. It is allowed to continue as it was. Radical or abrupt changes would be suspect because they would not be rooted in the rhythm that was originally found.

---

3. I gleaned this idea from *The Teachings of Don Juan* (1968), the first book Carlos Castaneda wrote about the teachings of a Mexican Yaqui sorcerer. I have much skepticism about what he writes but some insights I found useful. In this one, the sorcerer told the apprentice there was a place on the porch that was his, and when he found it, he was to spend the night there.

True Repetition acts like a movement meditation and draws dancers into an open, receptive, and relaxed state. It was ideal for starting our work sessions. Evolving Repetition is a more "athletic" and adventurous structure and certainly more interesting to watch. A year later, we started each performance with Evolving Repetition, calling it *From Now.*

Very quickly, as we assembled to work, five of the earliest exercises merged into one seamless whole and became the key to all the work that followed. Some of them went through subtle changes, and the name of one became the name of the combined five. The columns that follow should help make the evolution and the progression clear.

The Original EGAS		*The Duet (6.5)*
The Mind-Wash (3.2)	remained	The Mind-Wash (3.2)
The Mirror (2.4)	changed to	The Other (6.5a)
Hub Meditation (5.7)	remained	Hub Meditation (5.7)
Circles (4.1)	became	Each Alone (4.4)
A Duet (3.11)	became	Duet (6.5c)

In the column on the left are the early, individual EGAS that were so rewarding to do. Those on the right became, in essence, one EGAS with five parts. This entire sequence took its name from its climax, The Duet. On first reading, it may appear complex and not easy to follow. Actually, the five parts are bound together by an internal logic. Approach the progression step by step and clarity will emerge.

Should you, the reader wish to follow the development of this sequence with a specific image in mind, make one up now or choose one from the following:

- Someone always has to have their own way. You are that person or you are dealing with that person.
- Someone needs to live in a neat, orderly, predictable world. You are that person or you are dealing with that person.
- Someone is always busy and in a hurry and the other is laid back. Which one are you?
- Someone is a protector, shielding another from anything potentially dangerous or negative. You are that person or you are dealing with that person.
- Someone is leaving. You are leaving or you are the one being left.

The Duet 6.5

The Duet. Sit cross-legged, facing your partner, knees a few inches apart. Close your eyes and clear a space in your head with your breath.

After a while, you will hear me say, "Someone or something is doing something to or with someone or something."[4] Put this statement on a shelf of your mind to be dealt with later. Now do The Mind-Wash, only

4. This next paragraph is an almost word-for-word quote of the exercise Each Alone (4.4). It is repeated in order to give continuity to the description of The Duet.

73

The Other
6.5a

this time, when it is completed, that is, when your gaze returns to the face of your partner, instead of imitating each other, quite simply look at the other person just to see what can be seen. If one really looks, the longer one looks, there will be a constant flow of insights about the person observed, a wonderful experience for some and unnerving for others, for to see in this context is to be seen. This is called **The Other.** This "other" is the person with whom you are going to go on a journey. It may be the first time you have worked together or the twentieth; there will always be something new to be observed. What can you glean just by looking . . . looking?

The moment will come when you have learned what you can for now, and you are ready to take the "someone . . . something" statement off the shelf of your mind and do a Hub Meditation with it. You let your mind roam through literature, films, TV, your own life, finding as many relationships as possible that fit the statement until one dominates, until one is always there, regardless of what new ones come up in your mind. All this time, you are looking at your partner. These two actions, looking at your partner and looking for what will occupy the hub of your mind may seem too far apart. Wait. You may find that they reinforce each other.

If and when you find the specific "someone-something," you have a decision to make. Which role will you play? Who will you be?

After knowing which one, you face the critical question: if you are so-and-so, what is your task? What do you need to do with, to or for this other person? Once you know your task, you need to find a movement metaphor for this task. It is here that your imagination has its greatest challenge: finding a poetic movement metaphor rather than a literal action. One way you will be dancing (whatever that elusive word means), the other way you might just as well speak like an actor rather than go through the motions of an inefficient dumb-show.

Each Alone
6.5b

Once you have determined your role and your task, you are ready for the next phase of The Duet. Whichever one of you is ready first, indicate that to your partner by turning your palms up and resting your hands on your knees. When the other is ready, he.she clasps the upturned palms and both rise and separate, each to find a private place. Here you will become X, the person you found in your Hub Meditation, whose need is to accomplish a specific task. You do this through the structure called **Each Alone.**[4]

Once in your private place sit, stand, kneel or lie down, whichever is an appropriate place from which to become X. Above all, know that it is you who are doing this and not X. Do not for a moment try at this stage to "become" or look like your X. Doing this will create a banality. Above all, do not think, plan or plot how you will proceed. Call up the vision of X

4. This next paragraph is an almost word-for-word quote of the exercise Each Alone (4.4). It is repeated in order to give continuity to the description of The Duet.

doing what X does and immediately allow some *one part* of your body to perform that act—as X. In time, you will feel as if you have done that part, that it has become X doing what X does, and you will be ready to move on. Taking all the time that is needed, you will continue in whatever sequence your body tells you, body part by body part. As you do this, try to retain what you have done. Symmetry is possible but not necessary: the focus of activity might be the shoulders or only the right shoulder. Discard the rigorous logic of Circles and follow instead the dictates of your body and your feelings. Let them control sequence and timing. You may never get to body parts mentioned in Circles, and you may become absorbed in an area untouched by Circles. There will come a moment when all the body parts will become a unity and you will be X doing what X does.

Duet
6.5c

You are now ready to engage with your partner, with the Other. Without losing any of the character you have become, and deep within the danced truth of X, approach the other person, whom we will dub Y. Here you may face a decision. If Y is ready to engage, then each of you will proceed to do what you have to do, in dance. If Y is not ready, would X wait or barge right in? Decide. On the other hand, if Y is interrupted would she.he be pliant or resist by continuing with Each Alone until finished? This is the beginning of making choices as the person each of you have become.

Whatever the outcome, sooner or later the two of you will engage in the attempt to make something happen. There should be no terror of the literal, only of getting stuck in it. The literal can be welcomed but only as a springboard to a danced metaphor.

If you are having difficulty realizing your goal, be as flexible and resourceful as X is—or as rigid, depending on who X is. It may even make sense to change your intent because of what you are experiencing as X.

If you achieve your task, celebrate that and leave the floor. If your partner does this before you, then dance out your recognition of failure and leave the floor. If you try this and that and nothing brings you any closer to success, you, still as X, may give up and dance your acceptance of that failure and leave.[5]

As noted earlier, any reader coming across this material for the first time may groan, "How complex! How can anyone follow such a detailed and tortuous path—and still dance?" If this were the first structure given to any group, they would be dazzled and lost before they started. If one were to back off and look at The Duet from a distance, one would recognize structure after structure that has already been explained in detail and *danced*. These became the

---

5. In our early forays, The Duet would seem to go on forever. It was Charles Hayward who suggested that the choice of action made in The Other implied a task. Therefore, we could leave our partner and the floor when the task was accomplished. I saw that this was the solution and added the refinements of celebrating success or recognizing failure as part of the leaving process.

big bones of The Duet. The logic becomes apparent *after* one has gone through the process a few times. Then the entire sequence takes on a unified organic flow from beginning to end.

As a general procedure, immediately after introducing a new exercise, I will always review it, cutting out all "the poetry" and the "fancy stuff" which I tend to use in order to stir up the imagination of the dancers. Summarizing The Duet would go like this:

> Sitting facing your partner, you will hear "someone . . . something." Do nothing about it except to save it on the shelf of your mind.
>
> Do the Mind-Wash and when finished contemplate your partner. When you have done that, return to the "someone . . . something" and do a Hub Meditation.
>
> When you have found the dominating image, decide on your role and your task.
>
> Completing that, sign to your partner that you are ready to go on by opening your palms on your knees or, if your partner is ready before you, clasp his.her hands.
>
> Both rise to find separate areas in which to do Each Alone.
>
> When you have become X, find and engage with your partner. If you succeed in your task, celebrate that and leave the floor. If you fail, recognize that—in dance—and leave the floor. If after many different attempts you are convinced it is futile, recognize that—in dance—and leave.

Even reading this condensed version may still be confusing, and perhaps it would help to review the mental process through which I went in a duet with Ara Fitzgerald, a member of the Workgroup. The premise of that duet was "Someone is favored in almost every way: looks, health, wealth, position—the works. You are that person or someone dealing with that person."

By now the questions arise. How, for example, does each know what role the other has taken? Neither knows, no more than any of us in "real life" know when we deal with others, at least until later (sometimes much later), and even then we misunderstand each other. If this is true in life, then why should it not be so here in The Duet?

Second question: What if both take the same role—the same side of the implied dichotomy? How many times are two people united in a power struggle, each determined to dominate, or each longing to find someone to lean upon? The complementary relationship of opposites is not a general condition. It probably happens as often as similar types try to relate.

As I sat there looking at the sweet, clear-browed face of Ara, she became very wealthy and I became very ugly and poor. I found, out of the blue, a very powerful man—physically powerful—who had spent time in jail for theft and assault. A resentful man with a violent temper. I had achieved notoriety by writing of my childhood and history of violence. I was now a minor literary celebrity, and Ara and I were guests at a country estate. I was determined that she should come to love me and, because of that love, let me push her about and dominate her. Once she accepted my treatment of her, I would have all I wanted and could leave. I would have a victory over a "rich bitch."

Ara had found her role and task some time before me and her palms lay up and open, waiting for my grasp, for my decisions. She sat there gazing simply and directly into my face. Finally, when I was clear, I grasped her hands and we went off to separate parts of the studio.

When I found my "private place," I realized, as I stood there, that it was a cell—a prison cell. The first part of my body that became active were my lower abdominal muscles, which seemed to be writhing with all of their power and I was walking, *walking.* It was as if I were being led by those muscles up and down the brief length of my cell. For some reason, my feet were bare, in my mind, though I was actually wearing soft dance slippers. My attention then shifted to my feet, which worked harshly into the cold, damp concrete as if they held the angry claws of a predatory animal. That action slowly flowed into thighs that bulged with the muscles of a weight lifter. The power allowed me to perform sudden squats to a stillness as if waiting to spring. All this time, I was intermittently pacing my cramped space like a caged animal. Without warning, my mouth became alive—a stretched gash across my face which I constantly tried to make smaller by turning my lips inward. This in time activated my whole face, which was always on the verge of exploding out of control as I kept trying to keep it in rein, all the while pacing the cell. Then the attention shifted to the shoulders which felt massive and writhing like the abdominals. This action gradually flowed down the arms to the hands, which wanted to flail about but were always caught by fisting and lowering the arms so that they would be quiet for a while. Lastly, the back came into play, and its wish was to crouch, to duck, to avoid blows from somewhere, but the wish had to be concealed so the crouch was spasmodically evident but mostly suppressed.

I had "become X." As I looked over to where Ara[6] was dancing, lightly flinging her arms about as if they were little flags pressed into the wind. I realized that I had to put on a tweed suit over my anger and my ugliness. I did everything I had been doing but one could see little except that I was walking toward her with a slow held step followed by quick ones which were almost out of control. It resembled an erratic rhumba. The moment I approached Ara, she turned and circled me as if to observe me on all sides and to be observed by me on all of her sides. Pretending a cool stance, I alternately observed her closely and looked off as if there were other items of more interest to me. I went into a slide almost to the ground which I stopped with some show-off pushups into a sudden squat and then stood erect trying to tower above her.

Ara moved closer to me. "This was going to be easy!" Looking away, I

6. In this accounting I call her Ara, but I don't know who she was within the duet and I never asked her, in spite of doing this duet many times in the studio and in performance.

reached to her, drawing her into a ballroom stance and, leading with definite power, guided her about as if on a dance floor. She followed as if we had done this many times before, once releasing herself from my grasp to circle and return to my arms. The more we danced, the more brutal I became until I was sweeping her down to the floor, pushing her away and pulling her back, each time going further and further from her, pretending an interest elsewhere, not unlike the way cats will play with a cricket or a mouse.

Finally, I drifted off to the far end of the studio, confident that she would be waiting for me, so sure was I of my power. I was ready to leave the floor after "celebrating" my success, the achievement of my task. While I was strutting my power, I glanced back at Ara and instead of that flighty arm-flinging, she was pacing back and forth in a limited space with a strangely familiar contorted body. *It was as if she were going through the same agony I had suffered.* The similarity was so great, I was shocked into the most unexpected compassion and concern for her. Uncertain, I wavered there, not knowing my next move, and found myself falling in love with her.

Confused, I approached her cautiously and slowly began a dance of protection and cradling and loving—which Ara accepted and reciprocated. We ended with a fierce, yet tender, love duet which finally settled into a moment of emotional exhaustion, and we left the floor together.

I have no idea as to whether Ara had achieved the task she found during the Hub Meditation or whether it had changed as the dance progressed. What shook me was that for the first time I had set out in an improvisation with a clear direction and because of what I had experienced I not only took an entirely unexpected path, but went through a profound change in character. This duet first occurred during studio work, and because it came out so richly, we did it again and again until we were sure it could be performed for the public which we did, many times, because it "worked."

To sum up these last few pages: The Duet (6.5) became the cornerstone of our work. It was the most fertile, challenging and exciting structure of all. I realized its amazing power when I became aware that even when performing it in public, there was a long period in the beginning when we were "doing nothing," we were just sitting cross-legged and staring at each other. Nonetheless, the audience was mesmerized, glued to what was highly intense activity, albeit mental. Once again, I learned that if there is an active, honest, inner life, an audience will go with the performer.

The great leap for all improvisors, whether they are musicians, actors, or dancers, is the act of performance. Improvising in the studio, we expect failures along with the successes. We hope to gain the skill and the authority to bring good, strong stuff to the public beast that demands meat in return for the effort of finding out-of-the-way studios hidden in ancient factory buildings leaning together in dark streets.

We met four times a week in four-hour sessions. By the time we presented our first programs, we had spun at least fifty different EGAS out of those first three I had encountered so briefly with the Open Theatre. Why were some performed on this program and others never? Actually, in our daily work we didn't "look" for performance material. Instead we held to a twofold focus: first, to try in every way to gain the freedom to respond fully to the moment and to each other, and second, to seize the most fruitful dance metaphors for our response.

The first performances were in our studio at 550 Broadway, August 25 and 26, 1971. Describing what we did then will give a sense of how we were developing and how we structured our work so that it could be performed. A copy of the program:

THE WORKGROUP

Directed by
DANIEL NAGRIN

Lee Connor, Ara Fitzgerald, Charles Hayward, Daniel Nagrin, Saluka, Mary Anne Smith and Yung Yung Tsuai.
Music Director: Richard Steinberg.

Program

Mary Anne	Charles and Lee
Mary Anne and Yung Yung	Charles
Lee and Ara	
Ara and Saluka	
Daniel and possibly some others	
The Workgroup	Charles and Lee*

Intermission

The Other
Each Alone
The Duet
    The Workgroup
Rondo
    The Workgroup

The way of The Workgroup moves in a shifting balance between the poles of improvisation and structure. Therefore, the results are a product of the creative energies of all.

Music on tape: Coltrane; Nagrin; an anonymous English estampie.

*[This was Polythemes.]

In our studio, the Workgroup always performed in the round. We wanted to be *seen* doing what we were doing. We did not want to *show* what we were doing. Why show when we could be seen, unless it was our intention to look a particular way? Throughout the entire four years of the Workgroup, the only costumes we ever wore were the best-looking dance clothes we had. The brilliant costume designer, Sally Ann Parsons, helped each of us choose. Our work was never a matter of appearances. It was always about doing something. To perform with an audience on one side only, as on the proscenium stage, is a metaphor for showing, therefore our choice of performing in the round. We felt that the moment we showed what we were doing, rather than just doing it, we would slide into preconceived notions of looking good: looking beautiful, looking interesting, looking like no one else (innovative), or perversely, looking rough and gross, and so on.

I have only realized recently that this distinction between showing and being seen doing something is precisely what has marked almost all my work, both as a soloist and as the director of the Workgroup. It explains why my own work attracted only a limited segment of the New York dance audience and only a grudging and limited recognition from most of the New York critics of dance. Most of them wanted to be shown something. When they sat there looking at a dancer or dancers not showing anything but doing something, they, of course, couldn't see what I/we were doing.

A discussion of each item on that first program will clarify some of our methods and thinking.

Mary Anne. This solo piece never had a name other than that of the performer, Mary Anne Smith. Like every performance piece, it came out of an exercise. As part of a warmup for the earlier Percursor Workgroup, I used to give an abdominal exercise which I called The 5/4 Reach. From a supine position, arms spread wide, the dancers would swiftly reach up, the torso following the arms just as quickly, to arrive very erect on a slow count of "1," hold for "2," and then roll down slowly to the original position for "3, 4, 5." Some of the dancers would roll back down too quickly, arriving on "5" or before and get caught in a static moment. To make the point that the life of every fall is in the resistance to falling, I would ask the dancers to ignore the five counts and to find something up there—in their imagination or on the ceiling—that they wanted/needed to touch and knew they could never reach, all the while knowing they must return to the ground.

The first time I gave The 5/4 Reach to this Workgroup, I challenged them to work the contradiction of being compelled to fall and refusing to fall. They were beautiful as one by one they fell in slow motion, that is, until all but Mary Anne had finished. She was still up there, reaching.

I had made it an unwritten principle for myself that when I gave a problem to the dancers and someone was taking what seemed to be an inordinately long time to do it, I would not interrupt. I let them finish in their own

Mary Anne
6.6

time. Work in the studio was for research, and each of the participants had to be given the freedom to explore without the imposition of theatrical, up-tempo timing.

She hadn't moved as she kept reaching. We were all very quiet, and finally it became apparent that she was falling—but more slowly than any of us thought possible. It was even hard to see her move. The passion of her reaching upward gripped our attention. It may have been five minutes later that, completely prostrate, she released the mad upward tension in her fingers, letting them fall back. Actually, none of us knew how long she took but we were aware that we had witnessed an exciting dance. When it came time to make up our first studio performance, there was little question that *Mary Anne's Dance* would lead it off. A dance experience had led to a work that could be performed for an audience. Once I timed her fall during a performance. She took seven and a half minutes to arrive at a complete rest.

Mary Anne and Yung Yung 6.7

Mary Anne and Yung Yung. Both had the capacity to push a process to the limit just to see how it would work. I had raised the business of maintaining eye contact to a first principle. I thought that sensitive and specific interaction depended on knowing who you were dealing with and what was happening to them. One day I observed these two engaged in a swirling, twisting, turning duet, remarkable for the fact that they never lost eye contact—on the floor, turning, in the air or running. It had the quality of a good-humored duel. Both with their flexible spines were performing "barrel turns" as they spun away from each other, they bent their backs until their heads hung upside down for a moment, thus not losing sight of each other even for a second. Originally, they did this as a full duet, starting with The Other, and continuing with the Hub Meditation, Each Alone, and The Duet. I can't recall how they got to it in performance nor how they ended it, but this can be set up by telling a group about to engage in a Duet:

> "Someone, something cannot or will not stop looking into the eyes of another."

The beauty of this almost fanatical locking into an activity is how often it leads the dancers into virtuosic movement. It follows directly from Tamiris's challenge to "follow through."

Lee and Ara. I have always been fascinated by contradiction and think it is the key to performance resonance. Pursuing this interest, I set up "Someone, something cannot move but wants to—desperately." This was at an open workshop session on a Saturday. It was amazing how much intense movement slowly filled the room. Suddenly, I caught sight of Lee and Ara in the far right corner of the studio, dangerously close to the steam radiator. Lee was on the ground in a quivering catatonic state at Ara's feet, trying to roll to the wall behind her. She was trying to move forward but not only was Lee blocking her, she seemed unable to raise her feet because her legs were rigid.

Despite the fact that they got nowhere, I couldn't take my eyes from their deadlock. Their intensity and concentration were equally fierce. When the sequence ground to a halt for everyone, I asked Lee and Ara as they passed close, "Can you remember what just happened, not what you did but what started it?" Bemused, they nodded. A few weeks later, during a lull in the work, I asked them to go at it again, emphasizing that they were to return to their original images and intentions and not try to repeat anything they had done the first time. It was a powerhouse and funny-sad at the same time. It became a staple in our first season of studio performances, though it came out differently every time. Once, in performance, Ara, exasperated by Lee's quivering stubbornness, bent down, gathered up his stiff body in her arms, and marched off the dance space. The audience was surprised and delighted and, as we were to learn, all the women in the company took note. From then on, we never knew who would lift whom, the male or the female.[7]

Lee and Ara
6.8

Lee and Ara. "Someone, something cannot move. Wants to move. Must move, but cannot."

Contradiction is the electricity that lights up the theatre. Without it, we have nothing to say. With it, we are challenged intellectually, emotionally and physically to confront the mess and the glory of existence. In the years since, I have given this "someone . . ." many times, and always the studio rocks with motion and intensity.

Ara and Saluka. This is dim in my memory. The duet was the end result of a couple of months' work around two not so simple questions: What is male? What is female? How it happened is explored further below (6.12).

The Duet was compelling for an audience, even in those first days. When an evening's program started, none of us, including me, knew what the "someone . . . something" would be. During the ten-minute intermission, I would let about seven minutes go by, then separate myself from the group, go into a high speed meditation and wait until a "someone" would surface in my mind. The moment one appeared, I would assemble the dancers and tell them the "someone . . . something." Then, I would sort out three couples, the audience lights would go out, the performance area illuminated; after a pause the three couples would step out on the floor to find their own area to sit and face each other. The entire process of The Mind-Wash and the Hub Meditation, with its choices and decisions, could take a long time. I, who often made myself the odd man out, watched the audience. They were never restless, but rather showed the intense involvement of people who knew something vital was going on between those three couples. Though they had no way of knowing what was in the minds of the dancers, they were unquestionably drawn into the dance.

---

7. At that time, 1971, ladies did not lift gentlemen dancers.

When all the dancers had made their internal discoveries and choices, had separated, and begun their Each Alone, music would come on. This was usually a tape, twenty minutes or longer, which the dancers, from previous experience, knew would energize their bodies and release their imaginations. Watching this was not easy for any audience. First, there were six individuals, each transformed from a neutral, waiting stance to a new human carved by a succession of danced metaphors. This, followed by the couples engaging with each other, each with their own agenda, created a stage overloaded with actions and counteractions—all seen through dance. Two things made looking possible. First, the entire space was infused with the energies around a common theme, say, "Someone is leaving. You are leaving or you are the one being left." Second, most in the audience would focus on a single couple, taking occasional glances at the other two couples.

As I said, we were a special taste. Some who watched us felt as if they had never seen real people dance before. They were more aware of a life going on than a "dance concert." Others were quite upset. On occasion we heard, "I felt as if I was intruding upon what was too personal to be witnessed." We found our best audiences on tour.

Rondo (6.1). For music, we used an irresistible estampie played four times. Every member of the company had their own short choreographed themes for this music. We began with changing combinations of trios, solos, duets, and finished with the entire company—all to the same music. The last time, everyone burst into their own theme at the same time. It was a bit of a circus, but by this time, the audience knew us, our themes and our game of rondo variation. For one of our few directed activities, we all exited on the last few measures of the music. We would return for a bow, exit and from offstage, I would announce, "Now it is your turn to dance!" which was the cue for a medley of renaissance, jazz and rock tunes and for the audience to take to the dance floor, which they did.

Polythemes was the first of our more complex and extended pieces. It started with a statement followed by a question: Most humans have one or more circular patterns of behavior. What is yours? Each dancer was to find movement metaphors for this and choreograph such a circular phrase, a phrase that repeated itself endlessly. By way of example, I will give what I chose: The perfectionist sets out to produce an immaculate masterpiece, but perfection takes time and since there is never enough time, it is not finished when the moment of delivery draws nigh. The final product has to be frantically pulled together by temporizing and making do. I had a specific task in mind. Confession: I always start out with a plan of deliberate supercomprehensiveness. In sight of the deadline, I am transformed into a speed demon thrusting all the pieces together. Fortunately, I thrive under pressure.

To do the piece, each dancer (eight is best) must have already choreographed his.her own personal circular theme.

**Polythemes
6.9**

Polythemes. Set up a square space about sixteen feet on each side. Four dancers start at the four corners of the square. Four more stand along the sides, midway between the corners. Leave your place whenever you are ready and move to the center of the space. When your body comes in contact with another, close your eyes and you are in and doing Goldfish Bowl (5.1). Whenever you are ready to leave the others, find a space for yourself and begin your circular theme phrase. From here on, do your phrase continuously, but never leaving the square. If in the course of dancing it, you encounter another, you are to persist in the pattern and direction of your movement with no deviation, but you must not leave the square. The probability is that you will encounter someone who is impeding your motions. Your action is to persist in continuing your theme but never using force that would unbalance or injure the other. If you are blocked, you will attempt to disengage yourself while still asserting your theme. This activity—being blocked and working your way free—modifies your theme, permanently. Your phrase is now changed. Like a car that has been in a crash, you can go on but bent out of shape. The piece ends when the music ends. Again, the only limitations are swift and/or forceful movements which could easily inflict harm on anyone you encountered.

The music for *Polythemes* was the joint work of Charles Hayward and Lee Connor. Charles could play the saxophone, and Lee the viola. I asked each to find a musical equivalent of his own circular theme. I brought them one at a time into the studio to record eight minutes of his circular theme, neither having heard the other's music. They were rerecorded on parallel half-tracks. The weaving of the conflicting, longing, sometimes anguished melodies were intense and right for *Polythemes*.

Looking back from this distance, I can see the contradictory metaphors that kept that work alive in the repertoire for two seasons. Goldfish Bowl, when it is done sensitively, carries the sweetness of a group of people meshing with gentle physical intimacy, while the development of Polythemes is all about self-preoccupation, the disregard of all others and the damage that does to others and self.

That summer we created and performed one other major work: *Ritual for Seven*, later renamed *Rituals of Power*. The problem of power has always interested me, in its historical aspect and its all-too contemporary manifestations. It is the doorway for most of the pain coming into the world, whether among nations or intimate circles of family or friends. What follows is a summation of how we set up this work.

**Rituals of
Power
6.10**

Rituals of Power. All sit in a circle, big enough to observe all. (Recall, we were seven at the time.) Accept the premise that we are all guests at a luxurious home in the country.[8] First, all do a Mind-Wash (3.2). Then, after

---

8. The setting could be a business office, a royal court, a military unit, a fraternity house, etc.

simply looking at all the others in the circle, ask yourself, "Who are these people sharing this weekend with me?" As you gaze upon each other, new individuals will emerge from the faces and bodies of these dancers you know so well. Accept whatever surprises emerge. Everyone will create their own secret cast. Every group has an unspoken ranking of popularity, talent, power, and so forth. Who are you and where do you rank among all of these? Who do you think might look up to you? Who is your equal? To whom would you defer? Where do you want to be in the power-prestige structure of this group and what are you willing to do to get there? What is the dance metaphor, the physical metaphor for the task you have set for yourself? When you have the answers to these questions, turn your palms upward and rest your hands on your knees.

When the last person does this, she.he rises, leaves the circle and goes to find a place in an imaginary line that faces the circle, placing her.himself at the front, the middle or the rear, depending upon where she.he ranks her.himself. Then, clockwise, the next person rises to do the same and so on until all are in the line, self-ranked. There will be surprises and some gentle jostling as individuals negotiate for "their" position within this group.

When the group has settled into a line with a "leader" at the head, the "leader" walks to one side of the space and faces into the space. The person behind goes to stretch out prone and at right angles at the foot of the leader. Each person in turn does the same, a couple of feet away from the previous person. When all are in place, the leader steps across all the bodies to find his.her place to do Each Alone (4.4). Then the first person to lie down rises, steps across the bodies of the others, and finds a place to do Each Alone. In this order, one by one the others rise to do similarly. At this juncture we started the taped music.[9]

Rituals such as this one are critical in these improvisations, since they let the viewers in on the ground rules of the performance. The audience must gain a sense of the structure they are observing early in every piece. They will not know the specifics, but they will know enough to free their imaginations to attach their own meaning to the actions they observe. Every member of the audience will supply a different set of particulars. In this work, being in front is a metaphor for a social relationship, just as is stepping over another. With that initial bit of preset staging the audience finds itself working along with the performers.

Rituals of Power, continued: When you finish Each Alone and have become X, you move to engage one or more of the others in order to real-

---

9. This was a collage assembled by Lee and me. It had Tibetan buddhist bells slowed to half speed, Lee's running feet, a bit of Handel's *Messiah* and Libby's screaming—not all at once of course. It worked.

ize the task, the ambition you have set for yourself (unless of course your X is trying to be unnoticed). Your X may have a high or the highest ranking position in the group and yet wish to avoid it, to avoid the responsibility and the exposure it entails. Follow the needs of your X. The development of this stage of Rituals of Power is exactly like The Duet (6.5) except that now there are more than two people on stage. How many others you deal with depends upon who you are. One character might try to affect everyone, while another may focus on only one other. If and when you realize your task, you celebrate that in dance and leave the dance floor. Similarly, if you are convinced you cannot succeed, you dance that resignation and leave.

Rituals of Power had an astonishing development. The first performance was electric and tumultuous. Everyone found a strong character and the interactions were intense. In fact, it was here that the duet between Ara and myself first occurred. There were to be four more weekend performances, and when the second one approached, I began to wonder how we were going to return to *Rituals of Power*. During that week I ran the company through two of the other pieces, *Polythemes* and *Rondo*, and experimented with some new ideas but something stopped me from getting near *Rituals*. The night of the performance, before the studio doors had opened to admit the audience, I gathered the company and threw this at them:

Rituals of Power continued: You will sit as before, anywhere in the circle, clear your heads and go back to *Rituals of Power*, as you experienced it last week. What do you recall? What happened? Did you change? Did you change anyone? Did you succeed? Fail? What was left undone? What did you learn about these people? In reality, we have already lived a part of *Rituals of Power*, and tonight will be a continuation of what happened last week. As you sit in the circle, observing each other, you should ask yourself, "What remains to be done? Having lived through this and that with these others, what am I now going to do? What am I going to try to become?" The order in which you line up and lie down will probably change. Much will be different and some things the same. Find out!

Over the weeks of performing, *Rituals of Power* became a powerful dance novel. About the fifth week it ran into the ground because two of the dancers arrived at a static place. It mattered not what any of us did, they never changed nor responded to us and the piece fell flat. This raises a tricky issue. If their rigidity came from their own lack of sensitivity to the others and the limits of their imaginations, they had failed and so sank that performance and that setup. (We never returned to it.) If, however, their characters had evolved to a static place, and sadly people do, then as the I Ching says, "no blame." At the time, I was upset with this development, or rather this lack of development of a wondrous structure and secretly blamed the two dancers. Now, I wonder what really happened.

This raises a paradox and a potential flaw in how we dealt with improvisation and performance. The hard rule was that we were to find what was there, never to make anything interesting, beautiful or original. If we found something that was interesting, beautiful and/or original we were to hold on to it, pursue it, work it and, if it stood the test, to perform it. By its very nature, improvisation is unpredictable. It may go flat. *If so, so be it.* A tennis match between the two hottest players in the world can go flat. The 1993 Superbowl was a yawn. When you go to a sporting event, you hope for excitement and may get it—or not. Honest improvisation is no different. My message to audience and critics attending an improvisation performance is to accept the fact that it is an event which *may* deliver excitement. All that can be demanded of athletes is their skill and commitment. All that can be demanded of performing improvisors is imagination, poetry, good dancing and honesty.

I never ever again gave Rituals of Power as an exercise or as a performance piece. We went on to other projects. Still, I am convinced that with a dedicated group, skilled in improvisation, with a clear conception and experience with the duet structure, it can be an enlightening exercise and, equally, a wonderful performance piece that can continuously develop from performance to performance, like a novel.

We did not videotape it. We taped nothing at this time; we were not at all ready emotionally, nor were we sufficiently secure in our powers of imagination and honesty to be looked at and remembered by a ruthless and insensitive camera eye.

Though these were the pieces that were seen by our public, there were many more never seen by others which were equally important to us. Performing improvisation is a difficult craft that requires considerable honing. Here are the EGAS no one saw us do and yet made us stronger and clearer in our work.

Backs
6.11

Backs. All sit cross-legged, with your eyes closed, in a line facing the back of another dancer. Clear a space in your head with your breath. Whenever you are ready, reach your hands forward to touch the back of the person in front of you. With your hands study this back, the texture of the cloth, the skin, the configuration of the muscles and bones that can be felt. You will study not only to experience but to remember. When you think your hands have it, the memory of that back, drop your hands in your lap. When you become aware that the person behind you is no longer studying your back, with your eyes still closed, turn a quarter of a circle away on your bottom and now reach your hands forward *as if that person were still in front of you* and with your fingers relive the entire experience of touching her.his back, not merely to go through the motions of touching but to feel once again the cloth, the skin and the configuration of muscles and bones.

Do not be disconcerted if you find areas whose sensory life you cannot recall at all. In other places, the most you will have is the idea of moist skin or a nubby fabric, not the sensation. Do as much of the back, in the air, as you can. Then swivel back to face in the original direction, with your eyes still closed, and reach your hands to touch the back. If you encounter a shoulder, your partner is still re-creating in the air. Drop your hands and wait until you sense a movement back to the original facing. Then raise your hands again and go to the places where your memory encountered either a blank or only a general idea of skin or cloth.

Experience with your hands what eluded you, and when you think your hands have it, and the dancer behind is no longer studying your back, once again swivel a quarter turn away and go directly to the blank places and fill them in by experiencing the actual sensation of touching. When you have done all you can, drop your hands to your lap and wait until you hear an "OK," indicating that all are finished.

The person at the head of the line will need the qualities of a meditative saint: patience, joy in serving others and the capacity to be fully alive while doing "nothing." (Unless the group is large enough to form a circle.) The saint's eyes can be opened or closed as desired.

Backs is what the teachers of acting call a sense-memory exercise. Usually they assign mundane tasks like putting on clothing or sewing, without props. For students of the craft of acting, it opens the door to imagination, specific movement sensualities and the very spine of their work, *the act of pretending.* What is an actor? One who makes believe. One who takes a childhood game and turns it into an adult profession of being watched by others seated in a large room all facing in the same direction.

What teacher of dance gives sense-memory exercises? Actually many, but not consciously: "Carve the air." "Your arms are passing through water." "The floor is hot as you are doing the prances." Many teach this way and some do not, deliberately. They, and choreographers of this school, want their students and dancers to move without pretending anything, not emotion, not meaning and without any sense-memory games.

When Anna Halprin walked into a space bent over, carrying a wine bottle, all she did was place it on the stage floor and leave, still bent over, to get another wine bottle and repeat the task until twenty-four bottles had been brought in. She ended the dance by reversing the process. For her and for much of her audience the accomplishment of the task was sufficient. Yvonne Rainer had a group of dancers running in a circle, occasionally stopping to fall down and then rise to resume running. That was the dance. Dancers trained in the Merce Cunningham tradition are asked to do a movement simply and fully—period. I have found much to admire in the work of these artists even while I resist some aspects. The only point here is to *know who you are.* If your work does demand imagination and the game of pretending, deliberate sense-memory work will give all your performances a vital, living presence that breathes and changes with each new dance role and throughout the course of a single performance.

This matter of sense-memory brings into focus two radically different experiences in all performing, including improvising. One is what we have just been examining: what is imagined. The other is the palpable objects: props, sets, costumes, music *and the other dancers.* The ideal for which we reach is a full, unquestioned response to the object of our focus, be it palpable or imagined. Each presents difficulties.

One can present the problem in the form of a tricky paradox: the visible object is easier and harder to embrace than the imagined object which is easier and harder to embrace. The visible/tangible object's presence is a constant reality check *if* one observes closely, but so much is hidden from view. The whole point of art is that what we see is only a small part of what is happening. Every bit of our intelligence, sensitivity and imagination is challenged by what we are looking at. What is hiding beneath the surface? What are the mysteries that surround the metaphoric import of each gesture, costume, prop and piece of music? Then too, there is so much to see. What to focus upon? What is really important? What is relevant? To further cloud matters, there are our inhibitions which check or re-direct our attention and reactions.

As for the intangible object, undivided concentration is so much more easily achieved. Possibilities of response seem to be richer and freer. Negatively, the imagined object is all too easily reshaped as one goes along in the improvisation or performance of the role. Reshaping it may be caving in to one's inclination to ignore troubling or complex or forgotten aspects of the object. Such an improvisation loses its core and becomes self-indulgent. Reshaping the intangible may, however, represent a deeper penetration and understanding of the object which could be called poetry.

A dance artist must be able to regard the imagined and the palpable as one continuum in order to move fluently from one to the other with a clear respect for the reality of both. If a dancer ever becomes unable to conjure up the reality of the imagined world, she.he is getting ready to retire from the role of an artist.

What is male? What is female? At the time we were working, the air was thick with these questions. I had conceived an elaborate structure that would throw some of the problems, the confusions and the clichés on to the stage. Since the very meaning of the company was improvisation, it not only meant that I was not going to choreograph anything for them, it also meant that what they did had to come out of *their* hides and *their* insides. Here is the process that built **The Male/Female Dance.** The entire company, women and men, were involved in every stage of this work.

Find your private place on the studio floor, sit, close your eyes and clear a space in your head. Then do a Mind-Wash alone, without a partner. When you finish, the question you will drop into your insides is, "What is male?" Allow a parade of images and answers to pass through your mind and wait until one of them stays—until one of them is always there regardless of what new images come up. (This is the Hub Meditation [5.7].) Be certain you are contemplating a specific and not a generalization. Few questions are so often answered in generalizations as this one. "What is male?"

When the image comes close, when it becomes clear and specific, when what it does becomes apparent, become the image, become X. Start the becoming standing, kneeling, sitting or lying down, from wherever it is appropriate. The act of becoming X is realized by one part of the body at a time doing what it is that X does. You do not imitate X. You do not try to look like X. You only do what X does with one part of the body at a time. There will come a moment when everything will come together. You will be X. (This is Each Alone [4.4].) Celebrate that and then leave the floor.

When every one had left the floor, this part of the work was over for the day. The next day, I gave exactly the same structure to all, men and women, except for the fact that I rephrased the question to, "What is female?" On the third day we moved to a new level:

Go through the process of preparation: finding your place in the studio, clearing a space in your head, doing a Mind-Wash, and then return to the male or female image you had. Men return to your male image, women to your female image. Go through the entire process of becoming X again, one part of the body at a time doing what it is that X does. When you are "finished," when you have become X, come to a rest standing, kneeling, sitting or lying down.

After a while you will hear music. Listen to it as X. Find the place of X in that music. What is X doing in the world of that music? When you can answer that question, begin to improvise to the music until a phrase emerges that you can repeat, that you can analyze and even count. Now, do that phrase (A) twice and then improvise a new phrase until that improvisation takes a repeatable form. You will now have a complete phrase (AAB), that somehow comes out of the question, "What is male?" or "What is female?" Leave the floor and rest.

If you are a woman, when all the women have left the floor, you will be ready for the next stage. The last one to leave the floor now teaches her AAB phrase to all the women. All learn to do it twice in succession. As soon as this "teacher" says "OK, done," anyone who feels that her phrase would flow nicely out of the one just learned announces, "Next!" and she teaches her phrase to the entire group. As soon as all the dancers can fluently do both phrases in succession, she announces "OK, done," and another dancer sings out, "Next!" and so on until all the women have learned all the What is female? phrases. Finally, all the phrases are performend in one continuous flow, a short dance.

Meanwhile, the men are going through the same process. When both men and women are finished they dance for each other. Then the men learn the women's dance and vice versa.

To summarize the structure:

Men do their dance.
Women do their dance.
Men do the women's dance.
Women do the men's dance.
Men and Women mesh and together do both dances.

Finale in a circle: Each dancer steps out solo to do a favorite phrase learned from a woman or a man, and his.her own phrase. The last person does this once and then leads all offstage again doing a favorite and a personal phrase while the dancers following do their favorite and personal phrases.

The apt colloquial expression is that though "we worked our tails off," we neither finished nor performed any part of The Male/Female Dance. When we made our first program, I did remember that Saluka, in response to "What is male?" and Ara, in response to "What is female?" had both hit what appeared to be rich and fertile material, and I linked them in a duet with an arbitrary division of space. Neither could leave their own space while trying to reach and influence the other. Like most "good ideas" superimposed on material rather than coming up out of it and out of necessity, it was an interesting setup done by a pair of beautiful dancers and without weight or a future.

If any readers find possible excitement in The Male/Female Dance and wish to bring the entire structure to life, there is the problem of music. In the description above, there is the sentence, "After a while you will hear music." At this point we brought in our percussionist, Richard Steinberg, and I laid down a rather odd rhythmic framework based on a 7/4 bar: a seven-count phrase done twice and a seven-count variation, a total of twenty-one counts which made the *AAB* phrase. (I don't know why I chose this bar structure; I suspect I fell prey to one of my personal no-no's, trying to do something different.) To make your own Male/Female dance, I believe it would be appropriate to use a live percussionist to help build a simple, cool rhythmic score with melodic material added later, if at all. To start off with music, be it rock, romantic, classical, jazz or whatever, would bend the head of each dancer in the meditation on "What is male?" and "What is female?" Every one of those musical styles has a built-in answer to those two questions. Matters of length, bar structure, number of repetitions, and so forth, would be determined by the musical sophistication, taste and number of the dancers. If you do it, please invite me to a showing. At this distance, I realize that it never happened for us because, though it sprang out of improvisation and though all contributed to its movement, *it was, in its final form, choreography and not improvisation.* Our hearts were in a different place. The experience was useful nevertheless in that it drew us together as we learned each other's style.

Wind II was an elusive, lovely development out of Wind I (5.10).

Wind II
6.13

Four dancers assemble just outside the working space. Call them dancers A, B, C, and D. Dancer A enters the space to find the "right" place to be. Arriving, she.he pauses to absorb the feel—the impact of the room and all that is in it. When that feeling coalesces, Dancer A lets it emerge in one brief movement gesture, not unlike the spare single brush-strokes one sees in early Chinese Taoist paintings. They tended to be serene and elliptical. Of course, the feeling of the room may be something wildly different to Dancer A. The goal is not the Taoist quality but their economy of motion. The end of the movement is held, motionless. This is the cue for Dancer B to enter the space, looking only at Dancer A and finding a place anywhere but in front of Dancer A. What Dancer A did in relation to the room, Dancer B does in relation to Dancer A. "What is the feeling that comes off Dancer A?" is the question asked by Dancer B. When the feeling takes shape, Dancer B releases a spare gesture and holds the end of it, motionless, whereupon Dancer C enters looking only at Dancer B. Dancer C goes through the same process as Dancer B, followed by Dancer D. Dancer D has one added responsibility, to find a place where he.she can see Dancer C *and yet be seen by Dancer A.*

The moment Dancer D appears in the line of vision of Dancer A, the latter immediately absorbs all that is possible by looking . . . looking. when Dancer D becomes motionless, Dancer A does a spare gesture coming out of what is felt by looking at Dancer D and holds still for its last moment. This clues Dancer B, who has never stopped observing Dancer A, to release a spare gesture about Dancer A. And so the movement travels in stops and starts from dancer to dancer. All the dancers are motionless except for the one who is releasing the spare gesture. There is no rule about how long one should take to make the gesture after the dancer focused upon becomes still. Each should be sensitive to their own timing.

The "spare gesture" is stage one. Stage two occurs when one of the dancers—any dancer, while continuing to look at her.his person of concentration, receives a strong impulse to keep moving rather than becoming motionless after a brief motion. When that happens, whoever is focusing upon the continuously moving dancer must follow suit. Similarly, the next two dancers in turn begin to move continuously. Call this stage "continuous motion."

There is a distinct peril at this juncture. Becoming absorbed in the necessity of continuous motion, it is too easy to lose sight of the very spine of Wind II. It is all about *reading* the body and movement of another from moment to moment. The continuous motion embodies what each dancer sees, feels, senses about the other. Ideally, what the dancer *thinks* about the other should not be the focus. Conscious opinions and thoughts about others are always with us, to a greater or lesser degree. Here, we are seeking another level of awareness and response, poorly described as a *felt* awareness.

Stage three takes place piecemeal. At any time, any dancer can broaden her.his focus from one dancer to all. This means capturing the feel of the entire group at that moment or continuously shifting attention from one dancer to another. That action becomes the cue for the three other dancers to follow suit, each in her.his own time. Call this stage the "universal ad lib." It resembles Wind I (5.10).

Stage four also takes place piecemeal. At any time, any dancer can shift his.her attention to only one dancer, still moving continuously. Call this "continuous motion again." In this transition, the dancer chosen for focus can be the same as in the beginning, or any of the other three. With this freedom, it is probable that the symmetry of the beginning when one dancer fixed upon the next will not occur. Instead, it might be that three dancers choose the same dancer—who chooses one of them. There is one hard restriction. No dancer may choose a dancer who reciprocates attention, that is, there cannot be a pair focusing upon each other. That's a very different EGAS. If a mutual attention occurs, one dancer or the other must back off and look elsewhere.

Stage five can be called "spare gesture again." At any time, any dancer can shift to the single motion and become motionless. Whoever is "reading" that dancer must also make a single spare gesture and slip back into that first mode (like stage one), becoming motionless until she.he witnesses another spare gesture.

The end: sooner or later, one of the four chooses not to make any more spare gestures.

His.her observer can no longer make a move unless a motion is witnessed. Stillness gradually spreads to all four. They hold their last position, *each still looking at another*, until by mutual awareness they break and leave the floor.

Several notes about Wind II: Originally, the transitions from one stage to another were controlled by the director, me. I would clap my hands as a signal. Once I participated in Wind II, I became aware of how unnecessary and intrusive was this guidance. In the early stages, however, when the dancers are learning the sequence, an outside controller might be helpful. A variation on this EGAS is to have one of the four be a sound-maker, either a dancer with a percussion instrument or a musician who could move as well. That worked beautifully, a few times. On the whole, our studio work with Wind II was uneven. At its heart was the challenge to learn to "read" another dancer.

Despite the fact that we never performed it in that first year, I think it did help to heighten our sensitivities. It remained for a few years an "exercise" until, in the last year of the Workgroup, it entered the repertoire as part of a sequence called *Sea Anemone* (8.16). There it was fine and, in subsequent years, it proved to be a breakthrough for university groups having difficulty entering into the adventure of improvisation.

Another EGAS that we never performed but found to be a good warmup was **The Cliché.**

The Cliché | To a steady beat, either to music or an internal rhythm you set up, find a
6.14 | few of the moves you always do and work them into a short phrase which can be repeated. Once the phrase is set, continue doing it without changing. Then, whatever happens, happens. It might change itself or not.

Long before the Workgroup and long after, a collection of spare and evocative poems have been seeds for some of the most creative work in my classes. In a book of essays by Kenneth Rexroth, perversely titled *Assays*, I came across a collection of native American poems that were gathered by Frances Densmore.[10] I was caught up by their elliptic power and brevity, immediately sensing that they belonged to dance. At the time, I had the good fortune to have at my disposal the services of a young actor with a typewriter. At the rate of $1.50 an hour, Dustin (yes, Hoffman) typed out forty or so index cards which I have been using in classes ever since. A few of them:

> Strike you
> Our land
> With curved horns.
>
> In form like a bird,
> it appears.[11]
>
> Sometimes
> I go about pitying
> Myself,
> While I am carried by the wind
> Across the sky.
>
> The odor of death,
> I discern the odor of death
> In front of my body.
> He said, Unreal the buffalo is standing.
> These are his sayings.
> Unreal the buffalo is standing.

10. Kenneth Rexroth, *Assays* (New York: New Directions, 1961), pp. 59–68. Another rich source of evocative poems ideal for dance from peoples of Africa, America, Asia and Oceania is *Technicians of the Sacred*, edited by Jerome Rothenberg (Garden City, N.Y.: Anchor Books, 1968).

11. Robert Duvall, another young actor in the class, made a startling study for this one.

> Unreal he stands in the open space.
> Unreal he is standing.
>
> A voice,
> I will send.
> Hear me!
> The land
> All over,
> A voice
> I am sending!
> Hear me!
> I will live!

That was a movement class for a group of young actors gathered up by Dustin; they were graduates of the Neighborhood Playhouse where they studied with one of the foremost teachers of acting, Sanford Meisner. I tacked the cards on the studio walls saying,

Poems
6.15

When and if you find one that gets to you, one that strings you, one that changes your breath, learn it, drop it into your body and let the words come to life.

For about two weeks in the early days of this first Workgroup, the pillars and walls were decorated with about twenty of these. The dancers would, in their warmups, in breaks, while lunching, during an extended improvisation, pause to glance at them and then sometimes we would make them the focus of our work.

While writing this passage, I checked back to Rexroth's book and was struck by these lines:

> The intense aesthetic realization which precedes the poem is a realization of identity with a beneficent environment. Often this is focused in a dream or vision, waking or sleeping, after long lonely fast and vigil in the forest or desert. An aspect of the environment, an animal or a natural object or force, appears to the Indian, waiting in a trance state, and gives him the song, which remains his most precious possession and the pivot of his life forever after. (p. 58)

Despite the vast differences between the men and women who created those poems and the dancers of the Workgroup, I was and am constantly trying to make the same creative process happen. Our contemporary environment is hardly "beneficent," but that is our life and our world. I present the dancers with the creative paradox: lose yourself as you observe and interact with the world, with the other, with the object; in that "abandonment" of self, allow the poem to well up out of your inner being.

Like Backs (6.2), and Male/Female (6.12), the Indian poems were never used in performance, but the time spent working on them strengthened all our subsequent work. In retrospect, the Indian poem time was the most valuable of all. We learned from those poets how to find the metaphor that poeticized our dance and how to invigorate the vision and the imagination of the audience.

It also, taught us how to deal with the potential weakness at the heart of our method. The strongest substance has a vulnerability. A glass vase can gleam in its glory for centuries. One light tap of a metal hammer and we have a mess of shards. The plastic wrapping on four little peanut butter crackers will frustrate all efforts to tear it open until stabbed by the point of a nail file. If our intention was to be specific in all that we did and to have a specific identity at all times, what was to guard us against dancing linear, literal content? What could shield us from the most devastating question of all, "Why are you dancing? Why aren't you actors in a play and just speak what you have on your mind?" Getting caught in the literal and the linear was and is the Achilles heel of how we work. The answer? We never fled the literal but tried never to get stuck in it. We learned to bend it, stretch it, squeeze it, quicken it, transmute it to another part of the body, alter the "who"; we learned to make the literal a springboard to the metaphor. In so doing we were making motion poems, which could easily be another name for dancing.

It is time to pause to pin down this word, *metaphor*, not only to be clear as to how and why we are using it but to point out that a significant segment of dance abhors and avoids its use. What follows will lay bare the philosophic and aesthetic bones of how and why we worked, despite the fact that all about us in that time, 1969—1974, the winds were blowing in the opposite direction.

Jill Johnston talks negatively of dance "in which movement represents anything other than itself."[12] This is the classic put-down of metaphor by the ideologists of modern, abstract, formalist art.

Francis Sparshott waves his flag for purity: "Meanwhile, it may be claimed that at the hand of Balanchine, the traditional art of ballet has been reborn . . . as the art of pure dance that it always potentially was. Just as relief from the burden of representationalism has disentangled from extraneous tasks the pure art that painting always was, so relief from storytelling has set ballet . . . free to be the art of dance that it never managed to be before."[13]

In essence, these people have declared dance, as metaphor, dead. They ask: What is there to see, to experience, to interpret or to analyze except the movement and the shapes they fall into?

In a left-handed way this whole matter came up in an interview with Charles Hayward who was in the Workgroup and is now a film actor. He flew in from Los Angeles to help me review our history.

> CH: [That was] one of the most wonderful things we were constantly able to do in the Workgroup. We designed ways to again regain and retain the child.

12. *Movement Research*, September 1990, p. 2.
13. Francis Sparshott, *Off the Ground: First Steps to a Philosophical Consideration of the Dance* (Princeton, N.J.: Princeton University Press, 1988), p. 73.

DN: What you are saying casts an interesting light on large portions of the modernist and post-modernist movement. They lost the ability to play—to make believe—like children. They were terrified of make-believe. They tried to do what they thought was "real."

The mainstream of modern art, through all of the "isms"—abstract, non-objective, formalist, avant garde, post-modern—flowed away from the game of pretending, representing, having meaning, from playing. Most of it is humorless and none of it is tragic. I agree that it is often interesting to see someone walking or running, and to many of us it is equally interesting *and important* to see whether they are trying to get away from something or go someplace,

Webster's Unabridged Dictionary:
"metaphor: a transferring from one word the sense of another . . . a figure of speech in which one thing is likened to another, different thing by being spoken of as if it were that other, '. . . all the world's a stage.' "

Fowler's *Modern English Usage* (1965): ". . . our vocabulary is largely built on metaphors; we use them, though perhaps not consciously, whenever we speak or write." (p. 359)

The Lord is my shepherd . . . My cup runneth over . . . A heart of stone . . . Thy word is a lamp unto my feet . . . The long arm of the law . . . A stiff upper lip. There is no end to them. They weave in and out of every expression and every thought and every movement. What human gesture is not a metaphor? A handshake offers the hand that could be bearing a weapon. Hands clasped in prayer are a symbol of subjection—hands voluntarily tied together. Bowing diminishes one in size. Shaking a finger is waving a stick or a club. Thrusting arms overhead says, "Look at me! I won!" Posture is a metaphor of whom we think we are or whom we think we have the right to be. What is the Flamenco dancer saying with lifted chest, arched back and head high?

Consider the lexicon of "pure dance movements." The attitude that was so shrewdly stolen from Giovanni da Bologna's *Mercury* by Carlo Blasis is the perfect metaphor for being airborne while standing or turning on the ground. Mercury was the flying messenger of the gods. The line of the lifted back leg ascending to the curved upper arm is so powerful that it eliminates from our consciousness the supporting leg—and the dancer is in flight. To me, to Tamiris who schooled me in my beginning, the sheer elegance and physicality of an exquisite attitude is just one of the ten thousand ways of seeing and experiencing it.

Merce Cunningham raises a curtain on two men and a woman stripped down to leotard and tights. They stand in alert lifted positions in a small group upstage left, facing and looking straight out at the audience. In a moment they lash into a fury of brilliant unrelated moves in all directions, paying no attention to each other or the music. Who in any audience is going to speculate that it is really a ménage à trois? No one. Cunningham gives no false signals. The ballet-based moves, interspersed with a rare contraction

and arbitrary arm motions, immediately present the metaphor of people dancing, albeit it strangely by comparison with traditional classical dance—or
modern dance for that matter. "They," including Mr. Cunningham and his
colleague, John Cage, might shudder at my phrase "the metaphor of people
dancing," but does it not denote a sign, a statement, a conviction, a flag as it
were, a view of life, a philosophy, that of all the possible ways of dancing and
using dance, this is the way chosen? A group of highly skilled dancers exe-
cutes a set of given motions. Is not this choice, prepared with much labor and
care and presented to the public, a metaphor for a profoundly held belief?

If dance is truly alive it has a shimmer of the ineffable that distinguishes
it from dance that is lifeless. We know that we are looking at an unsuccessful
dance when all that fills our consciousness are the dancers, their efforts, their
costumes, the music, the lights, the stage, the person sitting in front of us, the
theatre and whatever else can be perceived at that moment. A dance becomes
alive when we are "hooked," caught up, drawn in, forget the bad seating and
join the dancers in their dance. We are not experiencing merely their motion
any more than a true performer merely experiences that act of moving about.
So, what is this "ineffable"? It is something more than a leg raised, more than
a motion. "More" is another name for poetry; the bones of poetry are
metaphors, and metaphors represent something other than themselves.

Every action, in or out of art, can be seen as a metaphor for something
else. Metaphors are what we do for a living. In improvisation, we are never
dangerously rough with each other. It is unthinkable to actually eroticize
another in a course of our work. And yet, we can do *anything* in dance as long
as we are doing a metaphor for it: murder, rape, the tenderest of gestures or
just plain hotshot dancing. We impoverish the depth of our artistic life if we
avoid dealing with any and all these impulses, poetically.

There are startling moments when the metaphor and "it" coincide. A
handshake, an embrace, a thrust fist are all literal gestures which have been
used in dance time and again with powerful effect, but only when they are
spare islands in a sea of evocative signs and metaphors. At other times, they
are banal, sentimental, trite and, worst of all, lacking in poetic vision. The
fear should not be for gesture, for meaning, for an inner life, for representation, but for slovenly and opportunistic attempts to be entertaining, to use
"accessible" as a cover-up for lightweight and the single-minded determina-
tion to be "successful." All these vulgarize and abdicate the dangerous and
difficult task of being an artist. The purists who shun meaning fail in the
search for the holy grail of purity in that whatever they do is drenched in and
expressive of a specific and precise attitude toward life and art and that if anything is dance crammed with meaning.

Every art movement is like a child in relation to what came before. Some
carry forward a tradition and some react violently against what was given as
truth and the only way. Consider this lyric from the most popular song in the
1910 musical *Madam Sherry*, written by Otto Harbach.

> Every little movement has a meaning all its own,
> Every thought and feeling by some posture may be shown.

The couplet is quoted by Ted Shawn in his book, *Every Little Movement,* and he goes on: "Current trends in life, politics and art provide the raw material from which the musical show distills its satires, 'takeoffs,' burlesques. . . . 'Every Little Movement' reflected the epoch-making new chapter which had been opened in the world of the dance. . . . with the advent of Ruth St. Denis and Isadora Duncan, a whole new approach to movement had come into the dance world—that at all times, dance should *express something.* The movement might . . . have dramatic, emotional, narrative content, kinetic or symbolic values—but certainly every little movement had to have meaning and not be performed merely as technique, as 'steps' or as an acrobatic spectacle."[14]

The subject of Shawn's book was then a new movement derived from the theories and the teachings of François Delsarte which influenced a whole generation of actors, singers and dancers. Delsarte believed that specific body positions carried specific meanings.

> Head raised but turned towards the object or person:
>   Abandon or Vulgar Familiarity
> Head (level) turned toward the person or object:
>   Favorable criticism or tenderness
> Head lowered but (turned) towards person or object:
>   Veneration or maternal tenderness.[15]

Detailed maps of fingers, shoulders, eyes and mouth spelled out precise meanings for each possible position—the bent back of the wrist pressed against the forehead surely indicated an overwhelming grief. Still, it would be bad history to dismiss this as nonsense and useless. The fact is that some very fine artists studied, used and believed in it. There is evidence that Isadora Duncan absorbed it, certainly Ruth St. Denis, and I can recall Martha Graham sitting erect and imperious in her Fifth Avenue studio and solemnly stating that the body was divided into three parts, the physical, the emotional and the mental. She touched her legs, "the physical"; her torso, "the emotional"; her head, "the mental." The same with the rest of the body: touching her jaw, "the physical"; her mouth and eyes, "the emotional"; and her forehead, "the mental." Every part of the body could be divided in this way, the arm, the hand, and so on. Pure Delsarte.

This system lent itself to naive, sentimental, simplistic story-telling and melodramatic posturing. At its worst, it produced shallow work in choreography and performance, succeeding only in creating a lexicon of cliches. At its

14. Ted Shawn, *Every Little Movement: A Book About Delsarte* (Broolyn, N.Y.: Dance Horizons, 1954), p. 10.
15. Ibid., p. 37.

best, it produced ravishingly lovely dances which were and still are strong and gratifying experience for any viewer. The best artists of this school created works that reflected deeply felt emotions and complex thoughts.

The reaction to the style typified by Delsarte took two roads. One, in the name of purity and honesty, discards all attempts at meaning, at representation, at metaphor, in favor of pure motion. The other took its lead from the great Russian theatre director Konstantin Stanislavski, who taught his actors *to do—not to appear;* not to indicate an emotion but to find the emotion through action. It was Tamiris who applied this to dance both as a method of choreography and of performance. It is this road that I found liberating and is the seed and root of this book.

Every artist in our time is faced with the choice of formalistic art or metaphoric art. Not a few straddle the fence or leap from one side to the other, unaware of the contradiction. Whichever way is chosen, both should be understood, accepted or rejected. Working through our choices was at the center of all we did in that first year of the Workgroup.

7 The Second Workgroup, 1972–1973

As the seasons go round in their perennial dance, one day the leaves fall and so do dance companies go through the falling away of dancers. New men and women come to fill the space, the time and the dance, each with their distinctive color, heft, terrors and fountain of energy. The company changes and the work changes, nowhere more than in a group that performs improvisation. The newcomers were Jack Deneault, William DeTurk, Donna Joseph and Lisa Nelson. We added a new category, associates. They participated in all the studio "research" but rarely in performances: Jana Fleder (now Haimson), Katie Fraser, Karen Geller, Imogene Horne, Anet Ris and Robert Ungar. The "old-timers" were Lee Connor, Ara Fitzgerald, Mary Anne Smith and myself.

"Old" and "new," each in their own way, added to the character and the development of the Workgroup. When the "old-timers" met for the first time after the late summer break, I threw out a question that went back to elementary school days: "What did you do on your summer vacation?"

What Happened? 7.1

Ara, go into the space. Now, tell us what happened in the last six weeks. No words. Call it **What Happened?**

It actually turned into a delightful afternoon, as one by one we rose to tell—with no words. We were learning to speak fluently with no words.

Auditions brought in the new people, and after we helped them discover the ways in which we had been working, we turned to new directions. I was excited. This was to be the step toward maturity as a company. We had unearthed some powerful fundamentals in that first year. Not only had we gained the skill and confidence to perform improvisation, we had found ways that could dig deeply within ourselves and within our audiences—and we were finding a loyal, core audience. I felt that now we could move forward and deeper into matters that mattered.

For several years, I had been developing an interest in ancient China. One story in particular haunted me, the life of the great historian of China, Ssuma Chhien. The emperor had ordered the death of a defeated general. Ssuma

101

Ara Fitzgerald, Donna Joseph, Daniel Nagrin, Lisa Nelson and Jack Deneault. *Photo: Judith Mann*

Fragment Rondo
(7.10). Daniel
Nagrin, Lee Connor,
Donna Joseph,
William DeTurk,
Lisa Nelson (hidden)
and Ara Fitzgerald.

Jack Deneault,
Mary Anne Smith,
Daniel Nagrin,
Donna Joseph,
William DeTurk,
Ara Fitzgerald (hid-
den), Lisa Nelson
and Lee Connor.

Chhien dared to defend his innocence and argue against execution, angering the emperor. As punishment he suffered an obscene mutilation and the pain of imprisonment. Suicide would have been the correct response, but his need to finish the history, begun by his father, prevailed, and after serving his sentence, he endured his shame and continued to write his great historical work.

In a way I cannot explain, this confrontation rhymed with the turbulence of that time of the Workgroup. It was a period of violent confrontations around the issues of civil liberties and Vietnam. Not a few people went to jail. I wondered about those who had risked so much for their own freedom, the freedom of others and the *idea* of freedom, spending days, months, years in prison.

We had bought about thirty urethane pillows to augment seating capacity for studio performances. They were four inches thick, cut with clean, right angles and could balance on edge. One day, I arranged all of them so that there were rows of two-foot-high enclosures or cells of about six feet by four.

Prison 7.2

Step inside the space furthest from where you are now. When you arrive, you have only one thing to deal with: the word *prison*. Whatever that word means to you and whatever flows from or away from that word is what happens.

On its surface, **Prison** is the simplest setup I ever presented to the company. What happened was anything but. Following are the jottings I have found scattered through the Workgroup notebooks of 1972.

> Prison Image—Remember Jack trotting
> Freedom
> What is it to be black?
> The Box
> Donna—the twitching
> Lisa—"aaah" and the crawling
> Read George Jackson—re being black[1]
> Jack—pillows piled up over him
> Punishment
> Bill—on back
> Connor—right hand
> Prison image

> Feb. 11 '72. We did a prison image
> When does my business become your business?
> and: when does it turn into art?

My memory holds images of dancers caught up in such intense absorption in dark and troubled places as I have never witnessed in all my dance time,

---

1. George Jackson was sentenced to one year to life for stealing $70 from a gas station. He was eighteen. Ten years later, still in prison, he had become a self-educated militant and the writer of eloquent letters published as Soledad Brother: *The Prison Letters of George Jackson*. He was shot and killed by a guard.

never in the studios and rarely on the stage. The notes above give but the faintest indication of the thrashing, the autistic cul-de-sacs, the fierce actions with no apparent purpose that went on in those cells. The company had slipped so quickly into the depths of the subject, I was certain we would build an important work out of this beginning.

Recognizing how difficult it was to sustain such overwhelming involvement, I staggered work on Prison with EGAS that were not so taxing. In spite of this precaution, a distracting note began to slip into the room each time we returned to work on Prison. A dancer might precipitously stop in midstream and leave the dance space. Another would beg off as not feeling well. Once, when I was reading from George Jackson's letters on prison life, one of the new company members began to mock and belittle the text in a way that I felt was actually an assault on me, and that was something I did not know how to handle. Then one day after settling down in the cells, ostensibly in the meditation that preceded almost everything we did, *nothing happened for a very long time.* The dancers mostly toppled over on their sides or simply stretched out as if taking naps.

The signs were clear. We had done four, maybe five sessions over a period of three or four weeks and now, the company was drawing back from participating in this work. I bowed to a defeat that hurts to this day. There is a phrase, "his admiration knew no bounds." I have enormous admiration for the dancers who were working with me then, but it is an admiration that has definite bounds.

What was the difference between them and me? The simplest metaphor was that I read the newspapers every day and most them rarely did. Many times, what is happening in the world around me moves me more deeply than my personal condition. Does this make me a better person than them? That's a judgment I withhold, though it may appear to be implied. Whatever, it was, in this arena, an enormous difference separated us.

Was this a generational gap? More to the point, it was a gap between me and most of the dance world—and for that matter most of the world of art. In the postwar period, much of dance and art moved away from a focus on humans toward a preoccupation with the materials of the art itself. In dance, the buzzword was *process. Content* was a dirty word.

It would be unfair and inaccurate to lump the company members with the formalists and the "process people." They were unusual in that they wanted to deal with content as humans, but the content had to be immediate and personal, whether serious or light. They shrank back when the horizon extended too far from home, the self. Perhaps they were closer to it than they knew, for this "far from home—far from self stuff," this word, *prison*, drew stronger responses than anything else they did before or after. Perhaps, for that very reason, they went, as it were, on strike, and Prison was dead as a project.

In what amounted to a retreat, we concentrated on the earlier pieces with one remarkable innovation, Quiet Dance. It evolved out of my attempt to steal some improvisational vitality from jazz. Jazz gains its freedom from the strict gridiron of rhythm laid down by the percussion and the bass and by the harmonic frame of the blues or the ballad. Our first attempt was pathetic. For some mysterious reason, someone had once given me a pair of fencing foils. I tied a red bandanna to the tip of each one, picked a rhythmically strong dancer (I think it was Lee), and gave him a simple rhythm waving the foils. He was to lead the pack of dancers anywhere in the studio, always adhering to the given rhythm. The "pack" were to individually do anything that related to that rhythm but was not exactly like it. Instead of the basic aural rhythm characteristic of jazz, we would have a basic visual rhythm for the improvisors. Aside from the chaos, Lee's arm tired very quickly, and that terminated our first shot at jazz.

But then, two disparate exercises blended in my mind. Very early there had been the Open Theatre game, The Conductor (2.5), in which a single person pours out rhythmic impulses to which two movers respond and interact. The other was Go Visiting, a recent development of Internal Rhythm (5.5). After the dancers gain an ease in getting to their internal rhythm, at anywhere from five to ten minutes into the exercise, I say:

Go Visiting
7.3

Continue what you are doing as I speak to you. When you hear me say, "OK, go," without losing one bit of your internal rhythm, go traveling, go visiting and see what the others are doing. You must not lose one bit of your identity—the rhythm that is carrying you along—as you move among the others observing them. OK, go!

After the dancers seem to have had a good tour of each other, I add: Continue what you are doing. I will put a question to you: "Who in this group interests you, positively or negatively? Either will do. Enter into the working area of that person and deepen your observation. After a while, you will become aware of one of several impulses. You may want to be influenced by that person or, on the contrary, want to change her.him in a specific way. Accept the possibility that the person who interests you may be focused on an another. That should not alter your purpose. If and when you succeed in absorbing what you wanted to take away or in altering the other, you can leave the floor. If you fail (you are left alone), recognize that in movement and leave the floor.

During the work on this EGAS, as I watched the dancers grouping in pairs, trios or quartets, I would occasionally see some who had found a vibrant rhythmic interaction. One day, glancing unhappily at the foils with their silly red bandannas drooping from them, the two EGAS meshed in my mind and there was **Quiet Dance.** After many tries and fumbles, here is the form that finally emerged. It may seem quite complex upon first reading and perhaps upon first doing, but the logic will eventually become apparent. It clearly owes something to Wind I (5.10) and Wind II (6.13).

The preliminary is to have all the dancers find their own internal rhythm as a repetition. That done, the director has all the dancers stand in a circle as one by one they step into the center to dance their own internal rhythm. Next, the dancers are asked to choose the one who they believe will best complement what they are doing. After they have chosen, the director asks each pair to show their juxtaposition by having one dancer start and then the other meshing in. The dancers are then asked to discuss which pair they thought had the most dynamic rhythmic interaction. Sometimes I would suggest a pairing other than the one the dancers had chosen. For the purposes of the Workgroup, with its goal of bringing these EGAS to a performance level, I threw my attention to what I considered the most vital combinations of rhythms. In the time that Quiet Dance was being created, this was with Lee and Lisa. His was very simple, powerful and verged on the ecstatic. Hers was quick, detailed, sensual and witty. Together they made a visual music.

The next preliminary is to chose a third dancer who will both blend and differ with the first two. Then it was Jack Deneault, who was tall and angular in his moves. The three were quite wonderful together, each vividly different and all sharing a common understanding of what they were into. Because Quiet Dance is a bit complex, I will use their names to map it.

Quiet Dance 7.4

Quiet Dance. Stage one: Lee, Lisa and Jack spread out along one side of the space. (In a theatre, along the back wall or cyclorama.) Whenever Lee is ready, he finds his place in the space and declares his rhythm. When Lisa feels that the space is saturated with Lee's rhythm, she enters, meshing her rhythm with his. When Jack senses that Lee and Lisa have filled the space with their energy, he enters the space in an improvisation *with no repetitions* that is about only one thing: what is happening between Lee and Lisa. Similarly, Lee and Lisa never lose sight of Jack and consciously use their repetitive rhythms to support, encourage or tease Jack. They can slow down, speed up, shift dynamics and so on. Whenever Jack is ready to end his ad lib, he shifts from a constantly changing improvisation to finding a repetitive rhythm that relates to what Lee and Lisa are doing. As soon as Lee becomes aware that Jack has begun a repetition, this becomes his cue to break loose and improvise with no repetitions off what Lisa and Jack are doing. Lee ends his ad lib by finding a new repetition that meshes with and complements Lisa and Jack. Lisa's awareness that Lee has begun a repetition is the signal for her to improvise with no repetitions around and about Lee and Jack.

Stage two: When Lisa is ready to end her ad lib, she finds a new repetition that feeds off the repetitions of Lee and Jack. All three are now doing repetitions which should create a new bit of interactive movement— "visual music."

Stage three, the "universal ad lib": Sooner or later one of the dancers tears loose from his.her repetition and is improvising freely, but still about the other two and what they are doing. This becomes the signal for the other two to shift into a continuous ad lib to, for and about each other. All three are improvising without any repetitions off each other.

By now it must be apparent that any dancer who is in ad lib time cannot permit her.his improvisation to slip into any repetition for this would confuse the other two by sending what appears to be a cue for the next stage of the dance. Every change is cued by slipping into a repetitive phrase.

Anyone who has improvised knows that continuously evolving movement is not easy. Repetition is not demanding, though it can have a beauty all its own. More to the point, it gives the improvisor a breather, a chance to regenerate the creative flow. Continuously evolving and continuously changing movement that relates to the other two dancers and has a sense of form rather than a mess of arbitrarily changing moves is no slight achievement. It is a special and specific skill within the craft of performing improvisation. All that is required is patience and practice.

Stage four: Sooner or later, one of the dancers opts to leave stage three, the "universal ad lib," and, gleaning from what the other two are doing, finds a new repetition. This is the signal for the other two to find a new repetition based on what they are seeing. When all have found a new repetition they are in stage four.

Stage five: Now comes the most subtle, difficult and exciting part of Quiet Dance, modulating to the end of stage five. Never losing sight of each other, all three begin gradually to make small alterations of their repetitive phrase leading back to their *original* repetition. This is easier for Lee and Lisa, who began Quiet Dance with a repetition they had found before the improvisation started. Jack has to recall the one he found upon ending his first improvisation. All are finally in their original repetitive phrase, and the dance comes to a close by a gradual slowing down to stillness. If all pay close attention to each other, the end will be sensed as surely as the moment the sun disappears behind the hill. There will be no movement at all, and at a moment all sense, Quiet Dance will end, breaking the stillness as they leave the floor.

Quiet Dance was the most abstract, formalistic EGAS we ever did, and it is easy to see why the dancers took to it with such commitment after the emotional turmoils of Prison (7.2). It was also quite successful as a performance piece.

Our first "big" New York concert away from the intimacy of the 550 Broadway studio was on April 4, 1972. It was a program we had been doing for about a year, and only Quiet Dance was new for us. Undoubtedly, the time spent on Prison and on recovering from its failure precluded many new works. That summer we did get a wonderful residency at Johnson State College in Johnson, Vermont, doing that same program. We did do one new work, a dance for the video camera, an architectural piece. We called it *Steps* because the camera followed us up three flights of sensationally designed steps many times as we revealed more and more of ourselves. Later a wonderful score by Oregon was put to it.

It was not until December of 1972 that we presented a program of new works.

December 21, 22, 29, 30, 1972
at 550 Broadway

Lee Connor, William DeTurk, Ara Fitzgerald, Daniel Nagrin, Mary Anne Smith

Associates Jana Fleder, Anet Ris, and Robert Ungar

Program

From Now
Recognition Ritual (Premiere)
Wind I (NY Premiere)
Relay Solo (NY Premiere)   Quiet Noise
Go 1-2-3-4 (Premiere)   Quiet Noise

Intermission

Quiet Dance
Signs of the Times (NY Premiere)   Tape collage
Fragment Rondo   John Dowland

Note re Quiet Noise: You are welcome to contribute sounds and rhythms with your voice or your key chain or sound-makers from the door table or finger snapping, etc., where indicated in the program. In Go 1-2-3-4, your cue to start is "Go 3" &/or "Go 4."

From Now was a wonderful way to start our programs. It gave a clue to the way we worked, who we were and, best of all, how different we were from each other.

From Now
7.5

From Now was Evolving Repetition (6.4) with a slightly different beginning. We would be grouped at the edge of the performing space and one by one would enter, find "our place," close our eyes and breathe deeply, waiting until an internal rhythm emerged. Each of us took off in our own time. We learned that ten minutes was an optimum time span, both for us and viewers. We created a tape on which each of us recorded the passage of the time. I started it, saying, "Go." After one minute, Lee's voice said, "one"; at the two-minute mark Ara said "two," and so on until at ten, I concluded with "OK." The sounds of the passing traffic through the massive windows that faced Broadway were also caught on that tape. In performance these sounds mingled with the actual traffic sounds, making a strange ambience of the recorded and actual.

A critical time in every temporal work of art is its first moments. It is there that the audience forms a sense of the style and the arena to which its imagination is being invited. Stylistically, From Now was a perfect introduction to our work. Each of us in our own personal rhythm declared our individuality and our own particular style. It established our focus as within the confines of the stage area, that is, we were dancing *for* the audience but not *to* the audience. We were dancing. In the context of that time, this was a major point that distinguished our company from others who were also performing improvisation, laced with many episodes of "pedestrian movement." We never shied away from "pedestrian movement" or the literal, but we never stayed there. Any casual or pantomimic action was possible at any time, but it was always a springboard into dance and danced metaphors.

Thus, as a company, we always danced. This distinguished us from others of that period like Yvonne Rainer's Grand Union or Anna Halprin's company who, at times, were involved with extended sections of "pedestrian activities." This comment is not meant as a putdown of those fine artists. It is only to clarify the limits we had set for our work. Basically, whatever we had to say was channeled into dance and danced metaphors. This of course is an opening for a discussion on what dance is, but the opening will not be pursued. Most readers will know exactly what is meant here. The professional word-jugglers of dance are always dying to talk about that, even though they too know exactly what is being said.

During studio practice, From Now was usually followed by **Recognition Ritual.** The former put us in touch with ourselves, but not with each other. All companies can gain from mutual sensitivity and awareness. With a company whose entire premise was bouncing off each other, the need was obvious. The convention when coworkers meet each day is "How are you?" and a return "How are you?" Groans and the litany of aches are exchanged, but in time the exchange slides into a formality with little learned about each other. Recognition Ritual was an EGAS to bring the exchange into the life we understood best—dance.

Recognition Ritual 7.6

All fill the space, making a large circle, pacing about, limbering up, and doing all the things dancers do getting ready to dance. Whoever is ready and willing steps into the center and really answers the unspoken question, "How are you?"—in dance. We'll call this person X. All the others will pay close attention to what X is "saying," having the option of responding to what they "hear," whether positively, negatively or indifferently. Responses range from lifts to touching to circling or to dance actions at a distance. There is no "ought." There is no proper response. Whenever X is ready to quit, she.he retires to the edge of the circle, and that will conclude the attention paid to X. Another person will step into the center of the group and "tell" us how he.she is. The dancers will again respond positively, negatively or indifferently. Each X holds the center for as long as needed. Recognition Ritual ends when the last person steps back into the circle's edge.

108

One unusual aspect of this EGAS was how many times the women lifted, caught and supported the men. By this time both men and women were becoming skillful and sure at improvising some astonishing lifts. At times it may have resembled the Contact Improvisation pioneered by Steve Paxton, because some of the dancers came in needing comfort and support—and they got it.

Wind I (5.10), which was so difficult for us when Paul Zimet first gave it to us, now assumed an authority and mystery in performance, making it an intriguing work to witness.

Relay Solo was a tricky development out of The Tandem Solo (1.8). Unlike Tandem Solo, we did not perform it to music, though there is no reason why it couldn't be.

Relay Solo
7.7

Relay Solo. Six to nine people sit in a circle, all with eyes closed, and all meditating on a specific idea for a dance. Whoever gets one first slaps her.his palm on the floor three times, thereby claiming the space and the right to start first. Call this person A. The floor-slapping opens everyone's eyes. Dancer A rises to enter the circle and, taking all the time she.he needs, begins a solo. All observe A closely. Whenever A is ready, she.he says for all to hear, "Now," stops dancing, and retires to the circle's edge. All rise and attempt to take off from where A said, "Now." Dancer A remains standing, observing. When A sees someone who is following through with what had been started, she.he calls out for all to hear the name of that person. All the others stop dancing, retire to the circle's edge and observe this second soloist. This person continues developing what A started and, whenever ready, calls out, "Now," leaving the center for the others to attempt to continue in the direction taken. For performances, we allowed for only four soloists. When the fourth person says "Now," all rise and try to *support* what D is doing, not to *do* what D is doing; this now becomes a group dance rather than competing soloists. The cue to bring the dance to a close comes from D, who stops dancing.

Go 1-2-3-4 had a few strategic and significant differences from the original version, Go 1-2-3 (3.6).

Go 1-2-3-4
7.8

In **Go 1-2-3-4,** the soloist gives all the cues verbally, not the director. He.she starts by announcing "Go 1," and begins an improvisation off the moment while the dancers seated in the circle are observing to sense and find the basic rhythm that drives the soloist. When ready to hear these rhythms, the soloist says, "Go 2." All beat out their rhythm audibly. The soloist tours the circle trying to find who has the best rhythm for what is being danced. Finding "the best rhythm," the soloist indicates the choice by clearly dancing in front of and to the "musician" dancer, saying, "Go 3." Now all the others in the circle try to mesh their rhythms with this one and move physically closer, thus creating an "orchestra" with a conductor.

To tie it all up, the soloist says, "Go 4," and all, in due time, rise, still beating out, clapping, singing as an orchestra led by the rhythm leader and now dancing with the soloist, who is still the focus of all. When the soloist is ready to end Go 1-2-3-4, he.she, still dancing, leads all off the floor.

What should be the attitude toward the soloist? In the original version, Go 1-2-3 (3.6), there was this: "Once you are meshing with your neighbors, shift your focus to the soloist. There are many choices open to you at this point. While keeping a musical relationship with your neighbors, your sounds can either challenge the soloist, support the soloist, mock the soloist, or whatever. Your attitude toward the soloist and what he.she is doing is what will shape the music/rhythms you and the others are creating." In the new version the "musicians," who are beholden to accept the leadership of the conductor, have two possibilities: sense the attitude of the conductor and support it, or contradict it if they have a different one, though maintaining a rhythmic relationship. This may appear to be tricky, but it can work. The music that fascinates me most contains widely differing but subtley interrelated elements that create the living tension I look for in all art (Bach is the most obvious and glorious example). This structure can open the door to dynamic music for the soloist's dance.

Since our company was never more than eight, that's as many as we ever used for performances of *Go 1-2-3-4*. There is no reason why it can't be done, both in performance and in the studio, with twice as many, or even more dancers. Great excitement can be added by inviting professional musicians to join; when the soloist calls out "Go 4," they can move about rhythmically and join in the exit, still playing their instruments. It makes for a great party.

Quiet Dance has been covered, but *Signs of the Times* was new, powerful and a bit of a concession to my need for dance that went beyond the immediate personals of our own lives:

Signs of the Times *7.9*

Signs of the Times. Find your place in the space and seat yourself. With your breath, create a clear space in your mind. (Time given for this to happen.) Wherever you go, wherever you look, there are signs saying things to you, informing you, ordering you, asking you, begging you. Do a Hub Meditation (5.7) on as many signs as you can recall. Which is the one that gets you the most? Which is the one that is there in your mind, regardless of what new ones you recall?

When it is clear that the hub is occupied, rise and begin to say the words of that sign silently, to yourself, at any tempo until it settles into a definite rhythm. As you are doing this, allow the body to follow the impulses, dictates, undercurrents, and the literal and the metaphoric elements of your sign. Gradually shape your motions and your words into a repetitive phrase. When you can do this with authority several times over, stop and go to the perimeter of the floor.

(Up to this point, what has been described is studio work that must be done before Signs of the Times can be performed for an audience.)

When the last person has left the working area for the floor's edge, from your position and in your own time, you can now utter your sign aloud for the first time, loud enough for all to hear, simultaneously moving through the motions of your sign. (In performance, the order would be set in advance.) After you fully establish the sound-motion presence of your sign, begin to take cognizance of the others, what they are doing and saying. Depending on how they affect you, the you that is bound up in that sign will select a person to interact with and what you want to do with, for or to that other person/sign.

For the remainder of the EGAS, the words cannot be altered or augmented with other words but can be rephrased rhythmically, intellectually or emotionally, depending upon what happens. The movement phrase can be dealt with in a more fluid way. Body contact, repetitions of single motions, altered dynamics, turning, shifting the phrase to the floor or into the air are all possible, but no radical movement changes should occur. You are finished when your intent in regard to one or more of the others is fulfilled or unequivocally defeated.

The company entered into Signs of the Times without restraint and good energy. For performances we made a haunting tape score: A good omnidirectional microphone was hung from the ceiling, and all the dancers lay on the floor, heads together and faces up toward the mike. With eyes closed, referring to no one but their own impulses, without any movement, the dancers muttered, spoke or shouted, each their own sign. For performance, the tape was cued in quietly after the first dancer spoke her.his sign three times and then imperceptibly went to an audible level, but never so loud as to drown out the live voices of the dancers. The double sound sources, taped and live, made for erratic, chance occurrences and gave the whole piece a dizzying tension that audiences found compelling to watch. Sadly, it was only one of two performance works videotaped—and not successfully.

For what it is worth, and they are definitely not meant as examples to be emulated, here are the "signs" that emerged for the dancers in the version that we did that season:

Anet:	"One line. One line only."
Bill:	"Don't tread on me, or we'll be back."
Ara:	"Liberty, 'till death do us part."
Lee:	"You're cockroaches, all of you cockroaches."[2]
Mary Anne:	"All this armor—all these weapons—useless."

Fragment Rondo. First, choose music that begs for dancing. We had all fallen in love with what Julian Bream did with his lute to the music of John

---

2. We had a tendency in the Workgroup to respect or rather to expect the illogical and the mysterious. No one ever thought to ask Lee Connor where he ever saw or heard of such a sign or slogan. I questioned it for the first time when I copied it this year from an old notebook.

Dowland. Picking four favorites, we prepared movement for it with a game taken from one of the earliest EGAS given by Tamiris, Stillness (1.1).

Fragment
Rondo
7.10

Fragment Rondo. Listening to the music, be in a position of readiness to move but don't, for as long as you can bear it. Move when you must and as little as possible, perhaps simply to another position—or perform just one brief action, a fragment. Continue until one of the motions seems to be the perfect emblem of what you hear in the music. Afterward, all show their "perfect" motion and all decide which are on the mark for which piece of music. (This is studio work.)

The "perfect" one turned out to be not so simple and is a good example as to how *Fragment Rondo* is danced. Listening to Dowland's most famous composition, *Lachrimae Antiquae,* Lee Connor and Anet Ris, then an apprentice, had started their "perfect emblem" from opposite corners of the space. They simply walked slowly toward each other and embraced. That was all, and it was lovely. In performance, they began with stillness, seeing each other from opposite corners of the space. Finally, a slow magnet drew them into an embrace. Each time they embraced, they flowed into an improvisation of leaving and returning until they come to another stillness at a distance from each other and repeated the same walk and the same embrace, which flowered into another improvisation and so on to the end of a six-minute piece of music that had no time.

To perform *Fragment Rondo,* put one, two, three and no more than four into the space. As the music starts each person in turn does his.her motion three times. The last person does her.his motion four times. All the others join in on this fourth time, doing their own motion, and then all spin our whatever flows from that moment. The dancers never lose sight or awareness of each other. Each one's improvisation will have its own arc of time, and when it finishes, the dancer returns to his.her fragment for refreshment, as it were, and swings out into another improvisation. As the music winds down, so do the dancers.

In performance, *Fragment Rondo,* like *Rondo* (6.1), was a suite in four sections. The first three were solos, duets, trios and or (rarely) quartets. For the final and fourth section all who had appeared earlier danced, using their own favorite fragment as a renewable fuse for more movement. This is easier for the audience to take in than might appear, since each dancer had been seen dancing a personal movement motif. What would be chaos on a first viewing becomes a mass of familiars, with audience members seeking out their individual favorites.

In the period that the Workgroup worked, the late sixties and early seventies, many efforts were made to involve audience in something more than observation and applause. We made a few tentative forays in that direction.

Quiet Noise was one of these. Once or twice on tour, instead of giving the "someone . . . something" to the dancers backstage just before they went on, I spoke it in the presence of the audience to the dancers as they sat facing each other in The Duet and invited the audience to share in the meditation on that "someone . . . something." Sometimes on the university circuit, we invited the audience to create characters for a duet. Lee was once given the role of a horny chicken (it was a risky business). In the December 1972 program we made the following insert:

A Note for an Experiment

There have been many forms of audience participation, both in ancient and contemporary dance and theatre. Old ways were built into shared community traditions. Contemporary forms have been innovative and often a challenge to an audience to search again for a community of feeling and understanding. Some recent experiments have been highly successful, others less so. All have suffered from a resistance by differing portions of the audience who feel self-conscious and resent being pushed into a role they do not choose.

The present structure of our work does not involve direct audience participation. However, tonight we would like to suggest an experiment in a subtle and private form of participation. All people at one time or another have imitated other's physical actions. The results are surprising. There are unexpected insights into the mind and state of being of the person imitated. Even imitating a part of the other's body gives a sense of what is going on beneath the surface.

Specifically, we are suggesting that when you find yourself particularly intrigued by the actions of any one of the dancers, observe her.his hands and imitate their configuration and energy. We think you may sense things that are not immediately visible to the eyes.

This is the first time we have suggested this to an audience. If you would like to write your comments on this experiment, or any other aspect of tonight's performance, we would be happy to receive them from you. Thank you,

The Workgroup

We might call it the **Exercise in Empathy** (7.11). It drew no noticeable response. Perhaps more went on than we knew, and perhaps little occurred because our interests and efforts were minimal in this regard. Only one response was successful and always quite joyous. We finished most of our evenings with *Rondo* performed by all the dancers. When they returned for a bow, I would announce, "And now it's your turn—your turn to dance." This was the cue for some infectious dance music, usually rock or some good jazz, and it worked! To juice it up, we would uncover a table with a few bottles of cheap red and white wine and a bowl of salty crackers. No one got drunk on anything but the music, the dancing and each other. I can still see a small, wiry, hairy man high up on the balls of his feet prancing ecstatically in his own world. I watched him go at it for at least half an hour with awe and a little envy. One can never be certain what it is that an audience takes away, but one thing I am sure; we aroused the dance devils of those who came to see us on the third floor of 550 Broadway. An hour later, a goodly portion were still dancing, as were many of the company members. Did our work create that overflow from him and the others? I think it did.

8 The Final Workgroup, 1973–1974

From the end of the 1972 summer, in Johnson, Vermont, to the beginning of the summer of 1973, when we returned to Vermont, just two new works entered our performing repertoire. Yet the notes reveal a prolific time of experiment. There were over a dozen new shapes of improvisation, some touched upon briefly and some examined in depth. Here they are, in no particular order.

When dancers work with each other day after day, inevitably they notice each other's style—the strong points and the limitations. **I Dare You** is all about limitations. It only succeeds with a group that has been working together for some time. Whenever I've set it up, either with the Workgroup or in later years in extended workshops and classes, the results have been fruitful.

I Dare You
8.1

One person leaves the room. The others try to identify the key limitation in the way that person has been working. Once there is consensus on this, the challenge for the group is to devise an I Dare You challenge that will help the person meet and overcome this obstacle. It must be stated in a poetically specific and nondestructive way, a way that will stimulate the imagination of that dancer. A literal statement like, "Improvise in a flowing, gentle quality," will come off as critical and beg for a generalized response. Once there is agreement, the dancer is called back and the person who contributed the most to the formulated I Dare You gives it to the dancer verbally. Time is left in the session for all to write down the *exact* wording of the challenge.

Allow a week for all the dancers to work on their I Dare You. By "work" is meant finding a specific image, a rich movement metaphor, and a loose construction around which the dancer can improvise. There is no pressure in this EGAS to create a piece of choreography, though many have done just that. Rather, it is all about encouraging the dancer to enter a new room, to experience a new way. When the dancers meet again, they each show what they have found within themselves. It may well be a quality that was there all the time but had never been exploited by the dancer. The group helps the dancer by commenting on how close he.she met the challenge of I Dare you.

The only notes I have for this EGAS come from a choreography class I taught at Arizona State University in 1987. Here are a few of the challenges:

"Become a length of lavender silk thread that is being used to crochet a delicate rose." This was given to the strongest dancer of her class, tall and powerfully built. As exciting as she was to observe, strength and power were the only qualities we ever saw her exhibit. Her study-improvisation was gossamer and yet strong as silk. Later she built a piece of choreography around this study and performed it with success at the student concert.

"Become a monstrous, brutal piece of construction machinery used for road building." This was a tall, elegant man who had a narrow image of what constituted beauty in movement: fey and floating. I think the I Dare You made him furious, and that only added to the power of an awesome study that was the best and most exciting dance I ever saw him do in the four years he spent dancing at ASU.

"Become a hard-hearted, egotistical, cocky, smart-assed, macho stud who's on the rampage." This was an exceptionally attractive woman who tended to cling fiercely to a banal idea of femininity in all that she did. Her study was a farcical, hilarious and outrageous blast, climaxed by making violent love to the floor. She appeared to have a giddy relish in letting go of her girly-girl image—at least for the length of that improvisation.

"Become a perpetual motion machine that never does anything twice." In all her choreographic efforts, this woman continually resorted to repetitions. Results: fair.

"Relive a tragic moment in Isadora Duncan's life as she reflects upon her children's drowning" was for a man who always smiled and kept his "cool" in all that he did. In a way, this was the most daring I Dare You, since it asked a man to be a woman—a mother—mourning. It was also the least successfully done.

The next four I Dare You's were given to people who all tended to keep everything they did in dance under tight control, infusing all their movement with physical caution and cerebral deliberation.

"Two stallions are fighting until death. You are the one who wins."

"You are a forceful wave coming a long way out of a storm at sea and finally blasting the shore."

"A wild creature, person, or thing without arms that destroys all things it can reach."

"You are a chicken which has just been decapitated."

Humorous challenges can be just as effective as profoundly poetic ones, as long as they charge the imagination of the dared one.

Your Secret Totem Animal was an improvisation I made for dancers who came to our workshop.

Your Secret Totem Animal 8.2

Six to seven sit in a circle with clasped hands. Close your eyes and empty your head. When you are ready for the next step, release your hands and rest them on your knees. (When all signify readiness, continue): There are many creatures in the world. Allow a parade of them to cross the stage of your mind. When one animal remains in view regardless of which others pass through, you have found your secret totem animal. Is it a real or a fantastical animal? Move in closely and observe all you can about it. When you feel you have a specific and vivid view of your secret totem animal, clasp your hands and open your eyes. Even though your eyes are open, you can still see the creature.

The last person to open her.his eyes will move to the center of the circle and begin to search for the inner spirit and the internal rhythm of the secret totem animal and to find a sound-motion repetition that contains them. This is a metaphoric sound-motion and not a literal pantomimic rendition of how the animal moves and sounds. All the observers will support and sustain the efforts of the person in the center with "quiet noise"—knuckle-rapping on the floor, tongue clicks, finger snapping, soft singing or humming.

When the center person has shaped a repetitive rhythm, she.he shifts focus to the others in the circle, seeking one to whom will be given the sound-motion of the secret totem animal. Upon choosing, the center person directs her.his motion to the one whom we will call the Disciple. The Disciple joins the Master in the circle and devotes all of his.her energy to learning not only the motion and sound of the Master's repetition but to absorbing the inner spirit and impulse of the Master. When the Master is satisfied that the look and the inner life have been felt and assimilated by the Disciple, the Master retires to the circle, leaving the Disciple to celebrate "coming of age"—the ability to go it alone.

After a respectful time the Disciple, in the most subtle and gradual fashion, begins to modulate bit by bit what was given into his.her own secret totem animal, finding its sound, its inner spirit and body rhythm. When that is achieved, the same process is pursued. A Disciple is chosen from among those who have not already been chosen, is taught, and left to become Master in turn. This continues until the last person is the Disciple. When he.she finds the true repetition of his.her secret totem animal, everyone in the circle becomes a Disciple, and all learn the final Master's motions and spirit. The dance ends when and how the Master brings it to a close.

I never gave this one to the company members. Did I fear they would think it too naive for them? Perhaps. The workshop dancers did lovely things with it, as did groups of actors to whom I gave it at a later date.

Four of my notes from that period are now mysteries to me. They are interesting, but there is no memory to back them up. Regardless, one day I will try what they imply.

Your Familiar 8.3

Your Familiar. "When you strike your familiar—freeze and then go into it, around it, rondo it." (I will choose dancey music.) When you hear the music, take off and have a time with it. If you find yourself in an all too familiar place, freeze, and stay with that position for a long time until it is impossible not to move and then go. (See Stillness [1.1].)

When that "go" plays itself out, return to the "familiar" and again hold the position for as long as you can, allowing all its implications and all the feelings it provokes fill you until you must move once again. Follow the rondo form of returning to the same "familiar" after each release comes to an end. After a while, you will know that you have wrung that "familiar" dry and that will be the time to leave the floor.

A variation of Your Familiar allows you the same beginning of an improvisation, halting at encountering a "familiar," and finally releasing the hold to continue improvising, stopping only when you encounter *another* and different "familiar," freezing there until that one boils over into a further improvisation, and so on.

What Are You Hearing? 8.4

What Are You Hearing? "What you hear outside/what you hear inside/ Build a structure—Music—what is on the surface—Add its opposite." There are two fascinating possibilities here: (a) listening to the obvious— music; or (b) listening to ambient sound.

a. I will play a short piece of music three times. Dance to what you hear. The second time, dance to what or who is inside, under, or behind the music. The third time, start on the outside, dancing to what you hear and working your way into the interior of the music; then dance with both.

b. Standing or seated, eyes closed, clean out your mind with your breath. In the ensuing silence, what can you hear? Absolute silence is too rare to even recall. Wherever we are there are sounds. What do you hear? Become what you hear. After a time, pause and go quiet. Listen to your insides. Do you hear anything or is there absolute silence within you? If and only if you hear something within you, become that thing. When it plays itself out, rest and wait as you listen to both the outside and the inside. When you are ready, start with one and, in due time, slip into the other. What will happen? Will they war with each other? One annihilates the other? Are you a duet? Does each change? Will they blend to become one?

Props Fantasy 8.5

Props Fantasy. "Set out in the space a kitchen table, chairs, a bed with linen, a toilet seat, etc. Go to the place that is meaningful to you—where your fantasy takes you."

In the entire time of the Workgroup, we rarely used props. In *Signs of the Times*, Mary Anne wriggled out of a leather jacket and Ara was blindfolded, and in *Prison* we used those polyurethane pillows, and that was as far as we went. I think the setup above, with all the literal props, could be a wonderful starting point, swimming away from those literals into the metaphors.

Mutter Music 8.6

Mutter Music. Seated on the floor, clear out your head with your breath. In the empty space of your mind wait until you hear a sentence you might want to but dare not say in public. Rise when you hear it and, standing still or walking about, begin to mutter that sentence inaudibly. Say it over and over again until the words begin to fade and all that is left is the feeling and the rhythm expressed in the flow of sounds. When the words have disappeared and only the juice is left, allow that to become the music of your movements. Many different moves can come from one set of sounds. Do you still need to make the sound as you move, or has the movement become the sound? I have an idea that many songs find their melody this way.

An idea I picked up about this time led me a few years later to make a dance for myself called *Art*. I visited the studio of a man who could have been an exciting dancer. He said he wanted to show me something. He got up, walked into the dance space and then, from nowhere, appeared to be flung half-way across the room by some violent force. Just as quickly he would rise and resume his quiet walking or standing still. Intermittently he would explode in a fury of motion or be catapulted across the room by an unseen force. He was a powerful man and probably had played some highly physical sports, for he knew how to improvise his falls safely. Later, I tried to get the company to play with this idea but only Mary Anne, who had been a gymnast, was interested. I did not press. In *Art*, I kept getting blasted and kicked about by an invisible force, all the while reciting in a calm and collected way about twenty-five differing and contradictory definitions of art.

Did I steal his idea? Of course. Did I make it my own? I thought so, and I hope creative dancers reading this book will do the same to whatever they find here that fires their imagination. Face it, the profession is like an infinitely long conga line going back to the invisible past.

Early Modern Dance 8.7

Early Modern Dance. Someone dancing is bent on throwing over traditional notions of femininity and granting for themselves the qualities of force—harsh lines and the freedom to move boldly. (I used Aaron Copland's powerful and harsh *Piano Variations* for this.)

In some of my setups, like this one, I was to trying to make something happen. By my own principles, I prefer to create an EGAS and then wait to see what will happen. This time, I hoped to see the company members redis- cover modern dance—no less! Ara and I came close. I, because I knew what I wanted, having seen it, and Ara because . . .? The others were baffled and hes- itant. I would like to rename this one and call it **The Spine of Style**. To set it up, whoever is the director would have the task of describing a "some- one . . ." by giving a verbal synthesis of a particular style, not only what it looks like but what those who created that style were doing. Example:

The Spine of Style 8.8

Someone who lives at the bottom of a society resents it fiercely and wants the world to know that she.he is actually the equal of anyone, no matter how high.

Could this make a roomful of dancers find the spine of the Flamenco dance? It's worth a try. Tamiris had a more practical way of finding a style: "Your clothes are tightly tailored around your waist. You have a high collar and high-heeled shoes. You are wearing an elaborate wig. Each hand is wear- ing several expensive rings." With an imaginative group, the eighteenth cen- tury in Europe came into view.

All through the time of the Workgroup, I continued to tour as a soloist, earning concert fees that supported us economically. The company never stopped meeting and working during my absences, and returning was always fascinating. That there was always something new was a vindication of the way we were working. The way of the Workgroup and the noncompetitive atmosphere kept the work and the ideas flowing and opening up. Ping Pong proved to be a vein to be worked in many ways. I came back from a tour to witness a kind of kinesthetic jai alai:

Ping Pong 8.9

Two dancers face each other about twenty feet apart. Either one starts by "throwing" a movement gesture across the space to the other. The receiver accepts the impact of the gesture into her.his body, letting it ride in and out of the body. The body change made by the thrown gesture shapes what is thrown back to the original sender, who continues the game of receiving and sending. The image to think of is the scoop-shaped jai alai basket which receives the ball only to swoop it back in return. This is not and should not be a mirror exercise in which the receiver returns what was sent. In jai alai, as in racket ball and in life, the receiv- er's response is a function of three factors: what was thrown, the nature of the receiver and the position of the receiver.

It was wonderful to watch the sensitivity the dancers had developed in differentiating between one "thrown" gesture and another, not only in dy- namics but in quality. One day, a week later, there was a lull in the day's work and I turned to Alain LeRazer, a new member of the company, and Mary Anne Smith.

Adam and Eve 8.10

"Alain, Mary Anne, do Ping Pong, only you are **Adam and Eve**. In the beginning you, Eve, who has never yet slept, are looking at Adam, who is asleep for the first time. After a while, Adam, you will wake and discover her for the first time."

It worked. It was one of the two new EGAS that entered our performing repertoire that season. The lighting was quite dim, they wore no clothing and it was quite lovely to watch them "discover" each other. I can't recall how they brought the improvisation to a close except that they kept the initial distance throughout.

Another note in the notebook: "Hamlet—Connor/King—DN/Queen—Ara/Ophelia/Laertes/Ghost—Allain/Polonius." I think it never left the notebook, but all through this period we maintained our contact with the Open Theatre. Paul Zimet would give us acting lessons, and one day he had Lee and me read and work on a scene from *Endgame* by Samuel Beckett. The next day Lee and I were about to go over the scene again when I said, "Why don't we do it our way, as a Duet?" Our "someones" were clearly defined. All we had to do was follow the exact route of The Duet (6.5) and we had a dance—and we did. It proved alive enough to be performed publicly many times. We called it **Ham and Clove.**

Ham and Clove 8.11

Ham is blind, and limited to a small space (a wheelchair in the play). He depends on Clove and needs a physical hold on him to control him. Clove is young, agile, and now, finally, rebellious, enjoying keeping out of Ham's powerful reach.

Any pair or group of characters that excites you, from the theatre, novels, films, soap operas to your own life are there for the using.

One studio EGAS, called **Compass,** took quite a bit of our time but was never performed publicly until that summer of 1974 when it became the structure of a dance for the videotape camera with the name *The Edge Is Also a Center.* That and *Steps* (see p. 106) made up the videotape *Two by the Workgroup.*

Compass 8.12

Compass. Five people are sent into the space to form a circle, with one person in the center, to be called "the center figure" (CF). Roles of father, mother, friend and lover are assigned to each of those on the rim of the circle. All are standing apart from each other, as the CF contemplates each of them in turn. When ready, the CF addresses them individually with one sentence or question and finally confronts him.herself.

Stealing from the videotape, these are what Lee Connor came up with: "Mother, why did you never let us love you?" "Father, have you ever seen my face?" "My friends, your judgments choke me." (For the videotape, a friend turned into friends and was played by two dancers.)

Wind I (5.10), performed as a part of *Sea Anemone*. Daniel Nagrin, Anet Ris, Ara Fitzgerald, William DeTurk and Mary Anne Smith (Lee Connor is hidden).

Ara Fitzgerald, Lee Connor and Daniel Nagrin. *Photo: Peter Moore*

Mary Anne Smith, Lee Connor, Anet Ris.

Recognition Ritual (7.6). An example of the spontaneous lifts that threaded through the work, none of which were ever rehearsed or repeated. Mary Anne Smith, Lee Connor, Anet Ris, Daniel Nagrin and Ara Fitzgerald support William DeTurk. *Photo: Peter Moore*

Lee Connor and Anet Ris in Fragment Rondo (7.10), dancing to John Dowland's *Lachrimae Antiquae.* Again, a vivid illustration of how hewing to a common task and context created coherent and elegant design without any conscious effort.

"Lover, why is it that when I embrace you, I fear that you will disappear?"

"I can taste truths, but they are not yet mine." There is no law that these statements have to be as tragic or as serious in their overtones. These were just what happened that summer. They can be flip, or mean, or wildly loving—whatever the CF comes up with.

> **Compass** continued: Each person, including the CF, takes the sentence given as the guide for a Hub Meditation (5.7), to visualize the person they are to become and to learn the task that will be the metaphor for that person's relation to the CF and the others. With this visualization and task in mind, each becomes that person. This is the Each Alone (4.4) part of The Duet (6.5) wherein the dancer becomes the person in the dance, transforming her.his body by doing part by part the core action of that person. When the CF finishes his.her Each Alone, he.she surveys the circle and on impulse proceeds to engage with any one of the others. Those not directly involved observe and react from their quadrant of the circle in terms of who they have become. Whenever the CF is ready he.she moves on to engage another of the circle figures. When the CF becomes involved with the fourth figure, the other three can at any time, in terms of the task they have discovered, engage with any one or more of the others, including the CF. Each of the five can leave the floor once they have fulfilled their task or once they have seen that their task is futile.

Compass worked well for us in the studio, but its awesome length made it a poor choice for public performance. It called for at least three duets to start and finish before all became involved. By that very token it was ideal for videotaping, since the camera could "lose" all those not directly involved in the strongest action. At Johnson State College in Vermont, there was a dining room of heroic proportions: a double height ceiling, great columns that could have come from an ancient Egyptian temple and mysterious pools of down light. The moment dinner was finished, we cleared the chairs and tables from the floor, and set up the lights. Shooting would begin after sunset and go to three or four in the morning. On the fifth and final day we worked until dawn and reset the tables just in time to sit down for breakfast. In editing the tapes, we had several choices for each segment—all different. To viewers who are unfamiliar with our work, it seems incredible that what is on the screen was improvised. It was.

During this 1972–1973 season we began the custom of toting to each performance an easel to support a giant sketch pad on which we would indicate the night's program. The printed program in the hands of the audience would have the following:

Tonight's Program Will Be Selected from the Repertoire:

a. Sea Anemone
       From Now
       Recognition Ritual
       Wind II
       Relay Solo
       Go 1-2-3-4
b. Wind I
c. Quiet Dance
d. Ritual for Two
e. Ritual for All
f. Rituals of Power   Rhys Chatham
g. Signs of the Times
h. Ham and Clove
i. Fragment Rondo   1. Dowland
                                                       2. DeTurk and banjo

On the easel, in heavy black marker, was written: "Tonight's Program," followed by a column of letters, say, "a, c, h, g, intermission, f, and i." The audience had to collate the program in their hands with the row of letters on the easel. We would select the equivalent of an hour and a half of dance plus intermission, our choices depending upon the space, the anticipated audience, our mood and what piece was in the best shape. We loved the flexibility and it kept our performances fresh, both on tour and in New York. We always opened with *Sea Anemone,* a poetic way of tilting the five dances as changing shapes of one organism with every EGAS starting up from the form of a circle and flowing one into the other without any of us leaving the floor or losing connection with all the others. It made for a strong program but, in truth, we had brought forth comparatively little new material since the previous year.

I was intensely aware of this when we returned for a second summer at Johnson State College in Vermont and felt the need to come up with something new for our concert in their beautiful theatre. The first quiet moment after arriving, early in June 1973, I found a table, pen and paper, and a view ringed by the far-off blue hills. In the brief life of the Workgroup, we had by then experimented with and/or performed more than ninety exercises, games and structures. That afternoon, all that experience came together to form the structure for a work that was to be the climax of everything we had done previously. *Hello Farewell Hello* was an evening-length work which the company embraced, practiced and made concrete in two weeks as if we had been performing it for years. It was about the cycles of love found, lost and found. The entire scenario is outlined in Appendix C to this book and lies waiting there for any who would like to bring it to life once again.

The dancers who helped to create this first performance of *Hello Farewell Hello* were Lee Connor, Ara Fitzgerald, Peter Lawrence, Alain Le Razer, Lorn MacDougal, Daniel Nagrin, Mary Anne Smith, Lois Welk and later on Sara Stackhouse. The first pair of musicians were Kirk Nurock (piano) and Bill Shimmel (accordion); the second were Charles S. Hayward (saxophone) and Martha Siegal (cello). A word about Sara Stackhouse: as I wrote earlier, my experience and needs gave me the conviction that the best dancers for what we were trying to create were people with an accomplished technique and *comparatively little performing experience.* Then, to prove me wrong, along came Sara Stackhouse, that glorious dancer of José Limon's last period. She spent this final season with us and performed improvisation brilliantly after a career as a dancer of carefully crafted choreography. So, what good are rules and experience? Very useful, as long as they're soft enough to be brushed aside at any time.

Essentially, *Hello Farewell Hello* completes the history of the Workgroup. We gave its New York premiere at New York University's Loeb Center and then toured it. Early in 1974, Swarthmore College engaged us for two performances, asking for two different programs. For various reasons, we did not have sufficient material. The solution? I would present a solo evening, a retrospective, as it were, of my works from 1948 to 1969. (From 1969 on I had been so deeply engaged in working improvisation as a performance form, there had been neither the time nor even a thought of creating new solos for myself.)

The company performance pleased some hugely and dismayed enough so that my solo evening was poorly attended. Despite that, the solo evening shook me, for I suddenly felt as if I had come home. I felt very good, and the small audience did too. From that time on, the company became secondary in my mind. A few dear and wonderful dancers were ready, as is the wont of modern dancers, to be on their own way, to do their own work. I had never quite recovered from the hurt of the company's resistance to Prison (7.2). I was ready to deal with the dreams, images and ideas I had ignored for four years in favor of the Workgroup. I had created the Workgroup to pursue a way and an ideal of performance consciousness and not with the idea of becoming the director of a dance company. It was a role about which I have always been equivocal. Being a director was merely a necessary part of that search.

I began to work on and tour the solo program while the company performed intermittently. On December 2, 1974, we began our last engagement, a five-day residency at State University College at Plattsburgh, New York, climaxed by a performance of *Hello Farewell Hello.*

It had been a good time, a productive time, and it was over.

9 On the Road Again, 1974–

Traveling back and forth across the country, I was hauling a trunk full of EGAS along with the equipment for my new solo program—costumes, tapes and props. Touring a concert program is exciting; new people, new stages, new cities and towns, each with their own colors, tastes and tensions, all charged and challenged me. Best of all, I was constantly meeting people who had been expecting and getting ready for my visit for months, sometimes a year. Their energy and openness electrified every exchange of ideas and movements. I was continually receiving as well as giving.

Wherever possible, then and now, I include a workshop in improvisation, and though most times I am limited to a session of two hours or even an hour and a half, I always ask to have it scheduled for three or four hours. Shorter than three hours is doing it the hard way. It is one thing to work with a group of dancers for months and years, four times a week in four-hour sessions; it is quite another to come upon a roomful of strangers and expect them in one session to understand and accept the ground rules:

no working to the mirror
no working to look good
no working to be beautiful
no working to be interesting
no working to be creative
no comparing self to others
but rather:
working to lose the self
working to find the other person
to just do

and, despite this mess of contradictions to everything they had always believed was dance, *to reach deeply into themselves.*

Happen it did and does, not every time, but many times; not for everyone, but for many. Most of the people I encounter have improvised, but few have ever experienced this expectation of deep personal involvement. I do not mean to belittle other ways of conducting improvisation. But most of it tends to be physical and/or cerebral and seldom opens the door to the emotions other than the physical and mental excitements that go with dancing. Interacting with others as the person you are will generate feelings: light, deep, confused, ecstatic or "heavy." How to make it possible for this to happen?

I never come with a clear agenda—a lesson plan. I arrive early and watch the dancers as they prepare for the class, stripping down to practice clothes, talking, stretching. I take in the ambience of the space, a factor which inevitably has a potent effect on the dance that evolves within it. I find that a brightly lit work space is inhibiting. Whenever possible, I have the space darkened a bit, sometimes radically. People feel less exposed and more likely to take risks when they are less obviously visible.

The first necessity in any session is to insure the safety and the freedom of the dancers' bodies. The easiest way out is to say, "Take ten or fifteen minutes to warm up." A terrible idea. The time is too short, too few dancers know how to do this well and too many will fill the time with chatting. Another way is to conduct a quick warmup: walking, then faster and faster, breaking into a run, slowing down to easy stretches, slow big body moves, extended arm motions, pliés, shallow and deep and so on. Strategically conducted, this works. I found another way. I called it **Gifts.**

Gifts
9.1

Pick a partner and face each other. The exercise is called Gifts. One will lead and the other will follow as in a mirror game. The leader has but one mission in mind: to get the other warmed up and on the way to dancing. That is the "gift," to free the other's body. The challenge is to fully take in who the follower is. "What does she.he need to get started? What is unique to this person, this body before me? Is there a nervousness? Would a bit of stillness be the right beginning? Would a formal, symmetrical opening center this person best? Are the shoulders lifted in a tense manner? Perhaps some easy shoulder rolls, lifts and drops would ease and lengthen her.his neck?"

Take your time to sense the specific needs of the person before you. Don't do what you think all dancers need—only what this dancer needs. You literally are trying to think yourself into his.her body. Can you really know these things? Never for certain, but you can guess on the basis of what you are seeing and sensing. All of us, whether we are self-aware or not, are constantly sending signals out to the world about ourselves. If you want to know about the other, the information is there right in front of you; if you really have to know, you will develop the skill. It is just that: a skill open to those who yearn for it.

When the leader has done a chunk of warmup work, he.she cues the other to take over the role of leader, and so Gifts proceeds, the roles changing from one to the other. It is vital that one of you does not dominate by hogging the role of leader.

There are two negatives that should be respected. If any of you, in the role of follower, is given a motion or sequence that you sense is beyond your capacity, that in fact might be dangerous for you, *do not do it.* Signal your reluctance to execute the move. The leader must respect this and go on to something else. The second negative says that the leader cannot do any move that loses eye contact with the follower for more than a moment. Any prolonged motions of turning away or bending far down or far back are oxymorons, a total contradiction to the whole point of Gifts. If the leader cannot see the follower, neither can the follower see the leader to follow. Nor should the leader continuously look away, whether at the floor, the ceiling or, more subtly, internally. Losing eye contact loses contact and the information needed to know what is happening with the other—the sacred other person. The leader's paramount responsibility is to be constantly aware of every change in the follower to know how to proceed.

The rules of a good and safe warmup are well known but worth repeating:

- Early stretches are wake-up stretches and not for limberness.
- Go from slow to fast.
- Go from simple to complex.
- Feet, legs, pelvis, torso, neck, arms, hands all need attention.
- Grandes pliés—deep knee bends—should be controlled, slow and limited in number.
- Introduce elevation late in the sequence.
- Introduce little jumps before big ones.
- Cool down should be followed by stretches for limberness.

Decide who will be the leader and start when you hear music. Use the music as you use the space you have for working. Find your freedom within your respect for the configuration of the space and for the contours of the music. Be sure to continue if there are breaks in the music or if you hear me call out suggestions. If the leader chooses to cover space, travel abreast, not "follow the leader," thus keeping eye contact alive all the time.

Go!

For obvious reasons, I have occasionally suggested that the dancers try to pick a partner who is close to their technical level, and yet I remain ambivalent about the suggestion. It immediately introduces the tension-creating factors of good, better, best and competitiveness, exactly when the aim is to get a large group of people relaxed enough to improvise freely. Still, there is a value here when people's technique is comparable.

I find it necessary to monitor this exercise closely. Every group has its own predilections, its strengths and weaknesses. Sometimes I note a plethora of waving arms and have to call out, "Continue what you are doing. Consider some big body motions." Or, hardly anyone has done plies and I say, "Think of getting to demi-pliés." I sense when they are ready to move ahead and call out, "If you haven't done big leg motions, now's the time," or "Time for little jumps," or "Time to travel, to cover space," and then "Whenever you are ready, cool down and stretch." All through Gifts, I stay alert for injudicious choices such as violent jouncing of hams on heels, jumps too early in the warmup, and so on, and will immediately enter the work space to talk quietly to the dancers concerned. (Normally I never speak during an exercise unless the structure requires me to call out the beginning of a new stage. The less aware dancers are of the leader the better.)

Sometimes I end Gifts by saying:

> Whenever you are ready, cool down, stretch-down and then take a moment to discuss with your partner what happened. What worked for you? Where did your partner really locate your need? Where was a need ignored?

When time is tight, I say:

> When you are both warmed up, ready to dance, let go of the leader-follower relationship and keep moving easily to the music on your own motivation as you both turn to face front. We will be ready to move on when all are facing front.

The wonder of Gifts is that it is perhaps the fastest and the safest warmup I've ever encountered. I've been opening workshops in this manner since 1974 and have never witnessed a serious injury. Additionally, it is a perfect introduction to the basic concepts of interaction, giving all attention to "the other" and the letting go of self-focus—these being the very spine of Work-group improvisation.

I am not one to press hard on the tools of charm and amusement when trying to engage the attention and the energies of a strange group of dancers and yet, in spite of myself, I early found two EGAS that could captivate and loosen up any group: Medicine Ball and Outrageous Travel. Both are spun out of Master-Disciple (5.9), the sound-motion exercise I learned from the Open Theatre:

Medicine Ball 9.2

Medicine Ball. Make circles of six to eight. In days long before the frisbee, it was the custom on beaches everywhere to stand in a circle like this and pass around a large, leather ball made heavy with stuffed rags. The game would start easily and slowly and, as it speeded up, part of the fun was to throw the ball in unexpected directions.

We are going to "throw" sound-motions. One person starts by "throwing" a short, impulsive sound and motion in the direction of any one in the circle. This direction must be unequivocally clear, even if it is made with the last gesture of the sound-motion. The receiver, without pause to reflect or evaluate, immediately repeats the thrown material *back* to the sender and then, without any hesitation or pause, throws her.his own impulsive sound and motion to another in the circle. That other repeats the ritual of reflecting what was given to the giver and sending out a personal sound-motion to a new person. This receiving and giving continues until you hear, "OK, let it wind down."

In doing Medicine Ball you must perform the two acts of reflecting and sending *without any pause* to think, to be "creative" or to reconsider any gesture or sound. The faster the exchanges go, the better. Start slowly to get the flow and sequence of the actions. As you gain confidence, build speed until you are all going as fast as you can.

One person in each circle volunteers to start. Wait for the cue, "Go!"

Medicine Ball is much more difficult to do well than it may appear. Few find the flow easily. The ritual of returning to one and then giving to another without pause can be very confusing and even unsettling. The ideal is an uncritical and immediate acceptance of what was given and an impulsive, unplanned and uncontrolled release of a sound-motion, both rendered as a seamless whole. It is necessary for the director or teacher to catch the evasions as they crop up. Few realize their own hesitations, even hairline hesitations, that slip in between receiving and reflecting or between reflecting and sending. I have to demonstrate what they do for them to recognize the flaws. I also call out cues to speed up. If there are many dancers and they really get into it, the din is such that it is a trick to be heard.

Outrageous Travel 9.3

Outrageous Travel. Form yourselves into parallel lines of six to eight, one in front of the other, at one end of the studio and facing the other end. The first person (First Person) in line crosses the space doing the most outrageous sound-motion travel possible. The others in that line observe First Person. Then the next person in line crosses the space, "becoming" First Person. This means not only duplicating what was visible—appearance and motions of First Person—but finding the impulse behind the motions and the sounds. Then, one at a time, everyone in that line does this. If what was originally done appears to be beyond your technical ability or strength to the degree that it might be physically dangerous for you, don't even try. Otherwise, throw yourself into it. Above all, do not attempt to be more outrageous, sillier or funnier than First Person; just slip into his.her skin and become him.her.

First Person observes all, seeking the one who comes closest to what was originally done. When the last person has crossed the space, First Person awards an accolade to the best one: a gentle double tap on the top of the head. This person becomes the new First Person, who now performs the most outrageous possible sound-motion travel with the others one by one attempting to "become" what they observe. If no one has come really close to what was done, First Person puts hands on hips and says,

"Tough," gives no one the accolade, and makes, in the opposite direction, a new outrageous sound-motion travel for the others to study and slip into.

The game continues for as long as the director chooses. In setting up Outrageous Travel, I start with one line doing it while the others observe. Wanting full energy from the dancers, I try to pick a first First Person who from previous observation appears to be lively and uninhibited. Paradoxically, first impressions can produce contradictory results. Almost invariably, the style and phrasing of this First Person is picked up by most who follow in the role of First Person, not only in the original example line, but in all the other lines. Let this very First Person plunge into a chaotic, violent and gymnastic Outrageous Travel and odds are that almost every subsequent First Person, in all the lines, will "on impulse" break into a chaotic, violent, and gymnastic Outrageous Travel. If the first sound-motion is a quirky, subdued and repetitive phrase, almost every First Person will follow suit. In the process of teaching and demonstrating anything, it is all too easy to find students creating an ostensibly personal pattern that was actually shaped by another, either by seeing the first student at work or by observing the teacher demonstrate. The point being made here is critical, so much so that I will recount a vivid experience that I first wrote about in *How to Dance Forever*.

A few years ago, I was having difficulty finding the address of a potential sponsor. Remembering that she had attended a concert the previous season, I dug up the guest book for that time but had no luck. It should be noted that during the concerts, the guest book was kept on the desk facing the elevator entrance to the studio. Beside it was a sign: "WOULD YOU LIKE TO BE ON OUR MAILING LIST?" Also, the guest book was unlined.

Convinced that I had missed her name, I leafed through the book a second time, but this time I was distracted by a startling observation. Every page had a pattern that was almost as consistent as a wallpaper design. On the first page, someone wrote his name and address in a slender, single line across the top of the page. All who followed gave the information in a straight, slender line across the page—fourteen names in all. The next page was topped by a bold John Hancock signature with his street address below, and city, state, plus zip code last, all occupying a third of the page. The next two people filled the page completely with the same configuration. And so it went. A small box containing the information in the upper left hand corner followed by a column of boxes was matched by a parallel column of small boxes on the right side of the page. There were a few exceptions—those who defied the style set by the first person. But, for most people, with no lines on the page and no indication as to where name and address should be entered, there was only the first person to go by. The question surfaces, who was the first person imitating—or were they?

These are not docile people but they are subject—as you and I are—to a phenomenon labeled by the psychologists as *imprinting*. "A learning process occurring early in the life of a social animal, whereby a behavior pattern is established through association with a parent or other role model."[1]

I hope it frightens you. It frightens me. In a way, it's the story of culture and tradition. *The first person sets the style.* How many critical choices in your life and mine have been decided by someone who got there first and how many were determined out of our own necessity and insight? How many were determined by imprinting? The shocker in those mailing list sheets is not only did people adopt the format established by the first person, but most picked up on the energy and the *size* of the letters. One would think these are too personal to be affected, but they were.

Observation is a great thing, important for all people as well as artists and having the talent to "become what you see" is part of the performer's craft, while becoming what you see *without realizing it or even worse, believing that is what you chose*, is sacrificing your individuality, unknowingly.

I promised you paradoxes and this one is a lulu. Being able to imitate expands your capacities when it's a deliberate, conscious act within the practice of your craft as an artist. Imitating unwittingly and believing you are making choices spontaneously when you aren't, is actually becoming the clone of what you see and of your peers. The latter hardly qualifies as a description of an artist and the former is in the practice and tradition of all art.[2]

In most workshops, I found it necessary to tell this story, long before I first wrote it down. If after five minutes it is apparent that unwitting imitation is taking place, it is worth stopping all the lines to point out what is going on.

On its surface, these two EGAS, Medicine Ball and Outrageous Travel are not far from kid games, games one might use to divert some very young children. Despite the fact that kids might not only delight in them but be great doing them, I regard these two as thresholds to the work in improvisation, performance and yes, to choreography. Here is the rationale I present to most groups:

Every artist travels on two legs. One leg is the skill of imitation and the other is the power to create personal and original expressions. Everything we do, from the first words we utter to the most recent technique class we take, we are absorbing by imitation. We blot up the world by imitation. The who and the what that is doing the absorbing is a mysterious complexity, but it is nothing without the envelope of experience. *What we do with the wealth of what we soak up is what makes us artists.* But, we are indeed impoverished if our skill and willingness to imitate are slight or inhibited.

In an early workshop at the State University of New York College at Brockport, I was giving Master-Disciple (5.9), for the first time a sound-

---

1. *The American Heritage Dictionary* (1985), p. 647.
2. Daniel Nagrin, *How to Dance Forever* (New York: William Morrow, 1988), pp. 201–03.

motion exercise involving imitation. I picked a very lively woman to start off. She woggled up to one model-height elegant woman roaring, "Cream cheese!" as she rocked about spastically. No matter how long and how energetically the Master repeated her outrageous sound-motion, the Disciple didn't budge a hair. Finally, I called a halt, asking the "non-disciple," "How come the resistance to imitating what was given to you?" Her answer: "That was silly."

In this game, it matters not whether the material to be imitated is silly, beautiful, honest, dishonest or whatever; it is to be imitated fully, *without evaluation or hesitation.* When Medicine Ball is done with speed and abandon, imitations become near miraculous: a delicate woman can pick up on the heft and power of a big man; a man's voice can of a sudden acquire a genuine female timbre. The beauty of these two exercises is that you plunge into a sound-motion that is not yours, that you may never have done—and yet you do it. You discover that you are not as limited as you thought, that in spite of your "personal style" you can do something you would think completely alien if you gave yourself time to think.

How is this possible? You do not "lose" yourself for an instant. No, but you do discover resources and qualities you never knew you had. You are presented with someone else's impulses and as quickly as a light turning on, out of the complexity of who you are and what you can do, a mosaic is assembled and you have "become" another. Being able to master this silly pair of exercises opens the door to the essential skill of imitation and reveals to you the knowledge that you are infinitely richer and more complex than you ever knew.

The more you protect yourself, like that elegant woman who would not deign to do something silly, the less nourished you are as an artist. The more you control your actions to preserve your "image," the more certain it is that you will do what you always have done—a dead end for an artist. The more you leap into these games, the more you will continually surprise yourself.

Why the sounds? You could argue, "We're dancers, not singers or actors." Answer: There is something untidy about the yelling, the grunting and the whispers and, precisely because most of you have no vocal training, there are no neat modules of vocal expression to which you can resort. As trained movers you are practically drowned in "neat modules of dance." The sounds mess things up and make it easier for you to come upon messy or, more importantly, unexpected movements.

As I traveled about, I gradually found ways to lessen my control over the development of an EGAS. One example that found favor and amusement from the dancers was a modification of Goldfish Bowl (5.1) called **The Schizoid Little Fishes of the Bering Sea.** As usual, the dancers receive the structure seated and with their eyes closed. (Standing and listening can be tiring, and lying down to listen can put some to sleep or drain energy from others.)

**The
Schizoid
Little Fishes
of the
Bering Sea
9.4**

When I say, "Go!" rise to your feet, your eyes still closed, and become a little blind, schizoid fish in the Bering Sea. You are conflicted because there is nothing you like so much as to be swimming deep within the pack of your fellow fishes; it fulfills a profound instinct that incidentally protects you from the big voracious squid who thinks the pack of you is a giant dangerous fish. But, you have a contradictory need to swim about freely and unencumbered by the presence of others, so you venture forth—only to be frightened by the risk of your tiny presence. In the middle of all the others you feel secure and at ease until the crowding pressures you to swim out alone and free of the others. Go where your instinct propels you!

The beauty of this setup is that it gives the dancers the freedom to clump with the others or to venture out alone, all the time with their eyes closed.

To the Mind-Wash (3.2), I added a Taoist touch. **Not Naming** is a lovely challenge which some dancers find quite helpful.

**Not
Naming
9.5**

In the course of the eye-journey, as your gaze travels down and up, devote your mind to seeing *without naming what you see.*

Most find this difficult, but some are able to achieve it intermittently and find it a transporting experience. When I give this exercise, instead of saying, "Your eyes go down to your chest, then to the floor, across to your partner's body . . . ," I simply pantomime with the tips of my fingers where the eyes should focus, from the tip of the nose to the upper part of the chest, and so on, thus directing the eye journey without naming anything.

In chapter 6 (pp. 96–100), I discussed the Achilles heel of working in the manner proposed in this book. A blanket of literalism will wreck everything. A superstructure of shining metaphors will illuminate the heart of our expressions. Very early in my contact with any group, I give, in one session, a pair of related EGAS that deal precisely with this problem.

**Gesture
Permuta-
tions
9.6**

Gesture Permutations. Pair off. If there is an odd number, make one a trio. Now, discuss with each other what you really think about Arizona. (Any place will do, the closer the better. After several minutes of this): Continue your discussion, but make no sound. Communicate only with gestures. (After several minutes of this): Now pause, and between you cull a short sequence of the gestures you exchanged, six to be exact. Person A makes a single gesture. B replies with the next gesture, A replies, B replies, A replies and B replies. Period. Finished. If you are a trio, keep it at six: A, then B, then C, then A, then B and then C. Finished. Once you have decided on the six gestures face me. (When all are finished and facing me):

Now go through the "conversation" of the six gestures three times *and each time you make your gesture do it as if it were the first time you ever did it.* Do it with the same conviction that you had before I stopped you.

Now do the six gestures three times as fast as you possibly can.

Now do the six gestures one time, moving more slowly than you have ever moved in your life.

You are a mammoth human made of lead and concrete. Do the six gestures.

You are actors in a silent movie. Go through the six gestures until I stop you.

You are underwater. Do the six gestures.

You are an ambitious courtier in the court of Louis XIV. He favors anyone who looks as if they might be an elegant dancer.

You are clowns in a circus.

Do the six gestures in waltz time.

You stammer and stutter painfully.

You have no hands and no arms. Communicate the meaning of the six gestures with your torso.

You can communicate only with your shoulders.

Only with your feet.

All your gestures are made of procelain. They have been dropped, broken and glued together this way and that, but not logically. Communicate as best you can.

Don't do any of the six gestures. Rather do what they feel like.

Manifestly, this list is potentially endless.

Gesture
Rondo
9.7

Gesture Rondo. Leave your partner or your trio, and in your own space and in your own mind, go over the three or two gestures you have been doing. Decide which one you want to continue working with, for whatever reason. When I say, "Go," you will do that gesture with as much truth and conviction as you did the first time and then, with no premeditation, allow *anything* to happen, from the most obvious, literal, banal association to the most esoteric muscular association. You may start on a physical impulse that leads to dramatic one that leads to whatever. Just let it flow and, above all, avoid "good taste." Just go. If and when the energy runs down, come to a pause and repeat the original gesture as simply and honestly as possible. Again allow anything to flow from it for as long as it does until it stops. Then again do the original gesture. Continue until I call out for this Gesture Rondo to end. Go!

After doing this sequence of EGAS, most dancers, instead of living in terror of the literal gesture—either sedulously avoiding it or feeling guilty of bad taste in being literal, even for a moment—discover that the literal gesture is a gold mine. The literal gesture becomes a source of a limitless range of movement. The tiny island of classroom moves to which most dancers think they are limited becomes one rich and useful area among many. Whatever we do and have done in our lives—from early morning to sleep and dreams, and from the earliest remembered days to this morning—is waiting there to be used in our dances: bent, twisted, turned inside out, stretched, shrunk and magnified. Every part of our lives belongs to us as dancers and artists.

As I pored over the notes from the time of the Workgroup, several times I came across the phrase, "possessed by a mannerism," but we never did it. It relates to Cliché Rondo (5.13), but it indicates a subtle shift of attention. I've never given what follows but I will one day.

Possessed by a Mannerism 9.8

Some dancers are haunted and even nagged by criticisms of one or more of their mannerisms: a Baroque arching of the hand, constantly gazing at the ground, a worried frown that accompanies every technical difficulty, hyperextending the pelvis in turns—the list can be endless. Actually most of us have one or more of these that cling to us like barnacles. They attract attention precisely because they usually are not at all pertinent to what we are doing. They are just there most of the time. We will call this next exercise **Possessed by a Mannerism.**

While seated, close your eyes. Clear your head with your breath. In the empty space that ensues, ask the question, "What do I always do in dance, regardless of the occasion? What is my mannerism? Do I have one?" If the answer is no, open your eyes and leave the floor. If yes, see yourself performing the mannerism in your mind's eye. When it appears clearly and vividly, open your eyes, rise to do it and, whenever you're ready, travel among the others to find one to whom you will show this mannerism. If there are an odd number of you on the floor, the last person can go to one of the dancers who has chosen to leave the floor or join a pair to make a trio. There will be four stages for this exercise.

First stage: Each of you in turn, demonstrate to your partner the mannerism you just visualized for yourself.

Second stage: Separate and find your own space where you will again "see" the mannerism. As you do this, begin to sense its inner rhythm, the motor that drives it. Once the rhythm is established, let it flood your body, let it move your body. Now, with this base, improvise a dance about the mannerism—doing it fully and consciously; doing it in different ways, in parts of the body where it is never done; do it to show it to the world like a flag; conceal it while still doing it; sense what the mannerism is trying to say or do. In short, dance to, for, about and against your mannerism. The only music for this exercise will be the inner rhythm you found.

Third stage: When you have done this improvisation, and you will know when you are done, find your partner and, if necessary, wait until she.he is finished. Now, taking turns, improvise once more for your partner the dance you did in private.

Fourth stage: When both have danced for each other, rest and talk to each other about what you saw in the other, what you learned about your mannerism and, if it is not too private, what you learned about yourself.

When you are next alone in a studio, do Possessed by a Mannerism again. In this private space and time, you may be able to delve deeper into what is really going on, where the mannerism came from and what it is really about. Undesirable habits need conscious attention without undue pressure or tension.

During a visit to California State College at San Diego, I went at the questions, What is male? and What is female? from a radically different angle. As before, each question was put separately on two successive days to all the dancers, men and women. On the third day, I gave out what came to be called **Inside the Outside.**

Inside the Outside 9.9

Sit, close your eyes and place your hands on your knees. Clear your head with your breath. When you are ready to go on, clasp your hands. (When all have done this): Yesterday, you did a Hub Meditation (5.7) on What is female? The day before, you did one on What is male? Recapture in your mind's eye what you found in these two exercises, first one and then the other. Now mesh them into one body and wait to see what will happen. What do you see? Is one image visible and the other present but not? Is one on the outside and one on the inside? Are both visible but is one dominant? So many possibilities.

When the mesh is completed, go to work on whichever is *on the inside*, using the technique of Each Alone (4.4). Do what it does to become that image. (This group had already gone through the sequence of Each Alone several times.) When you have finished, when you have "become" that image you are ready for the second stage: as X, go through another Each Alone, this time putting on the other image *on the outside*. We can call this outside image Y. Y is what X shows to the world.

When you have finished this double task, you are ready to look about you and take in the "world" in which you find yourself. You have one more question to answer before you go on. What do you as the complexity of X clothed as Y want to do—need to do—for, to or against the world in which you find yourself? Is there someone out there with whom you need to interact—or to avoid? Do you have a task? Once you have answers, retaining the full sense and presence of both X and Y, find the danced *metaphors* that contain this action. Now you are ready to do whatever you have to do, with or without others. As in Duet (6.5), if you succeed in your task celebrate that and leave the floor. If you fail, dance the recognition of that and leave the floor.

This one worked. There were many dancers attending this workshop, and that often makes for greater freedom because the dancers quite accurately assume that they will not be all that conspicuous among so many. The dancing was varied, animated and quirky. The duets went on for a long time and things happened—people changed as they danced. The talk afterward was full of wonderment at how completely they were caught up and how many emotional and intellectual surprises jolted them.

There's always a risk when the door is opened to deep and often conflicted feelings. Over the years, I've given out these two questions, What is male? and What is female? to about eight different groups, involving around two hundred and fifty dancers. Once, a few dancers wept bitterly, and another time, one was furious about the whole thing. (See the dialogue in Appendix B.) Most others were excited that they could be dancing *and* actually dealing with what really mattered to them. How sophisticated and how mature should the dancers be to attempt this stuff? I have no answer. I can almost always sense what is appropriate for a given group, but sometimes I slip. I only know this stuff is dynamite in the hands, bodies and minds of dancers who are open and willing to look at each other and themselves. They are the brave ones I salute.

Some EGAS have never been done as well as I dreamt they could be. The best Rhythm Circle (3.5) I ever witnessed was the first group for whom it was devised, those wild Texans in Austin. There were many subsequent attempts with others but only with modest results. The closest was at Connecticut College in New London where I added a flip which, in the right hands would make a sensational performance piece. After the dancers have learned and gained a facility with Rhythm Circle, I set up an overhead microphone with someone running the tape recorder and monitoring the level of sound. To the circle of six to eight dancers I gave **Rhythm Circle Performed,** first assigning a lead-off person.

Rhythm Circle Performed 9.10

When you hear me call out "Go!" the operator will put the recorder into the record mode. That will be the cue for you, the lead-off person, to begin to find your rhythm and start the action of Rhythm Circle. All should know this: every sound you make will be recorded. As in the original version of Rhythm Circle, when the rhythm travels around the circle to finally reach the original lead-off dancer or Master, all will join in to make a unison chorus of that last rhythm. When this last Master is ready, he.she ceases beating out the rhythm and rises to dance it, following its contour directly with no syncopation or counterrhythm. One by one, the dancers cease making the sounds and rise to join the Master dancing, also following this last rhythm closely. The moment the last dancer rises and there is no longer anyone beating out the rhythm, the tape operator stops the recording, rewinds the tape, and starts to play it from the beginning, monitoring the sound so that it is loud enough for the dancers and the audience, if there is one.

At this time, the dancers will have a full range of musical options: following the rhythm closely, making variations on what they hear or syncopating. Many kinds of interactions are possible, but the pervading concentration is the rhythm of the tape and what the other dancers are doing with that rhythm. Note that the recording will end with the last rhythm that came from the circle in unison and then gradually fade out to just one "percussionist." Use the fade to make an exit.

How I would love to see a group of rhythm hotshots tear into this one! The Rhythm Circle Performed could easily be a dynamic performance piece.

I was Visiting Artist at the State University of New York in Brockport for four or five years, and for improvisation classes I would ask each student to create and direct an improvisation structure. One night, a student named Jill Becker (who has since gone on to form her own company and perform in New York City) came up with one that I've never forgotten. Sadly, I have found but a few occasions when it was right to use it. I think it wants a group of dancers and musicians with a strong sense of community, which those at Brockport had. The very first time she set it up, it took off without a word of explanation from her other than to arrange the four or five musicians behind her, and the dancers (there were at least twenty) in a large semicircle facing the musicians. She named it **Celebration.**

Celebration 9.11

Her beginning was derived from many ancient rituals. From a jug, she poured something into what looked like a soup bowl. With deliberation, she came before the first person to her left, knelt, sipped from the bowl and then passed it to the person before her, who of course took a small sip. With a gesture, Jill indicated it was to be passed to the next person, which it was. It is a touching and a powerful metaphor when a large group partakes of a small amount of a liquid from the same bowl—and also a health hazard. I never used that part of the Celebration.

When the bowl had completed the circuit of the group, she put it on the ground before her and, facing the dancers, she placed an embroidered cap on her head. Rising, she said for all to hear, something like, "I celebrate my friend who is in Viet Nam." The dance that followed was just that, and the musicians supported her every move. The seated dancers got caught up in the action and sang or beat the floor with their hands. When she finished, she knelt before one of the other dancers, removed the cap, placed it on the head of that dancer, and retired to the edge of the semicircle. This one did not need to be told what to do. She took her place facing the group and, for all to hear, said, "I celebrate the daffodil bulbs I planted yesterday." When she finished, she selected a new dancer to take her place. That person said, "I celebrate my big, black Harley Davidson." Though I'm making these up, they give the sense of that group and that time—1970. I do remember mine: "I celebrate all of you— ten years from now." The entire sequence continued until everyone took center to dance their own celebration, while the musicians and the dancers made music and sounds to support the action.

I was amazed that this large-scale improvisation occurred with not a word spoken in explanation. It was an all-absorbing experience.

Take a Walk in Your Own World is an ideal EGAS for those times when a very large group shows up at a one-time improvisation workshop.

Take a Walk in Your Own World 9.12

All sit and listen with your eyes closed. When you hear music, that will be the "Go." You will rise and go for a walk in your own world—whatever that phrase means to you. That is stage one.

Stage two: When you hear me call out "Stage two," look out from the walking in your own world to the others walking in their own world. Observe as many as you can, but be certain that you lose nothing of the quality and the action of your own walk.

When I call out, "Stage three," that will be the signal to pick, from all the walkers you have observed, the one who interests you the most for any reason, positive or negative. When you have found that person, carry your walk close to them (but not in front), all the while observing that person very closely. There is only one restriction: you cannot pick anyone who picks you. One of you will have to give way and find someone else.

"Stage four" will be the cue to "become" the walker you have been observing. This will be tricky because that person's walk and motions will also change at that moment—she.he is doing what you are doing, becoming the person who interests them. So your task will be to remain close to the one who interests you, observe them closely and do what they *were* doing, not what they *are* doing. You will have to remember what you saw. By "becoming" I mean you take on for yourself not only what you saw the person doing but what you sense is the impulse that shaped his.her motions.

When you hear "Stage five," do what you see that person is doing *now*. This is easier and will lead to little or large circles of people doing similar motions. If a pair are facing each other and doing the same motion, they broke the ground rule by picking each other. If there is a "follow the leader" line with one at the head imitating no one, that one broke a rule by never picking an "interesting" person.

"Stage six." Still observing your "interesting" person, do what it feels like to be that person. This is not an imitation; this is not what it *looks* like to be that person but what it *feels* like to be that person.

"Stage seven." Gradually and slowly modulate your motions until you are back walking in your own world.

Take a Walk in Your Own World is best done to a piece of music at least twenty minutes long that has a driving rhythmic pulse, a continuous flow and without strong dynamic changes. Consider the composers Terry Riley, Steve Reich and Philip Glass.

Faces. The first version of this was Backs (6.11), in which all sat in a line, facing in the same direction, studying with the fingertips and closed eyes the back of the person in front. The awkwardness was that the first person had no one, unless there were enough to sit in a circle. In "Acting Technique for Dance Performance," a class at the American Dance Festival, I hit upon a most obvious solution and then, from nowhere, there appeared a follow-up which unexpectedly opened quite a few doors and windows. The very first instruction, which will shortly become clear, generally bemuses the entire group but all accept it without question:

Faces
9.13

Will everyone please get to a sink and thoroughly wash your hands? On the way, or returning, join up with someone with whom you will want to work as partners. When you return, washed, sit facing each other cross-legged, a few inches apart. Close your eyes. When you sit, avoid soiling your clean hands by touching the floor.

(The bemused go to wash, return as partners, and sit.) With your eyes closed, clear a space in the head with your breath. Anytime after I finish speaking, and whenever you are ready, reach your hands forward to touch the face of the person in front of you. With your fingertips study this face—the varied textures of skin and hair, the shapes of bone and muscle. You will study not only to experience but to remember. When you think your hands have it—the memory of that face—drop your hands in your lap. When your partner's hands leave your face, with your eyes still closed, turn a quarter of a circle away on your bottom. Now reach your hands forward into space *as if that person is still in front of you* and with your fingers relive the entire experience of touching his.her face, not merely to go through the motions of touching but to feel once again the skin, hair, muscle and bone.

Do not be disconcerted if you find areas whose sensory experience you cannot recall. In some places, the most you will have is the idea of moist skin or a hairline, not the sensation. Do not despair. Do as much of the face in the air as you can. Then swivel back to face in the original direction, with your eyes still closed, and reach out once again to study to remember the face of your partner.

If you encounter a shoulder instead of a face, your partner is still re-creating in the air. Drop your hands and wait until you sense a movement of returning to the original facing. Then raise your hands again and go specifically to the places where your memory had failed you. Experience and study with your hands what eluded you, and when you think your hands have it, once again swivel a quarter turn away. Go directly to the blank places and fill them in by experiencing the actual sensation of touching. When you have done all you can, drop your hands to your lap and wait until you hear "OK," indicating that all are finished.

(When all have done this, I add the following): When I give you a "Go!" open your eyes and rise to find a private space for yourself. Once you are there, without planning, without waiting to think about what you will do, begin to dance what it *felt* like to do what you were doing. Don't dance what you did; dance what it felt like to do what you were doing. Sit when you are finished. Now go!

(When everyone has done their private dance and is seated): Now go to find your partner and each of you show the other what you just did. After you have danced for each other sit where you are, facing in my direction.

(When all are finished): Now all come here and answer a question: What was the difference between the dance you did first, when you had no awareness that you were going to do it for an audience, when you had no audience in fact, and the second dance, the second version of what you did, when you presented it to your partner?

The ensuing discussion always reveals a vast variety of attitudes toward the problems of performance, truth and art itself. Some say they are heightened, energized, exhilarated and even gain a clarity of expression by the presence of an audience; other people become dismayed, disoriented and disappointed. Those having negative experiences claim to have lost spontaneity, become falsely theatrical, forgotten some good moves and, worst of all, lost the feeling that enriched the private experience. I ask, "Did you leave out some material because you thought it might not be interesting, or did you exaggerate some parts to make them more interesting?"

Almost everyone will admit to having left out material and also to speeding up all they did. Most artists do, though there are Asian artists and a group of postmodernists who make a virtue of extended time. Dance, like music and theatre, are artifacts that exist in real time. The question confronting every artist who speaks in real time is, How do I reveal the true time of what I am doing? Is it best seen, felt, experienced, impacted by compression, or its opposite, extension or in real time? There is no one answer. Every artist must beware of becoming a passive victim of a style, either of the time or what she.he has come to regard as her.his style. There is no general rule of rightness; the time-life of each phrase or dance makes its own rules.

For some, the changes from the "private" dance to the "public" dance for the partner were meant to increase clarity of expression and intent. The dancers feared that their solitary work was rambling, shapeless and unnecessarily obscure; it needed shortening, editing, speeding up, alterations of emphasis, or the addition of "something interesting." Even in that one unrehearsed "performance" for the audience of one, the original private exploration was regarded as a sketch and the "performance" as a "painting."

Another question: When you were dancing for an audience, for your partner, was there anything you did that was designed to make you look good, more attractive, more accomplished, something that did not relate to the task—what it felt like to study a face with only your fingertips?

This focus on looking good, on being attractive, which lives in the very bones of most dancers, is one of the curses of our profession and our art. To say, "I love you more than life itself," while concentrating on producing an exquisite tone of voice is an ethical oxymoron or to put it more crudely, hypocrisy. As for the loss of spontaneity, the loss of the feeling that enriched the private experience, this must be said: The climate of the creative process is turbulent and constantly subject to change. Those who feel they cannot function as artists unless they are always in full heat and flowing are in serious trouble. Similarly, those who constantly seek the cool, objective detachment that gives them complete control over all that pours out of them, are unwilling to risk the surprises that fill the life of an artist. For most artists capable of expression, there are periods of work where an intoxication possesses them and the work flows like a mighty river. *These same artists are quite capable of slaving away for long periods of time in the cold tunnel of creation, remembering, re-creating and laborious editing.* They willingly bear tedium and hours of detailed concentration that to an outsider would appear to be dealing with minutiae.

How many dancers have felt that in the heat of improvisation they flew past the limits of gravity—and in the cold moments that followed knew that they might never recapture that ecstasy and those elegant phrases? The artists that endure are the ones who patiently and stubbornly pursue the illusive, the ineffable moment and, in time, hammer out a shape that may not be precisely what they had lost but rather a lovely poem about it. The journey of artists is a gamble through the heat and ice of the creative process.

To close this section, I throw out a ruthless ethic about art. The greatest mark of devotion to the audience is not to create what they would like or expect, but rather for the artist to give all his.her devotion to the vision as it was found. That is the true gift to the audience, even though they might hate it.

10 Improvising Jazz, 1990

The summer of 1990 presented a window to an opportunity I had had only once before: a two-week jazz workshop. This was to be at Stanford University; the other had been at the University of Oregon in Eugene in 1962. That earlier one was a turning point in how I taught jazz: it focused on clearly and precisely structured jazz dance styles. The Stanford workshop centered on the creative use of jazz, and specifically in improvisation. A little history is needed to explain my excitement with this workshop, my experience with jazz, and what I mean by *jazz*.

As noted earlier, the improvisational processes of jazz musicians had a strong effect in shaping certain Workgroup structures. Ironically, our company members never did a jazz move, either in our studio sessions or before the public. On a few occasions we did use two fabulous stride piano solos, one by Leadbelly and the other by Cripple Clarence Lofton, as music for Rondo (6.1). Either piece of music could make the dead rise up dancing, but I was the only one in the company who had any jazz dance style. The others did lovely dance work, but not *jazz*.

The moment I got out of college, in 1940, I turned professional with a job in a summer theatre in the Pennsylvania Poconos, and it was there, in the person of Sue Ramos, that I came in contact with jazz music and classic jazz dance styles. By "classic," I mean "authentic" historical dance forms. She knew the Lindy and the Charleston, as well as blues and Latino dance.[1] I blotted up all I could from her and then, in the following year, at that summer theatre, I was hired by Helen Tamiris, for whom jazz was in the very bones of how she defined America. We worked together on Broadway and in films, and did a little TV, often using jazz dance. During that time I absorbed jazz wherever I found it—from Helen, at the Savoy Ballroom in Harlem, nightclub

---

1. American jazz and Latin-American music and dance are like adjoining bodies of water with a constant flow between them, each gaining colors and textures from the other without losing its essential character.

shows, other Broadway shows, old films with greats like Bill Robinson, James Barton and the Nicholas Brothers. I opened my eyes wide as a funnel and copied, imitated and improvised and improvised and improvised—but always for myself, always to find movement for my choreography and for the choreography of the Broadway shows which we worked. I never improvised for an audience.

All through this period, my focus was on classic jazz dance—traditional, historical jazz forms. At the same time, I witnessed the emergence of a great innovator, Jack Cole. Out of his East India dance training with Ted Shawn and Ruth St. Denis, jazz music and Afro-Cubano dance, he evolved a style which to this day defines what most people, in and out of show business, think of as jazz. This is the style that, with many variations, is taught today as jazz in dance schools and universities; it can be seen tonight on the floors of night clubs in Hong Kong, Paris and Manilla and on the stages of Broadway. My feelings about what Cole created? Mixed. It is powerful, compelling and driving in its energy. Cole himself always kept the stage or the screen alive with audacity and a great mix of wildness and control. Negatively, I always was repelled by the undercurrent of hostility and a viciousness in the pelvic thrusts. In the hands of some of the choreographers who have continued and developed this style, it all too easily transforms women into furious and contemptuous whores and men into toughs with but one thought in their skulls. Compared with classic jazz, it is rhythmically simplistic: a continuous hammering of eight to the bar. My name for this current style is Show Jazz.[2] From where I saw it, classic jazz was/is delight in the intracies of rhythm, humor, show-off, sheer joy in living—and, yes, with a sexy innuendo. Show Jazz, on the other hand, tends to have one focus: to deliver sex like a battering ram—most of the time. It would be naive not to recognize that there is something in the temper of our times that wants precisely this violent, bruising, and naive metaphor for the act of sex.

Am I scolding the times? I do it all the time. It explains why, despite my admiration for Jack Cole's originality, I never picked up on his style. I saw it evolve from its beginnings in the Rainbow Room, where Tamiris and I also danced. I admired Cole and his followers, some of whom are glorious dancers like Matt Mattox and Gwen Verdon. But for myself, I learned from watching the virtuosos of the Savoy Ballroom or James Barton—the "authenticos."

When I turned away from Broadway to create a solo program for the concert stage, I gave classes to earn money: modern dance technique, movement for actors and jazz. Because my jazz differed from Show Jazz, the class always attracted interest wherever I taught it—in New York, on tour and many times at the American Dance Festival.

2. None of these descriptions fit break dance or the new hip-hop style that has sprouted on MTV, particularly as performed by the men. Many of the women on the same dance floors collaborate in defining themselves as "sex objects," period. Hip-hop by the best is rhythmically dazzling and quite virtuosic.

In the 1962 two-week jazz workshop at the University of Oregon in Eugene, I came upon a demanding situation. The dancers were to meet five nights a week, three hours each night, a total of thirty hours! Each student would earn one college credit toward their baccalaureate. I felt an enormous responsibility. I had to teach them JAZZ, not just my jazz. Up to then, that was all I had taught: my style, my accretions, my inventions. In those two weeks, desperately trying to stay ahead of the class, I daily devised, remembered and stole enough to create a Jazz Lexicon—a basic English of jazz history—by arranging and teaching four different dances: a Cakewalk, a Charleston, a Lindy and a Blues. This then became the staple of what I taught and still teach as jazz in many workshops across the country under the rubrics of Jazz Dance Styles or Classic Jazz Dance.

Note that I wrote "arranging" and not "choreographing." I took the steps and styles acquired from many sources and put them together as "learning dances." They formed a basic dictionary of jazz dance history. Immodestly, I am proud of this achievement. Although dance is flourishing across the nation, hardly anyone else is attempting to preserve the classic moves or to use them as a springboard for their own work. Pepsi Bethel and Frankie Manning are among the last of the famed Lindy Hoppers teaching and choreographing. One should add the American Dance Machine directed by the late Lee Theodore.[3] Some teachers of tap dance keep the old steps alive—and that's it.

I go into all of this because although I was teaching Classic Jazz Dance Styles, I never got to teach the most obvious essential, jazz dance improvisation. Though I had given many classes in improvisation and choreography, none of them dealt creatively with this marvelously variegated jazz material. The four dances in the Jazz Lexicon are so complex, there is barely enough time to teach them in the six weeks of intense daily classes at the American Dance Festival or in the semester-long bi-weekly classes I taught at Arizona State University. There was never enough time to carry the learned work through to the next step—creation—by improvisation or by choreographing, at least not until the Stanford workshop, which would consist of a morning class in Classic Jazz Dance and an afternoon class in Jazz Improvisation (but not jazz choreography—that would have been one thing too much for the two weeks). After giving the students a two-day taste of the four dances, I let them pick which two they wanted to learn in the two weeks. They picked Lindy and the Blues. The afternoons were all exploration, work new to me as well as the students.

Well, not quite new. I scanned the history of the Workgroup improvisations, culling what seemed right for jazz and for these students. Every group

---

3. In fact, Lee Theodore once came up to Tamiris and myself during the intermission of a dance performance at the 92nd Street Y to proudly tell us that she had formed a company that would perform jazz dance improvisations. This was in the early fifties. That's all I ever heard of it.

has its own signature and footprint, and in teaching, I always work to sense with whom I am dealing. This bunch were bright, eager, good dancers, ready for adventure.

Before the workshop started, I spent hours of listening to different styles and tempos of vintage jazz music. The pieces I selected all had one qualification: they were irresistible—to me. To hear them meant I had to move. Another teacher would have found other music. Loving your material is the best way to teach.

In the first week we worked mostly with very short set phrases, usually of eight counts. The moves came from the dancers or me. The method of finding the phrase was similar to what I use when I work alone:

The Blues Sandwich 10.1

The Blues Sandwich. With your eyes closed, stand in your own space and clean out your head with your breath. When the music starts, listen to a good chunk of it. After a while, try to sense your inner response to what you are hearing. Is there within you a pervasive, repetitive phrase that is not quite like any you hear and yet runs parallel to the music? Fit what you find into an eight-count phrase.[4] If you find one, give it time to define itself. When it gains shape, let it come out in your hands, then let the feet enter the scene, still on that one phrase/rhythm/riff, and finally let it take over the entire body. Once you have danced it fully, repeat it until you are sure you will be able to return to it accurately. Once you are sure, leave the floor. (It may be necessary to play the music several times until everyone is finished.) When everyone has found a phrase, the music will stop. All return to the floor, and the music will start up from the beginning.

Now when you hear the music, you will use your riff, your rhythm, which by now has a set movement phrase, to create new phrases. The form is strict. Do your eight-count phrase twice, and then free-form for eight counts. Return to doing the eight counts twice, and then do another eight counts ad lib. This is the form that will carry you through the entire piece of music. *AAB AAC AAD*, and so on. (Most of the music, vintage jazz, was originally recorded for ten-inch, 78 rpm records which could not be longer than three minutes and twenty seconds.)

What do you do in the eight-count ad lib? Whatever: a movement or rhythmic variation on the original eight counts, a mickey-mouse of what you are hearing in the music at that moment, a feeling that spills over from the original phrase, a blind following of your body's impulses—anything that grows out of the original eight-count phrase.

The Blues Sandwich came after a few disastrous days. For the first class, I gave what I thought would be an easy introduction to the work ahead: an

---

4. The number of counts to a phrase will depend on the music and the listener, but the leader/teacher has the responsibility of choosing and of giving it for all to do. The freedom inherent in jazz improvisation rests on precise structures shared in common by the participants.

eight-count phrase (which I taught), followed by an improvised phrase of eight, alternating all through the music—*AB AC AD*. . . . The shocker was that the dancers sooner or later lost the eight counts, not, I learned, because they lacked rhythm but because they had no experience improvising within a specific phrase length. They could not respond freely to the music while keeping to a specific limiting count in their heads or their bodies.

I decided to assume nothing. We ran the music again, and this time, while they were doing their *AB AC AD*, and so on, I counted the eights aloud for all to hear. The second time, I had them all chant the eights aloud. Delightfully, their voices became a kind of jazz. They intoned it, sang it after a while, mischievous ones diddled with the rhythm of the simple downbeat counts, and everyone made a big deal out of returning to the first beat of their original phrase. To make that work, they had to do something to the last couple of counts before that downbeat. That was the beginning of a consciousness without which jazz just does not happen. It matters not how you know where you are in jazz music, but know you must—by feel, by melody or by counting.

It is precisely in this area that the whole problem of jazz dance improvisation hangs or, if it is done right, flies! Jazz musicians have almost a century of improvisations behind them. Every good jazz peformance contains improvisation. Improvisation is part of what defines jazz. Except for tap dancers, dancers have no such tradition. A jazz musician can walk into a session in Buenos Aires, London, Cairo or Biloxi and sit in on a happy time of music-making. They share a tradition and we dancers do not.

What defines the tradition for the musicians? Rules. Rules of time, harmony, known tunes to play with and rules of courtesy and precedence. A blues chorus has so many bars—twelve. A ballad has sixteen. As they play, jazz musicians have stored in their common memories, the sound of Louis Armstrong playing "Basin Street Blues," Miles Davis playing "So What?" and Duke Ellington leading his men in "East St. Louis Toodle-oo." No matter how far-out contemporary jazz musicians may be, whatever they blow, it is played out in front of an enormous tapestry of the past.

We have no past in Classic Jazz Dance Improvisation. At the Stanford workshop I was attempting to create the beginning of a little tradition. Precision and form were necessary, for without it, the dancers present would have no common ground for interaction, and interaction is another leg of what defines jazz.

A second shocker occurred when I tried to introduce syncopation. Noting that most of the dancers' phrases were rhythmically flat, I taught them on the second day a few of my own eight-count phrases with some fun syncopations for the Blues Sandwich. They were set to some wonderful John Lee Hooker blues. Again, I caught a shock. These well-trained dancers had little or no feel for the offbeat—and what is jazz without the offbeat? For an hour, to various pieces of music, we walked to one rhythm: a four-count measure clean on the downbeat followed by a four-count measure snapping out the offbeat. From then on, the offbeat, which is at the heart of syncopation, which is at heart of jazz, became a conscious tool of the dancers. Call it **The Offbeat.**

The Offbeat
10.2

1 & 2 & 3 & 4 & / 1 & 2 & 3 & 4 & / 1 & 2 & 3 & 4 & / 1 & 2 & 3 & 4 & /

There is a naiveté in music notation which many but not all musicians and many but not all dancers accept uncritically. Some things cannot be notated but must be felt—because they are part of the breath of the moment, the surge of energy, the sudden revelation that explodes in the middle of performance, and the recognition that hardly anything is quite what it appears to be. I am still talking about the beat. Being square on the beat or squarely on the middle of the beat is quite exhilarating when it happens *sometimes* and quite deadly when it happens all the time. One of my favorite assignments follows the teaching of the basic Lindy step. Once the dancers can do it with reasonable security, I throw the exercise **Before, After, and On** at them.

Before,
After,
and On
10.3

When you hear the music, go into the basic Lindy step, with no variation and a total preoccupation with being precisely on the beat. When you see me rotate my hands quickly, do the Lindy step a hairsbreadth *ahead* of the beat. When I make a slow spreading motion, drag the Lindy step so that you are continually a bit late. When I make an up and down chopping motion with my hands, drive clean down on the center of the beat. I will randomly redirect your attitude toward the beat.

(That done): Here's another piece of music. Make your own movement module of eight counts. When you have it under control and can repeat it endlessly, step off the floor. (When all are off the floor): When you hear the music, come onto the floor to do your module and play with it—before, after and on the beat. When does it feel right?

Whenever I teach the classic jazz dance course, I always add as a subtext the awareness of precisely this attitude toward rhythm, pointing out that a particular step can only have its quality realized if it is dragged, or that another needs to rush the beat, and how being square on the beat can be ecstasy.

Growing out of this toward a bit of creativity is Riff Cactus.

Riff Cactus
10.4

To the music you hear, and out of its nature and qualities, find a phrase of four, six or eight counts. When you have it under control, start to do it forever, meaning that you have no intention of changing it or developing it in any way. It just continues on its way *until it changes itself.* You could say this is a Taoist exercise. Well, it is. I use the word "cactus" because the exercise reminds me of the way a beaver-tail cactus will, after a long time, send out a bit of a bud that will grow into something like what it came from, but not quite.

When I worked on my solo *Jazz: Three Ways,* I found many of the steps in this fashion. It is very easy to make up steps, but who believes them? I prefer to have steps happen.

Some EGAS that I gave during the first week of the workshop aimed at freeing the imagination.

Who or What Is Alive in the Music? Find your place in the room, sit, close your eyes and clean out your head with your breath. Michelangelo would go to the quarries and spend hours there contemplating the great blocks of cut marble until he could see who or what was alive inside. When you hear the music, seek who or what is alive inside it. Your quest is a specific, never a generalization. When you find the who or what, let your attention move in close and learn all you can about X. Most of all, what is the inner rhythm that lives in X? The motor that drives X? How does that rhythm coexist and live within the rhythm of the music? The last question that needs an answer is, How long is this rhythmic phrase? You may hear a phrase of four or six or nine counts. It matters not, as long as that is what you feel; but before you go on, you have to make a conscious analysis and know its length. It would not be acceptable at this point to mush along with an indeterminate phrase length. Miles Davis was permitted, but not you, not yet. If and when the inner rhythm emerges full and clear, let it take possession of your entire body. Let it move you where it will.

Circles (4.1) starts the same as Who or What Is Alive in the Music? Now when you find the who or what, let your attention move in close, learning all you can about X. Most of all, What is X doing? Again, what is the inner rhythm that lives in X? How does that rhythm coexist and live within the rhythm of the music? The last question that needs an answer is, How long is this rhythmic phrase? When you know all you can about X—what X is *doing* and his.her rhythm phrase—rise to stand, still contemplating X. When everyone stands, we will go back to the beginning of the music and I will ask you to become X, doing what X does with your eyes, brows and your scalp *within the context of the found rhythmic phrase*. After a while, I will ask you to add your lips, tongue and jaw. Then your neck, your chest, your shoulders, your elbows, your hands, your waist, your pelvis/voice, your thighs/knees, your feet, and finally, your totality. Then I will ask you, as X, to go traveling and observe the others. Is there anyone your X wants to be near? To influence? To be changed by? Or to change? Stay on the floor until X is satisfied or until X knows failure.

Each Alone (4.4). The same as Circles, only now when you know all about X, become X one part of the body at a time, *deciding for yourself* the part of the body, the order and the time you spend with each part. You get no direction. You yourself will know when one part of the body is "done" and you are ready to go on. When you are complete, go traveling and seek the one who engages your strongest attention and do as you did in Circles. Above all do not neglect to locate the rhythmic unit that is at the heart of X.

These three EGAS, which were so central to the way of the Workgroup, work exquisitely in the context of jazz and very well in the order given here. They feed and reenforce each other. The startling result was that almost all dancers found a who or a what that moved, not necessarily with traditional jazz steps, but unequivocally with jazz style. The weakest results came from those who chose and stayed with literal gestures. Again and again it is helpful to note that in all of this improvisatory work, whether in the jazz mode or any other, the literal can be a generating seed if, and only if, it flowers into a danced metaphor. If the dancer hangs on to the literal gesture, to persist with the garden metaphor, it will all be dull weeds. Most of this group found movement with the feel of jazz *without trying to do jazz*. It was just there.

All three exercises hinge on the use of strong, driving music. The first can use one of the early three-and-a-half-minute pieces restarted the moment they end, but the second and the third need at least ten minutes of continuous music and more is better. Miles Davis, Charlie Mingus, and Sonny Rollins have recorded such pieces.

As in most improvisation workshops, I find Outrageous Travel (9.3) ideal for bringing a group to a place where they realize anything is possible—and OK; that being neat, precise, controlled and doing the expected are only a few of ten thousand possibilities. This time at Stanford, I missed the chance to really experiment with this exercise. I should have done it to jazz music and possibly to that rarity, comic jazz as performed by Spike Jones. As it happened, we did it without music and it did bring an open-ended, rambunctious spirit into the studio. Words being such powerhouses, capable of directing energies in a specific direction, it would be fascinating to see what comes out if one introduced the exercise as **Outrageous Strut** (10.6)!

Outrageous Strut 10.6

One whole session went to Cliché Rondo (5.13), using jazz tapes, of course. It barely touched on the possibilities and skirted a major difficulty. It is a perfect structure for jazz improvisation in every way, but poses a critical challenge. It has a classic variation structure, but only if the variations fall into specific and controlled time lengths. Recall the rondo structure: *AAB AC AD AE*, and so on. In the original version of Cliche Rondo done to lively preclassic music, no time limit was set on the variations. The *A* theme had a fixed number of counts but the *B C D* could go for any length of time. To make a **Cliché Rondo for Jazz** (10.7), the variations would best have precise time lengths in relation to the rhythmic and melodic structure of the music. This is not easy and demands considerable practice so that ultimately the time of the theme statement and the time of the variations are *felt* quantities. The tap masters have this skill. For us in classic jazz dance, it is a form waiting to be mastered. Recognizing one's cliché as something to be toyed with, examined and understood on many levels—intellectual as well as

Cliché Rondo for Jazz 10.7

emotional—opens up a treasure house of personal moves. Contained within and respecting the framework of a musical structure could be a glorious dance experience for the doers and for the viewers.

We never pursued the possibilities in Fragment Rondo (7.10). Here one could kick off from a specific gesture that seems to leap out of the music. John Lee Hooker sings a rather terrifying song, "Mad Man's Blues." An obvious gesture would be a metaphor for a specific threat. Duke Ellington's "Creole Love Call" could provoke a ripple from the waist up through the neck and arms, and so on. **Jazz Fragments** (10.8) is waiting to be tried.

Jazz Fragments 10.8

One that I never did in either mode, jazz or modern dance, comes off something that Tamiris set up in her choreography classes, Stillness (1.1). I think this done to jazz music having a powerful forward propulsion would kick off some strong jazz dance. Can't wait to try it.

Jazz Rhythm Circle 10.9

Jazz Rhythm Circle (10.9), derived from Rhythm Circle (3.5), is a natural for jazz improvisation after the dancers have developed a sense of what a jazz rhythm is. This could best be gained by some coaching sessions that focus specifically on music, with the help of an articulate musician who is wet with jazz. From such a person two things can be gleaned. First is the analysis of riffs, bottom rhythms, and breaks which can then be translated into physical movement with the hands, the feet and the entire body. Second is the clarification of the classic twelve-bar blues and sixteen-bar ballad structures. Once the foundation of a minimal skill with jazz rhythms is acquired, it would be time to attempt a Jazz Rhythm Circle. Recording each foray would give the dancers the chance to hear and analyze themselves with a bit of objectivity. "Was that *really* a jazz rhythm?" "What do I do to syncopate my phrase?" In the hands of dancers with authoritiatve, daring and inventive rhythms, this has all of the makings of a solid performance piece in which the music is produced solely by the dancers. See Rhythm Circle Performed (9.10). Here too, as in all Rhythm Circle exercises, it is helpful to leave the door open for those who have a significant difficulty picking up a rhythm for any reason. It should be made clear that there is the option to say, "I pass."

Inherent in authentic jazz style is the ability to isolate moves—to keep a still center when the rest of the body is going—and to have at any one time a wide range of body tensions co-existing. The hands can float lightly while a foot stomps, or a hip can slide way off center while the arms are carved strongly overhead like a Spanish dancer rippling castanets.

Jazz Isolations 10.10

Jazz Isolations. When you hear the music, freeze. When you hear a body part called out move it only, following the ground beat of the music. When you hear "Freeze!" do so, and wait to hear the next body part called out.

During the Stanford workshop, I gave a few versions of Quiet Dance (7.4), with two dancers and then with three dancers, with music and without music. Not one hit that wondrous moment when "it's really happening." This structure grew directly out of my attempt to transpose to dance what the jazz musicians did when improvising: a supportive group supplies a base for a soloist to "take off." In the history of the Workgroup, there were only three who could perform magic with Quiet Dance: Lee Connor, Lisa Nelson and Jack Deneault. Over the years, I have given this as a structure many times and very rarely does anything "happen" except in the "universal ad lib." Theoretically, it should work. The questions are: Does it need much experience and practice? Does it need dancers who have a heightened sensitivity with the game of playing with dance shapes? Does it need a sense of physical humor? Lisa Nelson brought that into the work and the two men seized upon it. It should be a natural for a happy trio imbued with jazz moves and rhythms working in silence. Maybe someday—we'll call it **Quiet Jazz.** (10.11).

Quiet Jazz 10.11

Speak in Lindy and **Speak in Blues.** For these exercises, I used two pieces of music, Benny Goodman's "King Porter Stomp" and John Lee Hooker's "Bluebird," one for its jump sound and the other for its blue sound. The exercises followed the same sequence, in three stages.

Speak in Lindy 10.12

Speak in Blues 10.13

Stage one: You have learned a mess of Lindy (or blues) steps. When you hear the music, dance away, but only use the Lindy (blues) material. You can bend the steps—slowing them down, speeding them up, spinning them, carrying them into the air or into the ground, going hard or soft. (After playing the music a couple of times):

Stage two: Sit and listen and listen until you know who or what is alive in the music and what X is doing. When you know—the specific—rise. When all rise, the music will be cued up to the beginning. When you hear it, become X, doing what X does in Lindy (blues), *because that is the only movement language X knows.* (After running the music a couple of times):

Stage three: When you hear the music again, become X doing what X does in Lindy (blues) and go traveling; go visiting and see who the others are and what they are doing. You will be seeking the one who gives you a buzz—negatively or positively. When you find her.him, do what you need to do for, with or to that person—in Lindy (blues). When you succeed or realize you failed, dance that statement and leave the floor doing the Lindy (or the blues).

The same sequence can be pursued to a cakewalk, Charleston, and so on.

Make a Jazz Phrase relates to the original, Make a Phrase (see HFH.3 in Appendix C), but has enough of a change to be described separately.

Make a Jazz Phrase 10.14

Gather in groups of three. Jazz music is filling the space. Individually, make your own phrase of eight counts to what you are hearing. In dance, you are asking the other two, "Can you do this jazz?" When the three of you have made the eight-count "Can you do this jazz?" phrase, show it to the others, decide their order, and then learn what the other two have made. When all know and can do the entire three phrases without a stop at least three times in sequence, come and show it to me. At this viewing, stylistic or slovenly phrasing may be critiqued.

After my critique, you are ready to do Make a Phrase. It develops in this fashion: Do the three phrases together once and in a line. Do it again and begin to face each other, like points of a triangle. When you start the third time around you are in open-ended time, meaning you can do what you will to each movement: repeating, stopping, slowing, speeding, turning, on the floor, in the air or exactly as it was in the original. There are only two restrictions: you must maintain the *exact* order of the three phrases, and *everything* you do is for, with or to one or both of your trio. The end of the music will be the end of your dance.

Make a Jazz Phrase needs an extended piece of music—nine or ten minutes or more—with a solid, driving beat and a fairly clear music structure. For this workshop, I used the early version of Miles Davis's "So What?"

In the Stanford workshop we did Make a Phrase twice. The first time, I set it in the usual form (see 16.5) where each person on a swift impulse creates a phrase. As soon as the others learn it, the next person adds a short phrase and then the third person adds a phrase. In two such circuits, six short phrases were accumulated, learned and performed.

The work was soft and uncertain, first because the form was new and second because I did not stay with the requirement of a specific number of counts for all the phrases. The second time Make a Jazz Phrase was done, the challenge "Can you do this jazz?" charged it, and each person worked separately to create a precise phrase of equal length before showing and teaching it to the others. That version was done on the last day and turned out to be a triumph. Fascinating and tricky rhythms vied with complex moves, and the interactions were responsive. In addition, it brought up the question that hovered over the whole workshop, "What is this Jazz?" In the critique that followed each trio's showing, this question was raised for discussion by all.

Definitions are always treacherous and yet we risked it. These are the words that emerged. Together they form a loose profile: jazz dance plays with a beat; it is shot through with breaks, riffs and syncopations; always some part of the body is still; some part of the body is always moving; it rarely stops cold, completely; it is sexy but the sex is mostly insinuated, not slammed; there is an undercurrent of humor; the spine may be lifted slightly but it is rarely tight or completely straight (meaning that a jazz dancer has a slippery hip); it's almost always on the feet and rarely on the floor or in the air. This comes close to what I said earlier: "classic jazz is delight in the intricacies of rhythm, humor, show-off, sheer joy in living—and, yes, with a sexy innuendo." When the moves are looked at through this viewfinder, it should not be too difficult to separate Jazz Dance from Show Dance. The latter is usually marked by hard, controlled bodies and hard, insistent, unsyncopated rhythms. Sometimes it is very good and sometimes it is very vulgar. Good jazz might be naughty but never vulgar.

The day before the end of the workshop I took a risk. Without any introduction other than "Who or What Is Alive in the Music?" (10.5), I played a cassette of "Coming Together" by Fred Rzewski. To my ears, it is one of the most powerful works of our time, though it is not definitively jazz. It is driven by a torrent of rhythms and the voice of a very good actor intoning a letter, over and over again. The letter was written by a prisoner in Attica one year before that New York State prison experienced one of the worst and most controversial prison riots in U.S. history. He died mysteriously in that riot. The letter describes his positive view of how he is keeping himself together and getting stronger in spite of the place he is in. None of the dancers had ever heard the music. What they finally did was not "jazz," but almost everyone hovered closely around the content of the letter. I once had a director, for whom I was doing some choreography, ask me why I had done a certain piece of staging. "I don't know," I replied. He said, "Good." I don't know why I gave the dancers this trip, but it was good. The work the dancers did was more than good, it was powerful—and nobody questioned the reason. One of the Stanford faculty has since gone on to create a solo out of that experience using the same score.

In a way, I do know. I think too many artists and too many in the audience are in collusion to turn their faces away from the dark. They prefer to pretend that the bright, the lively, the upbeat, the fun times, the successfully romantic and trivially tragic are the fit subjects for art. It puzzles me that jazz, an art shared by blacks and whites but certainly birthed by the black community, is almost never serious, never tragic. This art, created by a people whose very presence in America is evidence of the rawest crime conceivable, is almost always happy. True, the spirituals and gospel music possess grandeur and dignity, all the while referring subtly to oppression. But jazz amuses, delights and intrigues whitey because most of its practitioners want to amuse and delight. I wonder what whitey would think of jazz if it were tragic, sharp-edged and full of fury?

Why is this relevant to improvisation? I believe in context. I believe that technique is philosophy and that implicit in the games, structures and exercises presented here is a moral stance. If craft, inventiveness, virtuosity, success and being amusing, delightful and intriguing are what it's all about, what happens to *the other*? If interaction and paying attention to the other are central, we are on our way to decency—and jazz has riches that have yet to be minded.

PART II Practice

11 Teaching, Directing, and Performing Improvisation

Scattered throughout the preceding chapters are various ground rules for dancers, teachers and directors who are working with improvisation either in the studio or for public performance. The following paragraphs summarize and expand those ground rules. At the end is a suggested sequence of EGAS for learning and teaching the improvisations of the Workgroup. This progression allows the inner logic of the way of the Workgroup to appear clearer to the students and dancers working their way through the improvisations.

The director/teacher has enormous power, particularly in channeling the minds of the dancers/students toward expected results. I myself am always very careful in choosing the words and phrases that introduce a new EGAS. For example, in guiding dancers through the "entire" body in Circles (4.1), I have never said "with the genitals," not because I am particularly modest, but because the one position I choose not to take is to be manipulative. I deeply hope no one who directs these exercises uses them to push people around, easy as it is. I feel my role is to open up *areas* of imagination, and not *subjects* of imagination. I will say "someone/something loves," not "someone is lusting." I leave love to become love of country or love of ass or of daffodils or whatever. I don't want to know anyone's image, only their dance. I feel my teaching is strongest when the subject of imagination is determined by the individuals who work with me. An arm, a chest, a foot, has a generic abstraction when it is mentioned. The emotional or metaphoric connotation of each is a highly individual matter, but in our present culture there is absolutely no way of saying, "Someone is loving someone or something with her.his genitals" without forcing the participants to eroticize whatever they are doing. That should be the prerogative of each individual and not something which I or any teacher should force into the consciousness of an entire group.

Too many people who teach improvisation set up the exercises in such a way that the results will be close to what they want to see happen. This to my mind is destructive of art, destructive to the creative impulse, and anti-thetical to the role of the teacher. Along with bringing the tradition of one's craft to the students, one must proffer the tools of creativeness which make it possible to deal with a changing world. My premise is that the role of the teacher is to disappear. We teach because we are going to die and others are going to take our place. The aim is not to re-create oneself. The aim is to encourage the fluidity and fertility of those who will live in a world differing from ours when we are gone.

By its nature, improvisation is open-ended. Anything can happen within a carefully constructed framework of rules. Who will predict with certainty the outcome of a tennis match or a game of golf? No one. Who can play a good tennis match or great round of golf? Only those who know and follow the rules. Not to know or follow the rules of tennis or golf or a particular impro-visation is not to play tennis or golf or dance an improvisation. Let one dancer ignore one rule and everyone involved will be confused, uncertain or feel betrayed. In sports, it's called cheating. In dance, we have yet to find a name for it.

On rare occasions, I have heard dancers grumble about how very complicated some of the EGAS are. I suspect that many think this, although few articulate it. Do I have a defense? Not really. I can only try to explain that the Workgroup and I were engaged in snatching up chunks of life and living and transforming them in ways that could be danced. Life as it is lived is compli-cated and often a mess. So be it.

One could claim that impersonal, formal and abstract improvisations are considerably simpler precisely because they seek to simplify what is not sim-ple. I don't know—and that's a different book.

Conclusion: If you choose to use and experiment with the material pre-sented in this book, know the rules and follow them. Better still, change them for your own needs or create entirely new ones; but once launched on an improvisation, use the rules to find freedom of expression—don't trash them.

Once an improvisation is underway, on only rare occasions do I speak up. If I have to interject a comment, I precede it with, "Continue what you are doing," and then make my remarks. The one exception is Gifts (9.1), where I will pace the warmup by noting, for example, that the group as a whole is bogged down with arm waving and needs some big leg motions to keep it moving.

I think most teachers have a word, a phrase, a slogan that lies at the heart of what it is they teach. More times than not, Anna Sokolow, upon viewing the creative work of her students, will say, "More!"—and that serves to make her students plumb deeper. Helen Tamiris's key demand was, "Follow through!" Actually, the two were saying the same thing. Too often, the student offers work that is honest and goes in a brave direction, but it is tentative, it is only skin deep. Like an arrow, it points toward honesty and bravery but never arrives.

Once, in a Hawaii workshop, I took off on this "follow through" matter: "You go up to a certain point and then stop and I don't know whether it's politeness, whether it's the assumption that you are going to fail anyway, that you're never going to get what you really want—but I promise you that if you do follow through on what you're going for, in order to get there you'll reach not only a truth but virtuosity. You'll reach intellectual and emotional places you've never touched before, and you'll find yourself performing physical feats you never imagined you could do. You're much richer and more powerful than you realize."

The most common failing in improvisation is having a tumultuous, vibrant inner life and not acting on it—not dancing it—not finding the movement metaphors to express what is going on inside. Many students assume that the internal experience is sufficient: "if I *feel it*, that's enough." I became acutely aware of this one semester when I taught at Arizona State University. I had students keep a journal, describing each day's work, adding personal experiences and impressions. I asked for them at the end of the term. Journal after journal contained the same shock: what they wrote, what they experienced in their minds, was full of poetry, immeasurably wilder and more exciting then anything they did in class with their bodies! They did not have the skill or the temerity to "follow through." They thought—and then did less than they thought. After that experience, I had journal sheets handed in every week, so that I could monitor what was happening and make adjustments accordingly.

Where is the problem? Even if we don't look at the mirror, we carry it with us. Its obvious name is *self-consciousness.* We continually practice self-censorship, afraid of looking freaky or aggressive or of revealing too much or *departing from the norm.* Everything I and any other teacher of the arts is begging for requires a departure from the stultifying norms that reduce art to entertainment and kitsch.

As I said earlier, never fear the block but rather welcome it, for it may be hiding what is truly significant. When you slam into a block, confront it, tease it, play with it, run around or under it, waltz with it—but never back off, and never stop because of it.

Correction. Sometimes you will find yourself stopping for any number of reasons: confusion, uncertainty, fear or just plain physical exhaustion. There's nothing wrong with that, *as long as you deal directly with stopping.* When stopping becomes a part of the dance, it has its own excitement and meaning. I knew a talented composer who to my mind had a flaw: he couldn't stop. I suspect his prolixity was a way to avoid confronting the matter at

Practice
....

hand. He wanted to *look* as if he were dealing with it when actually he was busy running around it. In dance improvisation this is the evasion of more than one dancer. Some dancers never stop moving when moving is not the issue but rather a means of avoiding some central problem.

Just as in tennis there are the grunters and the serenely quiet ones, among dancers there are the silent ones and the noisy ones. The gates are wide for noise in some EGAS, such as Medicine Ball (9.2), Outrageous Travel (9.3), and Master-Disciple (5.9), but in others, vocalization, violent breathing and foot stamping can rattle the concentration of other dancers. This is particularly true in the rhythm series (5.3, 5.4, 5.5). As soon as the director/leader is aware that someone is beating out an intrusive river of sound, a simple command can protect both the silent and the clangorous: "Continue what you are doing. If what you are doing is highly audible, transpose your sound into motion. Though apparently silent, lose none of its force or its quality but let it infuse your dance."

After outlining the structure of an EGAS, it is not unusual to have a participant say, in a worried way, "But if we all imitate the person we have been observing, won't we all end up doing the same motion?" Actually, that is only one possibility out of many. Anticipating or, worst of all, planning, leads to forcing the work into an expected direction without responding to what is actually happening. On hearing the setup of a new EGAS, it is well not to look ahead, not to anticipate, not to formulate a plan of action. When you are given a direction or a new EGAS by a director/teacher, do it without analyzing or questioning it or evaluating it. You can and should do that later, but not before or during. At first hearing, enter into everything without analyzing, questioning, evaluating or anticipating.

As soon as serious dancers become aware of the new "ethics" of improvisation as developed by the Workgroup, it is an easy matter for them to slip into a state of unremitting anxiety about being pure and honest. They find an excitement in the challenge of trying *not* to be beautiful, to be successful, to be liked by the audience, but rather hewing rigorously to the task at hand. The anxiety arises from detecting the slightest infringement of these new noble commandments and whipping themselves, mentally, during an improvisation.

The discomfiting and brutal fact, which almost every performer lives with and too few teachers acknowledge, is that no performance is completely free of one or more of these sins. Some performances are worse than others. The honest but professional performer is not destroyed by such lapses. They are no different than a dancer keeping his.her balance. "Keeping your balance" means the constant loss of balance followed by a quick correction to return to center.

A performance with integrity consists of bouncing off every distraction and every "lie" back to the object. An awareness of the lie gives a hint as to where the truth may be found. A parabolic reflector, as in an ellipsoid stage light, sends all the light rays to a fixed point. The distraction, if it is recognized as a distraction, reflects back to the task. While you are submerged in the act of improvising, you will inevitably become aware, at one time or another, of slipping off the track, of a dose of phoniness, of falseness, of (horrors!) breaking a ground rule. *Don't waste a second berating yourself or bathing in guilt at your lack of integrity.* Just kick off and return to focus on your task. When the EGAS is over, your self-criticisms, if you have any, will well up and will be the result of what happened. That is the time to analyze what transpired, never *during* the improvisation. Take guilt along on an improvisation and the concentration will shift in exactly the wrong direction—to the self, the failed self. Mentally scolding oneself is a way of gaining purity through recognition of guilt, but it leads to lousy improvisation and dull dancing.

A young violin prodigy was asked in a TV interview whether she ever made mistakes. Answer: "Of course, everybody messes up sometimes." To those of integrity who demand absolute purity, and uninterrupted stretches of honest expression, my advice is, "Forget it." Invariably, there will be the bad moments, the "mess-ups," the vain moments, the self-hating moments, and the innumerable distractions drawing one away from the object of the internal task. *Actually, they are part of the subject.* They are part of every performance, even the best, but only if the artist catches the falseness and uses it unhesitatingly to leap back to the task at hand without wasting one ounce of energy at self-flagellation.

The best rules deserve a contradiction. When improvising, don't do anything to which you sense great resistance. If at any time, before or during, some part of you utters an adamant "No!"—quit. It would be too bad if that occurred before you even got into the work, but if the negation is too strong, don't resist it. In your own time, you should track down the reason for the block.

For example, doing the Hub Meditation (5.7) the center of your mind may be occupied immovably by someone of a sexual nature different than yours. For some, to "become "this person may be an unacceptable horror. Try not to flee from any surprising, shocking or unwelcome image. It may contain a subtle metaphor unrelated to hetero- or homosexual predilections. Most of us have more than one kind of identification, some of which are of the opposite sex but without any aura of sexuality. There are teachers, public figures, parents, etc., with whom our strongest feelings and hopes are strongly hooked even though they happen to be of the sex with which we do not identify.

The work we are engaged in will, at times, touch upon deep and sensitive areas of one's being. In fact, it is hoped that will happen, because if the material is not important to the artist, why bother? And yet, a participant in a class, workshop or company may encounter something within that is too painful or confusing to deal with. Everyone should have the right to chose when and under what circumstances they are ready to confront the difficult place. Forcing people to "face reality" is intrusive and a good way to drive them away from the work. Worse, it may encourage them to dissemble and pretend they are facing the disturbing matter.

In directing improvisation, all objections and expressed uneasiness should always be dealt with respectfully and specifically. Some suffer a fear of uncertainty which can easily be transmuted to hostility to the work or the director. Improvisation is a risk and by that token, about uncertainty, and it is possible that some will never enter its game willingly. Compelling participation from the unwilling is absurd. No one should have to take any risks they do not choose.

In a talk with Charles Hayward reviewing material for this book, he pointed out that we had no mirrors in the Workgroup studio during our first year and that this had disconcerted many of the dancers who came to work with us. One of the most important strictures that I lay down with any group is, Never use the mirror. (The only exception is when a dancer becomes a narcissistic X whose vanity requires constant checking in the mirror.)

The mirror is the vortex that sucks every dancer into banality, prettiness, audience seduction and playing it safe. If you focus on what X is doing, you're in business. If you keep glancing in the direction of the mirror to know what you look like, it is near impossible not to try to look better. I defy anyone to glance at the mirror without a swift and unthinking adjustment of the face or body. Using the mirror, you might do something quite beautiful, and if you are very careful, look nice, and work to have everybody love you. Guaranteed you will please many people and do this work abominably. Whatever personal originality springs from your involvement in the work at hand should not be known by you, nor improved by you. Underlying this constantly glancing at the mirror is a lack of faith and a lack of belief in oneself.

This concern for self-image is seriously aggravated by photo sessions, videotaping, or filming. How often have you looked at a photograph of yourself and said, "That does not look one bit like me!" The bitter problem is that we can't change what we see in the photograph the way we can shift our expression or body appearance to something more pleasing the moment we catch sight of our image in the mirror.

I recall meeting Tamiris in Grand Central Station after a long day at the NBC studios where I had been doing a TV show with a folk singer. One look at my expression and she asked with concern, "Daniel, what happened?" "I saw myself dance for the first time in my life. I saw the first kinescope of the show."[1] In the back of my mind was a grim voice saying, "Quit man. You're awful. Who would want to look at that?"

In a similar episode, twenty-odd dancers from the Workgroup Workshop, who had been dancing together weekly over a period of a couple of months, dwindled to four after seeing themselves videotaped *improvising* (see chap. 4).

I made one wise decision. We worked for half a year before anyone saw us. The first performances of the Workgroup took place in the studio for an invited audience *with no critics invited.* I let a year go by before exposing the company to critical review.

At the conclusion of a most successful first summer at Johnson State College in Vermont, three of the company members wanted to quit, claiming that the uncertainty of performing improvisation was too much for them. In a talk with Joe Chaikin, the brilliant director of the Open Theatre, he expressed surprise, a bit of awe and a large measure of doubt when I told him that we were performing improvisation. To paraphrase his thoughts through my memory:

> Performing improvisation is very hard. If you do a bad performance of set material, you can reassure yourself that the next performance will be better—that you will be able to recapture your belief in yourself. With improvisation, there is nothing to repeat and do better. If you blow it—tough—there's no going back.

Similarly, a photo, a videotape or a film once done, do not change. The lesson? Postpone photo sessions and videotaping of improvisation until the dancers have enough experience and self-confidence to know that what they are doing has value, a different value than just "looking good." Preparation, rehearsals, classes and workshops must take place in private. In my experience, nothing will either inhibit the dancers or, on the contrary, provoke exhibitionism faster than being watched by anyone not participating. *No guest observers of studio work.*

Performance of improvisation for a dance audience is possible, desirable and potentially as rewarding as any dance experience, and like other dance forms it must be preceded by a long period of practice. There is no denying that performing improvisation is difficult. It is an art form that is young in our culture. It requires a specific talent, an enormous amount of integrity, many hours of work in the studio before public exposure, a company that is bound together by trust in each other, and a director who can maintain the delicate balance between ruthlessly weeding out the false and meretricious and giving the dancers the freedom and the courage to take risks. If jazz musicians can do it, we dancers can do it. They've been at it for almost a century. Give us a little time.

---

1. In the early days of TV, before videotape, shows were recorded by filming the image on a TV screen. It was called a kinescope and it was technically awful. My comment was an exaggeration, of course; I had seen myself dance many times—in the mirror—that silver heaven where you can fix up what you see.

Just as debilitating as looking in the mirror is pausing in one's work to see what the other dancers are doing. To drop concentration on one's own task to observe the others, even for a moment, is to risk losing not only energy but, worst of all, belief in the reality of one's imagination. Make no mistake. What we imagine is as real as the sweaty clothes clinging to our heated bodies, but it is a fragile bit of reality and cumbles easily. Looking away is like awakening from a dream-filled sleep to find that your dream is thin smoke vanishing in the daylight. Look away at the others in the improvisation and be certain that returning, if you can, will be difficult and forced.

Improvisation is nothing if not a gamble. Once upon a time, a man came to a Workgroup Workshop who was wild, took great risks, got away with them, moved well in an awkward, personal way. After a few sessions, I asked him to work out with the company. In a month or so, we invited him to join. The irony was that the longer he danced with us, the less I believed him. What had seemed so genuine, startling and personal began to look unconvincing. It took me too long to recognize the destructive process to which he was committed. When he found something good, something that worked—and he had the theatrical savvy to spot that, he never let it go, performance after performance. Instead of doing, he was fishing for what would be effective. He was against gambling and thus against improvisation.

Anyone involved with improvisation must be willing to risk failure. Priming the mind-heart, practicing, being in great shape, setting up ideal conditions—all help make success more probable, but none of them guarantees success. Any attempt to force a result defeats the living reality that makes improvisation what it is. Injecting formulas for success means not responding to the moment but dredging up something irrelevant out of the past.

The comparison with athletics indicates a parallel. If in one tennis match rushing up to the net proved to be a successful ploy, a master baseliner could nullify that tactic in the next. A great player doesn't get caught in a style or try to be interesting.

Nothing is more destructive to the heart of improvisation, which is spontaneity, than for a performer to find a "goodie" and then stuff it into every subsequent performance. The rule is, never *try* to repeat. If a familiar lovely phrase or an exciting set of known moves bubbles up out of the flow, fine, but never drag them into the dance like a child insisting on taking along the little red boat every time he.she takes a bath.

Risk is the concomitant of improvisation and of every game and sport. There is no guarantee that a match between the best of the best will be thrilling, be it in tennis, football or chess. Similarly, improvised dance can reach a level of intoxicating excitement—or not. It is critical that games of all kinds be played with a purity and honesty, meaning that excitement and theatricality should happen and not be deliberately created. Play the game and dance the dance.

In the Workgroup, what interested us most was what happened between people. We wanted to know who was doing what to whom and why. We didn't probe *how* they were doing it but what was going on with these people. We didn't speculate on the space in which our movement took place, the time it took or the force behind a movement. Those to us were matters ideal for filling out a rainy Sunday afternoon when we might have nothing to do, but that never happened with us.

A note about open workshops. Any workshop where the director does not know the participants very well holds potential danger. Good improvisation is a difficult art, but some believe the opposite. Among those who think it should be easy to do, some have limited sensitivity to the needs and feelings of others and some have a streak of the nasty. Under the cover of spontaneity, I have witnessed a vicious push to a running dancer which brought me to my feet to catch the victim before he slammed forward on his face. Another time, from too far away, I saw a woman who had leaned her waist back on a man's supporting arm only to be lifted quickly, dropped and caught just as quickly. The sharp catch over-bent her back. I was beside them soon enough to stop his obvious intention of repeating the gesture. I came down hard on the man, and he had enough sensitivity never to return. The woman fortunately recovered from a painful muscle strain by the next week. For any one directing improvisation, whether it is with a professional group, a workshop or a class, the rule is *en garde*. The director's responsibility is never to take eyes away from the dancers and certainly never to leave the work space while improvisation is in progress—and look out for the crazies.

The closest I come to superstition is to avoid self-congratulation, fearing that it will set off a chain of disasters. Risking that irrational fear, I will take note that I've been directing these improvisation sessions since 1969, with only three minor accidents. I would guess that a well-conducted improvisation session is physically safer than dance classes, rehearsals or performances of choreographed material. I have no certain explanation other than that the freedom offered by improvisation allows people to work around their limitations, be it their level of skill, fatigue or previous injury, while set material makes its demands regardless of limitations.

It is not surprising that dancers entering this world of "becoming someone," react with confusion when the "someone" that emerges out of the Hub Meditation (5.7) is themselves. Some think it must be a wrong turn. Almost all are uncertain how to "become themselves." It should be a snap, for you are you, but that is an oversimplification. If a specific image is at the heart of how we are working, then a concomitant is a specific action. If you find yourself at the hub of your "someone," you must also know what you are doing, what you are trying to make happen. In Each Alone (6.5b), prepare yourself to do what must be done. If it is to teach someone a dance phrase, then choreograph the phrase. If it is to avoid another's attention, then make yourself invisible. (This is possible. I've seen more than one dance student do this.) If it is to seduce another, then do what you need to make yourself irresistibly attractive in their eyes, and so on. Above all, do not try to look like yourself.

When an EGAS calls for partners, the director faces a delicate decision: whether to select partners personally of ask the dancers to choose their own. Certainly, with a group new to the director or with large groups, leaving choice to the dancers makes sense. With the Workgroup, I tended to do the pairing and, looking back, I think my choices were good in that they generated strong work. Some pairings actually challenge the dancers in a productive way. If the choice is left to the dancers, they may play it safe, stick with "friends," or unwittingly upset some dancers by avoiding them. If the responsibility rests with the director, none of this happens. Both ways have value. The people, the moment and the director's style should decide. (In appendix B I say the opposite.)

A note about the designation "director." When I led the Workgroup, I never took credit as a choreographer for the manifest reason that I was directing, leading, casting, pacing, conceiving forms, arranging and structuring the EGAS, but not choreographing. We all, at one time or another, choreographed short thematic pieces which became the seeds for improvisations, but nothing else was set. Not a few viewers, however, thought they were looking at rehearsed and fixed dances.

The amount of time required for a Hub Meditation (5.7) varies radically from individual to individual. Often, almost the entire group will be standing with their eyes closed, ready to move ahead, waiting for a little bit of forever while the last one or two dancers search for their image. In a learning situation, I tend to let it go on for as long as it takes. I respect dancers who are not glib and do not respond to pressure to get on with it. I encourage those who are standing and waiting, their eyes still closed, to go even more deeply into the specific details of their image, to understand that it is three-dimensional, to go around and look at it from behind, from the side, from the top and the bottom, to know as much as they can because the more they know about their specific image, the more profound will be their work.

Ending an improvisation is a complexity. In rehearsals, workshops and classes, I let the dancers finish in their own time. Many times I have had to point out to dancers that they stopped working even though they had further to go; they left the floor the moment they realized all the others were leaning up against the walls, finished and watching! Not wanting to be conspicuous is as beside the point as trying to attract attention. Any reaching for theatrical timing in the context of studio work contradicts the very premise of the Workgroup's approach. I let it be known very early that there is no such thing as a dancer taking "too much time."

Performing improvisation for a public is another matter. In this situation, I am opposed to any attempts to speed up, for any reason, the beginnings and the middles of a performed EGAS. The rule we did find after some very "honest" and insanely prolonged endings was: If you know you have arrived at the last phase of an improvisation, that there will be no significant new development, and you know that its impact has been felt by the audience, tie the knot and get off the floor. It is possibly the only time we consciously allowed audience awareness to affect what we did.

Very early we developed an uncanny sensitivity whenever an EGAS demanded that all the participants finish together. We could swirl away for any length of time and just as abruptly know, all at once, "Here it is, the end," and all would come to a pause and exit.

In studio work, I tend to make all endings into beginnings—of productive thinking. Some of the challenges that get thrown out at different times: What happened? Was there anything of which you should take special note? Was there something you should return to in your own time? Was something in there the seed for choreography? What did you want to do that you did not do?

If the work involves two or more dancers, I will ask them to talk over what happened. What was good and stimulating that the others(s) did? Where did you feel that one or more slipped into a self-focus and lost sight of the others or strayed from the rules? In discussions such as these, I ask the dancers to perform a blancing act, that is, not to be so "nice" that what they say is evasive or so carelessly "honest" that they are pointlessly cruel. This injunction appears to be simple on paper but is, in truth, a complicated problem for teachers as well as for students who are mutually evaluating each other's work.

A ritual at the end of every EGAS of any depth or complexity or newness consisted of my calling the dancers to a central place on the floor and asking, "Well, what happened? Any notes from the underground? Complaints? Confusions? Ideas? Criticisms? Something unusual happen? Speak, but avoid going into your personal specific images. We're talking about structure and how to deal with and use the material that bubbles up in these improvisations."

I wait for the dancers to speak first, and then I offer my questions, make my comments and criticisms. Throughout my direction of the Workgroup and the workshops of 1969–1974, I was very careful not to overdirect the dancers. Almost all our decisions were arrived at by consensus. Lacking that, I made the final decisions. I relied very heavily on the discussions we had after each improvisation to guide future work. Some spoke a lot, some not at all, despite my pleas for all to participate. I tended to hold back criticisms of the improvisations much of the time. Perhaps too much, but I hoped their own evaluation of themselves and each other would develop the keenness of their observations and their taste.

Also, I had a serious weakness as a director. I dealt very badly with negative attitudes from any company member. The best directors are not rocked by hostility; they know it can arise at any time, and they know how to handle it by rerouting the negative energy or simply dumping the difficult one. I, however, would be thrown and sometimes weakened by doubt. Years later, in the preparation of this book, when I asked dancers who had been with the company to comment on their experience, one complained that she never got enough feedback from me to know how she was doing.
Since the Workgroup, in my teaching and in the workshops on tour and in residencies, I am much freer in expressing my observations, always making it known that what I offer is subjective, to be heard, accepted or rejected.

Dancers learn by observing each other at work. After everyone is given the structure of a particular exercise, much can be gained by dividing the group into doers and observers, pausing when the doers are finished to let the observers make comments before becoming doers who in turn are critiqued. Watching others, and hearing their comments about one's own work, develops insight, taste and a greater awareness of what the work is trying to achieve. Many a dancer who was sidelined because of illness or injury has, after watching a session, come to me wide-eyed, "Oh, I learned so much, just watching."

Keeping a journal is a must for anyone in the arts. If one ventures deeply into improvisation, the experiences are so complex and fleeting that to rely only on memory would be at best to retain blurred impressions of limited value. This book would be an anemic outline without my notebooks covering daily work since 1969 and the transcription of fifty-three cassettes recording years of classes and workshops.[2]

Novelty is a perennial delight. There are more than one hundred EGAS in this book. A group meeting twice a week could do all of them in half a year—without repeating one. That would be too bad. Most of the EGAS can be repeated profitably. Time and again, students who have worked with me in several workshops or classes will say how much more meaningful a particular EGAS was the second, third or fourth time. The structure may be the same, but if it is a true improvisation, what goes into it and what comes out of it will be different and "novel" each time. Miles Davis played "So What?" many times and always with a difference.

2. See *How to Dance Forever*, pp. 112–13.

At the opposite pole of doing what has been done is the necessary readiness to come up with what has never been tried. Invention purely for the sake of originality reduces creativeness to vulgarity. A director alive to the shifts and currents of each moment will, without any great effort, come up with new EGAS.

In chapter 7, I described the second Workgroup meeting together for the first time after a late summer break. I felt we couldn't just plunge back into what we had been doing. We needed a place to start from, for we had certainly all changed to some degree. If that was the case, who were we? And so I heard myself ask Ara and then the others to "tell us what happened to you this summer. No words." It was a bit of a kid game. We never did it again, but it served to bring us together and get us going.

This brings to the front one of the most delicate and exciting aspects of teaching and leading these improvisation exercises: how the leader/teacher sets the timing and rhythmic flow of each session. Knowing how to sequence the EGAS, knowing how long to stay on each problem, knowing when to go into a detailed, follow-up discussion, and knowing when it is best not to say anything—these intuitions are the glory of the good director/teacher and cannot be taught. One learns to choose, do and pace these exercises by paying attention, and paying attention, and paying more attention to what is happening with the students, the dancers, the actors, the musicians—with whomever you are working and also the very air, light and space of the studio.

Improvisation, yes, but where does sheer dance technique fit into the picture? We started most sessions with a technical warmup and a workout that stressed endurance and air work. Sometimes I led, sometimes company members, most of whom were good teachers. Improvisation as a component of teaching modern dance technique has been used by some of its seminal figures. Mary Wigman built her technique classes on improvisation. Every class had a specific focus which was developed, partially by her direction and partially by challenges to the students. A movement in an odd rhythm, say a 5/4, might be given, and then students would be expected to come up with their own phrase in 5/4. This would occur within the context of a continual flow on the diagonal rather than pausing to allow students to work it out in their own time. Elements of this tradition were carried forward by Hanya Holm and her heirs, Alwin Nikolais and Murray Louis. Helen Tamiris would sometimes give a technical sequence and then, just before we started, tell us to continue after what she had given us. "Continue," in this context meant to regard the last moment of the exercise as a seed that would flower out of what had gone before. In my teaching, I have at various times thrown improvisation challenges into the flow of a technique class.

- Phrase individually: A number of moves is given. The dancers do all of the movements in their own order, phrasing, number of repetitions and emphasis within a limited time frame, say sixteen counts.

- The Improvisation Sandwich: Give a short technical sequence, followed by an equal amount of time for an improvisation on the given moves. Then the students return to a short phrase of given material, followed by an equal amount of time for a technical improvisation. In 1968, at a workshop in Idyllwild, California, I gave a long jazz sequence in which I set every other eight counts, leaving all the "clear" eight counts for the students to improvise. It was a strange and fun sight to see the mass of them alternately beating it out together and then the turmoil of taking off on their own.
- Follow the Leader: This is what every dance class is, but here, each student gets a chance at leading off a diagonal in moves of their own creation with all the others following. Best done at high speed with little time for thinking.
- A Glimpse of the Outrageous: An outrageous and/or complicated move is demonstrated by the teacher full out, but just once. Dancers dance full out an impression of what was seen so briefly.
- Questions to be Answered in Movement: Why do you dance? Who or what is jumping and why? Who or what is leaping and why? Who or what is turning and why? Who or what is falling and why?
- Leading: lead with different parts of the body while walking, running, leaping. Example: leap leading with the toes or the knee or the pelvis or the chest, and so on. Turn with the leading energy coming from the arms or from shoulders or from the head. The challenges are not demonstrated but given verbally, and thus each dancer comes up with a personal variation on the idea. The permutations for each category of movement are as variable as the parts of the body and the bodies meeting the challenges. This one fully explored can open up new areas of movement and virtuosity. When a particularly brilliant or beautiful phrase is seen, get all the dancers to learn it.

Finally, the leader, the director/teacher, is most successful when the group takes the bit, when it gets so deeply involved that the director/teacher is no longer present in their consciousness. When the absorption in the task is so complete, there is no longer any thought or any awareness of the honcho and, least of all, any desire to gain approval from that direction.

The totality of this book is focused on improvisation by a group of dancers. What about a soloist? Ironic, for I myself have performed eight dances that were to a greater or lesser degree improvised: "Sweet Woman" in *Jazz Changes* and seven dances out of the twelve that made up the 1976 evening called *Ruminations*. Are there different rules and/or techniques for a soloist? There may be, but because I do them it has never occurred to me to analyze what is taking place. A quote from a few words that led into "Someone," a solo from *Ruminations*: "By the very nature of a soloist's work, she.he spends many long hours alone and yet for me, the space is never empty, in fact, sometimes it's thronged."

In chapter 4, The First Workgroup, there is an examination of the tangible and the intangible in the work we do. As I examine this problem, I realize, in retrospect, that in my work as a soloist I have dealt almost entirely with the intangible. I may appear to be alone, but in my mind there is quite often another in the space. I rarely use props. Does this indicate that a dancer working alone could use this book as a reference point in improvisation? I don't see why not. Many EGAS would be awkward, but then, what wonders are there for the imagination to concoct? Without being aware of it, I have probably been creating exercises, games and structures all along. Because I did not have to communicate them to others, I just did them, without naming them.

A Sequence for Learning and Teaching the Improvisations of the Workgroup

The following sequence allows the logic of the work to emerge. It can lead dancers over a period of time from simpler to more complex structures and, most importantly, to a deeper involvement of self in the act of dance. When limited to a single session or a short workshop, experience will help to make a judicious selection.

Gifts (9.1)

I find that Gifts is easily the best initial exercise for a group totally innocent of improvisation or for a company that has been doing it for years. First, it is rare that at the beginning of a session all the dancers are safely warmed up and ready to dance. Gifts is most amazing in that it is the fastest, most efficient warmup I've ever experienced. It does need dancey music: Renaissance dances; Bach's Well-Tempered Clavier, book I; Brazilian carnival music; Flamenco singers with guitar; Louis Armstrong. Choose your own, sensing who and where your dancers are. Second, a more subtle value is implemented because in this very first EGAS the central focus is the other, the sacred other person. Reaching into the needs of the body before them, each dancer who is leading is learning to pay attention to the other and possibly forgetting the self. It is the ideal beginning.

While we are at this juncture, it is a good time to mention an apparently minor point which is not minor. It is a good practice to request that all students participating in improvisation wear knee pads. In my classes, those without knee pads can watch but not dance. Whenever I, myself, want the freedom to plunge into any impulse, in the air or into the floor, I wear not only knee pads but also a heavy sweater to cushion the craziest actions. Not protected, I will unthinkingly avoid a whole range of excitements and virtuosities.

Practice
....

Goldfish Bowl (5.1)
Blind Journey (5.2)
The Schizoid Little Fishes of the Bering Sea (9.4)
> This is an alternative to the Goldfish Bowl—Blind Journey—Goldfish
> Bowl progression. Either sequence is a good beginning, to be followed
> without a break by, "With your eyes closed, go find a private place.
> Be certain there is room around you and remain standing." This can
> lead directly into the Rhythm Series.

Rhythm Breath Rhythm (5.3)
Series 1 Pulse Rhythm (5.4)
Internal Rhythm (5.5)
Evolving Repetition (6.4)
True Repetition (6.3)
Dedicate Your Motion (5.11)
Go Visiting (7.3)
> I rarely give Breath Rhythm and Pulse Rhythm more than once. They are
> used to set the stage and the understanding for Internal Rhythm. That, in
> turn, becomes in subsequent sessions The Repetition. In either of its
> forms, Evolving Repetition or True Repetition, The Repetition is used as a
> way to enter into the work with a cleared mind. It serves as a movement
> meditation and runs for at least ten minutes. Whenever the dancers do
> not need Gifts because they are all warm and ready to dance, I have set up
> a ritual in which, as they enter the studio, they go in their own time into
> the space, clear their heads, find their Internal Rhythm and slip directly
> into Repetition. At this juncture there is no music because it would
> intrude on the personal expression of an internal rhythm. Occasionally,
> when the dancers are deep into a Repetition, Dedicate Your Motion can
> be interjected. Go Visiting can be the tail of a Repetition. Another mind-
> sweeper is Spinning, which can be used to precede a Repetition.
>
> Members of a sect of Muslim Sufis use whirling as a way of achieving
> an ecstatic trance. For dancers, it acts like an emotional and intellectual
> centrifuge, throwing off distractions and leaving a clean center from
> which to begin the work of improvising.

Spinning **Spinning.** Spin in place, at any tempo, for as long as you can. Pause, and
11.1 then spin in the opposite direction for as long as you can. Then, in the
stillness, find your Internal rhythm. Those of you who know the secret of
spinning interminably without getting dizzy may be interrupted by my
asking you to bring it to a close.

Sound Medicine Ball (9.2)
Motion Outrageous Travel (9.3)
Work Master-Disciple (5.9)
Solo Singer (2.1)

172

Solo Dancer (2.2)

The first two in this group are good for all levels: raw beginners in creative work and in improvisation as well as professional dancers. Master-Disciple is a very good experience, but best left for an intermediate level of work. Solo Singer and Solo Dancer are fine for dancers, but particularly when there is a mix of dancers and actors, dancers and singers or all three.

Rhythm Series 2

Ambient Sound (1.5)
Conduct a Picture (1.7)
Rhythm Circle (3.5)
Rhythm Portrait (3.12)

Depending on the talents and problems of the group these are useful in the early stages of work, but after Rhythm Series 1.

The Middle Period

The Mind-Wash (3.2)
The Mirror (2.4)
A Duet (3.11)
Cliché Rondo (5.13)
Body Contact (1.2)
What Happened? (7.1)

The first three of this group can be given as one continuous sequence. The focus of this first form of A Duet is simply the other person. For it, the instruction is simply, "Within the context of the music, dance to, for and about the other person. Along the way, try to make something happen, either to you or your partner or both. When it happens, leave the floor. If you partner leaves first, dance a recognition of being left and then leave."

Second Stage of the Middle Period

Backdoor (5.6)
Hub Meditation (5.7)
Circles (4.1)
Hot to Cold to Hot (4.2)
Faces (9.13)

Each of these introduces important principles and ways of working that pave the way for more complex EGAS and performance pieces.

The Mind-Wash (3.2)
The Other (6.5a)
Hub Meditation (5.7)
Each Alone (6.5b)
Duet (6.5c)

This sequence, called The Duet (6.5), is the key to what the Workgroup did. From it flows an understanding of self, the other, a new way of dancing, a new way of performing improvisation, and other more complex structures. Good for studio work as well as for performance.

Practice

Adam and Eve (8.10)
Exercise in Empathy (7.12)
Celebration (9.11)
Fragment Rondo (7.10)
Compass (8.12)
Rhythm Circle Performed (9.10)
Signs of the Times (7.9)
Prison (7.2)[3]

> To bring these before a dance public, two things must take place. The dancers involved must first find a profound connection within the structures and make the work come alive in the studio. Each piece must be tested many times to be certain that it is fertile for this particular group—that it bears repeating and thus is viable for public performance.

A Performance Progression

Sea Anemone
From Now (7.5)
Recognition Ritual (7.6)
Wind II (6.13)
Relay Solo (7.7)
Go 1-2-3-4 (7.8)

> This is a sequence that can be performed from beginning to end without interruption, each segment building off the configuration of a circle. (Chapter 8.)

Hello Farewell Hello
The Inarticulates (HFH.1)
Processional (HFH.1a)
Museum (HFH.1b)
Wind II (HFH.1c)
Pygmalion and Galatea II (HFH.2)
The Picadors' Walk (HFH.2a)
Ariadne's Dance (HFH.2b)
Make a Phrase (HFH.3)
Hello To Now (HFH.4)

> This is the big one. It fills out a complete evening and needs the involvement of two musicians who are not only good but good at improvisation. (Appendix C.)

Many improvisations. Twice, once in a New York workshop and once in a class at the Arizona State University, I taught by following the chronology of

---

3. Performed only once with a gusty group of lithe, young acting students at the National Theatre Institute in New London, Connecticut. If any one out there is caught up in the idea, I leave it on this list as a challenge: go make your own structure.

how all of this happened, similarly to the structure of this book. It had a logic, it worked and incidentally helped lay out the bones of the book. For anyone who wants to work their way through our history, know that that course is viable and has its own excitement.

12 Playing Areas, Lights and Costumes

In all improvisation work, except for public performances, I choose subdued light. It is easier to maintain concentration, the dancers are less aware of those dancers with whom they are not involved, and it opens the door to mystery—and mystery is our business.

I fell upon our performance style lighting by accident. For the very first performance of the Workgroup in our studio at 550 Broadway, I was setting the lights, which were all 150-watt reflector floods clamped illegally to the pipes of the sprinkler system. They were perfect for our space, for the ceiling was only twelve and a half feet high. I had twelve of them hung and asked one of the company members, Mary Anne Smith, who happened to be on the floor, to move through the space so that I could judge how well and how evenly we were covered. As she moved about, I found several dark holes and was about to do something about them when Mary Anne interjected, "But it's wonderful to be able to go in and out of bright or dark areas." The moment she said it, I realized a bumpy stage was right for us.[1] The lesson learned, I never worked for an evenly lit stage, whether at 550 Broadway, in open spaces or within a proscenium. Wherever we were, I designed a balance between light that defined the body and light sufficient to reveal facial intelligence.[2] We never went with the fashion of violent washes of side light that reduce the face to a mask of fluffed up cheeks with black eyes crowding the bridge of the nose. Intense side lights do define the body, but they cancel out the individuality and personal expression of the dancer.

---

1. Months later, I came to realize she almost invariably gravitated toward the dark areas. More than once after a performance, I would launch into, "Now Mary Ann, what's the point of all those years of pliés if you're well-nigh invisible?" In spite of this predilection, she was a stunning performer with a wild and individual way of dealing with everything.

2. In the Workgroup, I was the only one knowledgeable about lights and sound, having toured from 1957 on without a tech director. I learned what I needed to know and did it. I tried to get the others in the company interested. They pretended interest, humored me and helped a bit, a very little bit.

During our first summer residency at Johnson State College in Johnson, Vermont, we did a performance on their magnificent stage, with the audience onstage, half off-stage right and half off-stage left. For this performance we did Rituals of Power (6.10), and I pushed the concept of bumpy lighting forward. I called it "passing clouds." The stage was divided in three bands of light reaching from up- to downstage. All through the twenty to thirty minutes of the piece, there was a slow but unceasing roll of strong light intensity from stage left to stage right followed by a band of subdued light. Sadly, I never saw it because I was dancing under the "passing clouds."

The tech sheet we sent out to the program sponsors read as follows:

The Workgroup

Technical Requirements

Onstage

We want a table about six feet long, a pitcher of water with no ice in it, a supply of drinking cups, a wastebasket, a roll of masking tape, a number of chairs and a low bench.

Performing Area

The best way to see the Workgroup is in the round. Our ideal space is an open one, 33–35 feet in diameter with two rings for sitting on the floor and two rings for sitting on staggered chairs, allowing for about 250 viewers. Additional seating on bleachers or 13" to 14" risers around the outside should allow easily for another 250 if a crowd that large is expected.

Even if you have little or no portable lighting equipment, performing in such a space with available light is preferable to a formal proscenium presentation with the audience in rows out front.

If your stage is large and has clear offstage space, it is possible to bring the audience onstage as in the alternate diagram. If you want to do this, be sure to send us the requested diagram of the stage with dimensions as soon as possible.

We can of course perform on a proscenium stage and have done so successfully in the past. However, the nature of our material is such that it is best experienced in the more intimate setting of in-the-round performance.

Lighting demands for such a setup are minimal: a dozen spots totaling 6000 to 7000 watts, four light poles, a portable dimmer and an electrical power source to match these needs. Most theatre departments have this equipment, or it can be rented locally at a reasonable cost. If available light in the space is bright enough and can be concentrated on an area 35 feet in diameter, theatrical lighting could be dispensed with altogether. No screens would be necessary. The Workgroup brings its own sound equipment. The only requirement aside from the lighting mentioned is an even, resilient wooden surface without splinters and providing enough traction for dancers, i.e., not slippery—not waxed.

There was never any question in our minds that our work would best be seen in the round. On the road, the sponsors and we usually agreed on using a gymnasium. The disadvantage of gym spaces is the probability of less than good sound. (The light plot we used for working in the round is at the end of this chapter.) Occasionally, there was no alternative to performing within a proscenium with the audience out front. Unquestionably, it bent our heads in the wrong direction. The premise upon which our work stood demanded that we respond to the issue at hand, *which did not include an audience.*

A major factor giving each performer his.her distinctive profile as an artist is how the presence of the audience is regarded. For people who work in the theatre, it may well be that the weightiest object in the universe is that yawning black hole out there crawling with living creatures. One of the most beautiful dancers in modern dance history was Louise Kloepper of Hanya Holm's company. Backstage, she struggled to control her stomach and had to be pushed onstage. The mythically great pianist, Vladimir Horowitz, at the height of his career withdrew from the tension of performing in public for over ten years.

The simple spatial fact that all the lookers are on one side and all the performers are on the other tends to force theatre artists to shape what they are doing to be seen from a specific angle: being seen becomes a major factor in their work. But there is a mass of artists who resist that consciousness from the depths of their guts. In the first week of my first professional job, putting on makeup by following the example of my neighbor, I heard from the far end of the dressing room the magnificent voice of an actor named Jack Berry boom out, "and Benno Schneider says the shortest distance to the audience is through the other actor." I may have nodded in assent, but I did take note.

When the Workgroup first encountered performing on a proscenium stage, our resolution was to ignore the spatial imperative of "front"—where the audience was. We successfully concentrated on each other and the task at hand, but I soon recognized that one small adjustment had to be made. We decided that if at any time we became aware that one of us was directly downstage of the other, we were, in a reasonable time, to get out of the way, and that was it. There were no further concessions to the proscenium situation.

The irony of performing in the round is double. At any time, any two dancers are always blocking each other for a few people in the audience. Also, it is inevitable that bounce light will illuminate the spectators ringing the performing area. Thus, wherever any dancer looks, there are a few rows of audience visible. Concentration on the work and the other dancers will neutralize the presence of the audience.

179

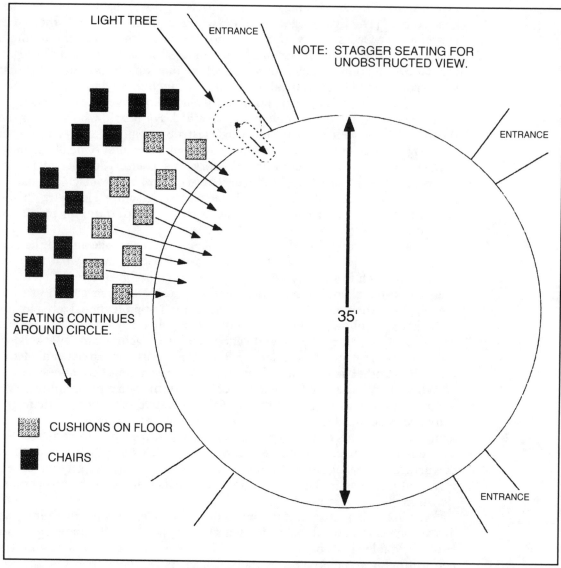

Seating Plan for In-the-Round Peformance

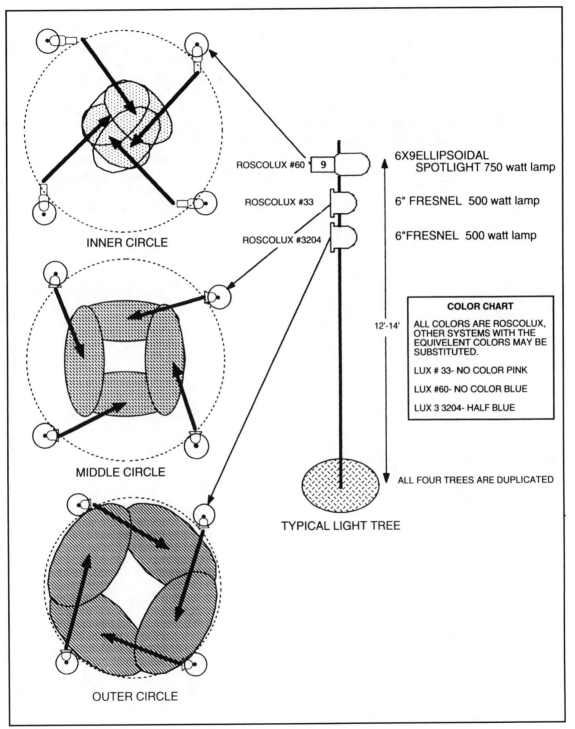

INNER CIRCLE

MIDDLE CIRCLE

OUTER CIRCLE

ROSCOLUX #60

ROSCOLUX #33

ROSCOLUX #3204

6X9ELLIPSOIDAL
SPOTLIGHT 750 watt lamp

6" FRESNEL 500 watt lamp

6"FRESNEL 500 watt lamp

12'-14'

COLOR CHART

ALL COLORS ARE ROSCOLUX,
OTHER SYSTEMS WITH THE
EQUIVELENT COLORS MAY BE
SUBSTITUTED.

LUX # 33- NO COLOR PINK

LUX #60- NO COLOR BLUE

LUX 3 3204- HALF BLUE

ALL FOUR TREES ARE DUPLICATED

TYPICAL LIGHT TREE

Light Plot for In-the-Round Performance

Practice

We never wore any designed costumes. For one piece, Signs of the Times (7.9), there were a couple of props: a handkerchief across Ara's eyes and a leather flight jacket for Mary Anne. How did we dress? Each of us went to Sally Ann Parsons, the costume designer who has done all of my dance clothes since *The Peloponnesian War* in 1968. We took our best practice clothes to her for her approval, and if she felt they did not do us justice, she bought or built what she thought was needed. It worked. No one ever commented on our clothes negatively or positively—which from our viewpoint was just fine. All danced barefoot, except me. I used a soft tan shoe because I work better with a shoe, and no one noticed the difference. None of this is meant to indicate how any other improvisation dance company should appear.

13 Music, Musicians and Improvisation

What needs music and what does not? Your taste and style will answer that. For every improvisation session, whether for myself alone or for a group, I always have at hand a fistful of tapes which may or may not be used. In the earliest workshops, before the company was formed, I regularly invited one or more musicians to attend, not as accompanists but as participants. I can recall Erik Salzman, Rhys Chatham, Michael Sahl, Charlemagne Palestine among others. For a while, a young percussionist, William Steinberg, was literally a paid member of the company. A few who visited the workshops were fine vocalists, among them a countertenor, William Zukov. The results of this mixed bag were as beautiful as they were hair-raising.

Under ideal conditions the Workgroup and every workshop would have had a complement of a few musicians as members. In the less than ideal conditions that prevail, musicans and dancers may at times come together for special projects, but be warned: dancers and musicians operate under radically divergent codes based on the economic realities that shape each of the professions. The most devoted musician has one supreme loyalty, the gig, slang for a job that pays. The dance market does not offer intermittent jobs that pay very well for a few hours.[1] The music market does. Dancers tend to make commitments that are not easily broken. You can form a dance group that pays little or nothing, and if you inspire conviction that the work is important and cuts to the gut of the dancer, he.she will do grinding work-work for money at the craziest of hours in order to be able to stay with the group.

Present musicians with a project that excites them profoundly and you'll have them working with full energy and devotion, until the almighty gig comes along. Then, with a genuine show of regret, you will hear, "I'm devastated, but you see, there's this gig. Gotta go." To grow a hardwood tree, you

---

1. This may not be the case on the West Coast, meaning Hollywood, where there is sporadic work for films and TV.

need time, continuity. To shape an aesthetic with the sweat, the minds and the hearts of people, you need continuity. Many dance companies have been built and are being created at this very moment with much faith and minimal resources. I doubt whether this is the case with music.

As the I Ching says so generously, "No blame." That's them and this is us. We each do what we must. I go into this because it is all too easy to begin a noble idea and too, too difficult to bring it to fruition, particularly if it depends on first-rate, professional musicians—unless, of course, there is a guaranteed budget that makes this "ideal" project the gig. This is not a resentful recital; it's just the way it is.

It can be helpful when one or more of the dancers is also a musician. Lee Connor and Charles Hayward taped a terrifying score for Polythemes and Charles after leaving the company, rejoined as one of two musicians for *Hello Farewell Hello*. Bill DeTurk, who was in the second Workgroup, was an accomplished banjo player, and for a while we did Rondo to his infectious strumming. These couplings of talent are too rare.

Thus, here is the warning. Never stop listening to scores new to you. Have a monster library of recordings at hand. In the matter of improvisation, either in the studio or in public performance, it is too much to expect musicians who have spent comparatively little time with you to be working the same mode, in the same style, with the same ground rules, or with the same rigor. On the other hand, nothing can compare with the electricity generated by the interaction of dancers and live musicians, *if* it is a true interaction based on a shared understanding and time, lots of time. If a choreographer gives professional musicians a prepared score, they need no more than a few hours to give what is wanted. A company that improvises would need much more from a musician.

Very early, long before the Workgroup, I carried about with me on my tours of master classes and residencies a list of improvisations focused on music. Along with this, I always had a tape of wildly divergent, brief chunks of music guaranteed to get dancers moving.

Using Music for Improvisation

- Isolate and work only one part of the body. (I would call out the body parts.) A precursor of Circles (4.1) and Each Alone (4.4).
- Follow (or oppose) the melody, then shift to a focus on the basic rhythm of the music, and finally dance between the two, bouncing from one to the other.
- Follow (or oppose) the dynamics of the music.
- Listening to the music, find a short movement riff and do a rondo.
- Use the challenge of the "I dare you" as your line of work. (Give yourself a challenge of doing what is unfamiliar or difficult for you.)
- For the length of the music, pose a single technical challenge (turns,

balances, speed, endurance), or a combination (turns that go into the air).
- Don't dance; watch the others.
- Work with a partner, sharing a problem or an "I dare you." One of you dances. The other observes, takes notes and gives you suggestions and criticisms. Then change roles.
- Keep a notebook. If you find something special, note it, save it, work on it and, if you want, teach it to all.
- Dance to the previous cut while listening to another piece of music.
- Dance only to the highest or lowest sounds in the piece.
- Sense and do the inner action of the music.
- Who or what is alive inside the music? Become what you find and do what X is doing.
- Perform the action of the music or of X in different parts of the body.
- Music—what is on the surface? Dance it. What is hidden but there, under the surface? Dance it. Dance between the two and bounce from one to the other. Dance both at the same time.[2]
- Move . . . dance . . . listen for the sheer delight of it without taking mental notes or any "useful" purpose.

For Musicians Only

When I think of musicians in the context of improvisation, I have some sadness and a little bitterness. At the root of the sadness is an unrealized vision. Briefly, I am convinced that, with few exceptions, the mass of the material presented in this book can be brought to a rich life by musicians without a dancer in sight. There is a way of making music that may very well be the original raison d'être of music expression. It is a reasonable guess that in those far-off days the sounds that came to be music were produced primarily in order to make something happen, not to make music. Some of that force survives, but the brunt of "serious" music making today is music about music. If musicians were to try the way of the Workgroup, they would find a way to make a music that in the climate of today would be a fresh statement, albeit an ancient one.

In the ensuing pages of this chapter there will be listing of all the EGAS now reoriented toward the needs and necessities of making music. None if it will make sense for anyone who has not read the book thus far. None of it will work significantly if the musicians attempting it are anything less than good. None of it will work if the musicians do not plunge into this work risking at least a period of a month or two of exploring unfamiliar terrain.

Musicians venturing to do this work will have to continually anticipate a problem that dancers rarely face. A roomful of dancers can exist, each in a separate world, without disturbing one another, unless the work of one or

---

2. Not so strange. We do this most of the time.

more is intrusively audible—and then I have them transpose their sounds into motion. Musicians *hear* each other. That fact should be used to make what they do more beautiful, not drive them crazy. To get around this, many exercises can and should be done one at a time at first, each person listening to and learning from the other. As soon as more than one is making sounds, commonalities need to be predetermined—of time, mode and/or the use of a conductor.

To pursue the elusive matter of "ideal" conditions. If any group of musikers get caught up in this idea, try to get a leader who relishes the gamble of improvisation and has sufficient taste to hear when you are on a productive track. I am certain, or at least hopeful, that among the newer crop of music directors or conductors or even opera directors, a good one might be found. Above all, find a leader who has the openness to listen to all of you and the taste and the authority to make decisions when a consensus is lacking. Many exercises will need a conductor. Work with a sound technician in a space where what you do can be cleanly and accurately recorded. Without hearing what you have done, and without evaluations, growth will be hard.

Now to the "little bit of bitterness." Believing that the way of the Workgroup could be adapted for musicians, I sent out a call in 1971 to the many who had worked with us and offered a workshop for musicians only. A collection of hotshots gathered at our Broadway studio. They met for two evenings a week without a dancer in sight—except me. After some initial fumbles and the gradual discarding of the traditional mind-sets for the making of music, just as something strong, different and exciting began to be heard, a thinning process began. The gigs came and a couple of musicians left, but good new ones took their place because they heard that something was happening up there on the third floor of 550 Broadway. But with new ones you have to start from the beginning once again. It's a complexity to tell a musician, "Don't make music. Do something to someone with your music." To shape a new aesthetic with the sweat, minds and hearts of artists, you need continuity. About six weeks of this and I could not see the point. The net result? Some wonderful letters from that group which I later used to bolster a grant application to work with Creative Associates, a new music group based at SUNY Buffalo. I won out over some formidable competition— and lost the whole project to an economy wave raised by Governor Nelson Rockefeller.

Is it possible to ever give this way a real go? Perhaps someone out there has the answer. Meanwhile, musicians, read on.

A Sequence of EGAS for the Making of Music

The code:

* Musicians would move/dance, whatever, *without their instruments.* (This implies no anticipation that their physicality would be expected to

compete with dancers' skill, quality and sheer quantity of movement. Moving within their own limitations, the musicians will simply open their sensibilities to the musical work ahead by moving about.)

** Musicians would be working with their instruments and not expected to move about.

*/** Both motion and music would be expected.

? = doubtful or probably not

Gifts (9.1)**

How does a percussionist "read" the needs of a flautist warming up? And vice versa?

Rhythm Series 1

Breath Rhythm (5.3)*
Pulse Rhythm (5.4)*
Internal Rhythm (5.5) */**
Evolving Repetition (6.4) */**
True Repetition (6.3) */**
Dedicate Your Motion (5.11) */**
Go Visiting (7.3) */**
Spinning (11.1) */**

Can one move and make music? I've rarely seen musicians who do not move while they make music. What is asked for here opens up the possibility of finding, from within, richer movement than the few patterns that most musicians click into early and rarely change over the years.

When the musicians are deep into a Repetition, Dedicate Your Motion can be interjected. The tail of a Repetition is Go Visiting and is possible with those who can make music and stroll about while those who are immobilized, as it were, like the pianist, the multi-instrument percussionist, a harpist, and so on, should be visited. Another mind-sweeper is Spinning, which can be used to precede a Repetition. Can any musicians do this and make music? Find out.

Sound- Motion Work

Medicine Ball (9.2) **
Outrageous Travel (9.3) **
Master-Disciple (5.9) **
Solo Singer (2.1) **
Solo Dancer (2.2) */**

The first three can be music alone. Solo Singer can be transposed to have one musician in the center and all the others relating musically to that solo voice. What have we here but a concerto form for improvisation? As for Solo Dancer, I can imagine that almost every group of five or more musicians has at least one who is agile enough to improvise.

Rhythm Series 2

Ambient Sound (1.5) **
Conduct a Picture (1.7) **

Practice

Rhythm Circle (3.5) ★★
Rhythm Portrait (3.12) ★★
    Every one is a set-up for musicians.

The   The Mind-Wash (3.2) ★
Middle   The Mirror (2.4) ★
Period   A Duet (3.11) ★★
    Cliché Rondo (5.13) ★
    What Happened? (7.1) ★★

    The first three of this group can be given as one continuous sequence. The focus of A Duet is simply the other person. For it, the instruction is simply, "Make music to, for and about the other person. Along the way, try to make something happen, either to you or your partner or both. When it happens, celebrate it musically and stop. If your partner stops first, play a recognition of being left and then stop." Until these three work for the musicians, it is better not to move too far forward.

Second   Backdoor (5.6) ★
Stage of the   Hub Meditation (5.7) ★
Middle   Circles (4.1) ★★
Period   Hot to Cold to Hot (4.2) ★★
    Faces (9.13) ★/★★

    These introduce the next set of principles and ways of working that pave the way for performance pieces. For dancers, Circles is based on a schematic division of body parts. Musicians doing Circles would have to agree on which schematic divisions they would concentrate. There are at least a dozen modes: Lydian, Dorian, Aeolian and so on. There are the major and minor scales. There is music in a 2, a 3, a 4; there are paso dobles, waltzes, marches and many more. Getting a potent image and inner action and shifting from one time pulse to another or from one musical mode to another would extend the range of expression and help the musicians gain the power to find the musical metaphors needed. Initially.

The Mind-Wash (3.2)★
The Other (6.5a) ★/★★
Hub Meditation (5.7)★
Each Alone (6.5b) ★★
Duet (6.5c) ★★

    This string of work is the key to what the Workgroup did. From it flows a new way of performing, improvisation, insights into self, the other and more complex structures. Good for studio work as well as for performance. If you can make music out of this, the point is made and my hope and belief are supported.

Take a Walk in Your Own World (9.12) ★★

    Try this with a large group of musicians.

188

Studio	Seeing Through the Eyes of Another (5.12) *
Work to be	Dawn Chorus Rite (4.6) *
Given at	Stillness12 (1.1) **
Odd	A version for musicians: Clear the head. Wait until there is a sound in
Intervals to	your head. Hear what it will do and where it goes—but don't do it for as
a Group	long as you can. When you do, do as little as possible and return to still-
Fairly New	ness, waiting for the next sound to appear, and so on.
to the Work	Lose Your Head (3.7) **

Your Familiar (8.3) **

Possessed by a Mannerism (9.8) **

Why Do You Dance? or, Why Do You Make Music? (5.14) **

The Minnesota Duet (3.1) **

The Chord (2.3) **

The Conductor (2.5) **

Your Secret Totem Animal (8.2) **

Whatever Happens, Happens (4.3) **

Yoga Mirror (3.3) *

Not Naming (9.5) *

Ping Pong (8.9) **

The Tandem Solo (1.8) **

Pygmalion and Galatea I (5.15) **

What Are You Hearing? (8.4) **

The Spine of Style (8.8) **

Early Modern Dance (8.7) **

The Indian Poems (6.15) **

Tell a Dream (3.8) **

Tell a Poem (3.9) **

    None are simple. All can create the conditions for music.

Advanced	I Dare You (8.1) **
Studio	Inside the Outside (9.9) **
Work	The Male/Female Dance (6.12) **
	As one of our early company members used to say when confronted with
	a setup that promised to stir the depths, "Heavy!"

Advanced	Rondo (6.1) **
Perfor-	Wind II (6.13) **
mance	Rituals of Power (6.10) **
Work	Quiet Dance (7.4) **
	Make a Phrase (app. C, HFH.3) **
	Ham and Clove (8.11) **
	Adam and Eve (8.10) **
	Celebration (9.11) **
	Fragment Rondo (7.10) **

Practice
....

Compass (8.12) **
Rhythm Circle (3.5) **
Prison (7.2)**

> To bring these before the public, two things must take place: The musicians involved must find a profound connection within the structures, making the work come alive in the studio. Each piece must pass the test of many passes to be certain that for the group it is fertile, that is, it bears repeating.

A
Perfor-
mance
Progression

Sea Anemone
From Now (7.5)**
Recognition Ritual (7.6)**
Wind I (5.10) **
Wind II (6.13) **
Relay Solo (7.7) **
Go 1-2-3-4 (7.8) **

> These six are a sequence that can flow musically from beginning to end without interruption, each segment building off the previous one. (Chapter 8.)

Hello Farewell Hello[3]
The Inarticulates (HFH.1)?
Processional (HFH.1a)?
Museum (HFH.1b)?
Wind II (HFH.1c)
Pygmalion and Galatea II (HFH.2)**
The Picadors' Walk (HFH.2a)
Ariadne's Dance (HFH.2b) **
Make a Phrase (HFH.3) **
Hello To Now (HFH.4) **

> I cannot conceive how this could emerge as a coherent full evening work of music. The starred pieces could be realized musically. More to the point is the dream that this hypothetical group of musicians would after a time of intensive work bring forth their own "big" creation.

....

3. See Appendix C.

Appendixes

Indexes

Appendix A.
Helen Tamiris

Young, she found interpretive dancing in a settlement house on the Lower East Side of New York. As World War I ended, she joined the ballet of the Metropolitan Opera House. A few years of that was followed by dancing in Broadway revues, tours on the movie-vaudeville circuit and nightclub appearances. Dissatisfied with all the dance training and dance culture she had experienced, she went into the studio and a year and a half later emerged with her first solo concert in 1927, one year after Martha Graham's debut and a year before that of Doris Humphrey and Charles Weidman. The language of her body, infused with the energy of her time; the contemporary music, Debussy, Gershwin, Negro spirituals; her themes, human and immediate; all were the hallmarks of what came to be known as the modern dance. In her lifetime, five names were always credited with the creation of modern dance in America: Graham, Humphrey, Weidman, Holm and Tamiris. As a dancer she was a breathtaking panther and as a choreographer she was always probing and searching for new forms to express her central concern for human dignity.

After World War II, she turned to work, with great success, in the field of musical comedy; choreographing Broadway shows and a few Hollywood musical films. Finally, in 1960 she returned to the concert field to form the Tamiris-Nagrin Dance Company.

In addition to her astonishing beauty and power as a dancer, and her innovative choreography, she had a brilliant mind capable of searching analysis, exquisitely clear exposition and some of the best teaching I've ever observed. We were married and together for over twenty years. (*How to Dance Forever*, pp. 267–68.)

Appendix B.
A Dialogue

In chapter 9, On the Road Again, I refer to a day when several dancers wept during and following a session in which images of male and female were called up. In the last few years, I have, with the dancers' permission, tape-recorded the discussions that followed these exercises. The one transcribed below occurred in Hawaii, and the talk that ensued the next day cuts to the heart of our art and our responsibilities as artists. The tape begins quite abruptly, somewhere after we started. Objections had been raised against experiencing a raw emotion in the context of performing, either onstage or, as in this case, in an improvisation in the studio.

DN: Have you never experienced a raw emotion onstage?

Student A: Not like that . . . not to that extent.

DN: Do you feel there's something wrong with a raw emotion onstage?

Student A: Onstage we should be presenting a remembrance of what was, not presenting the actual act.

DN: A question: If an improvisation led you to experience wild happiness, would you raise this issue?

Student A: I really wouldn't run around onstage and jump about and smile and be happy all the time either.

DN: You are not pursuing the logic of what I asked. Let us say you did an improvisation that provoked in you a spontaneous burst of laughter or a flood of joyousness, and say that you worked this same improvisation as an exercise one, two, three, four, five times and it always provoked the same responses, would that then be something that you would think suitable for improvisation?

Student A: Yes.

DN: And if you did something that consistently provoked rage, would that be suitable for improvisation?

Student A: If it provokes some thought on a part of the audience . . .

DN: I'm not talking about the audience, I'm talking about you. If the performance experience calls up from you laughter or great joy in an improvisation is that a raw emotion which could be acceptable or not?

Student B: I think it's acceptable but I think the performer has to have a certain amount of skill.

DN: Skill aside, if the performer were to experience it, would it be acceptable or not acceptable?

Student B: I think it's acceptable.

DN: Then what about rage?

Student B: I think that's acceptable.

Student C: I have to question the distinction between the character and the image of ourselves. The concentration should be on the character.

DN: In our improvisation structures, I don't assign you a character. You create the character.

Student C: No, I know that . . .

DN: You're not possessed by something outside of you.

Student C: I don't think that's what I said.

DN: Yes, but that's what is implied, that here you are and over there is the character. No, you create the character. It's your creation, assembled out of yourself.

Student C: But, I'm not approaching him as myself but as the character that I've created.

DN: Right, but the question at hand is, if you created a nice, warm, loving character instead of that raging person, would we be having this discussion today?

Student C: I don't know. So I created one that's full of rage and I want to discuss it. So what's wrong with that?

DN: Nothing at all. What happened asks for exactly this kind of dialogue. I have yet to hear an answer to what I've been asking: Do we have a different set of artistic rules for something that involves rage? Is that what you are saying?

Student C: I guess so, but I never presented something like that.

DN: You're saying two things at once: that this was a new experience for you in the context of dancing, of performing dance here in the studio. But what troubles me is the other statement. You feel that rage or genuine grief may need a separate set of rules. I find that shocking and, by my code, unacceptable.

Student C: I think that maybe there is a way to deal with a piece that provoked so much emotion—raw emotion—onstage or here in the workshop. My question is, could we present what we did yesterday by working through it numerous times? Then there would be a possibility that we might be more in control of our raw emotions. You see, yesterday, I broke character from the image that I had.

Student A: Why, because you were weeping?

Student C: I broke character by crying because *I* was crying, not the character. I think that through the discipline of creating over and over again, the possibility would be less for me to show that raw emotion onstage.

Student D: Would that be acceptable?

DN:	Acceptable or not acceptable you're still not getting to the point of my first question.
Student C:	I don't think you are understanding what I am saying, Daniel.
DN:	I really don't. It sounds as if you were dealing with something that isn't nice—something that has to be tamed, civilized.
Student C:	No. I'm not saying that at all. I'm just saying that revealing something so strong isn't comfortable. [The speaker's voice was quite shaky at this point.] It produced a discomfort not only in us but those watching us. I mean those strong emotions are a lot more uncomfortable than joy and happiness.
DN:	Now we are getting closer. Personally, when I find myself in the Comfortable Theatre, I want to leave. The only kind of theater I want to enter gives a rich stew of the comfortable and the uncomfortable. I'm interested in theater that splits me wide open; a theater that makes me ashamed of being a human being; a theatre that confuses me; a theater that makes me want to start my life all over again; a theatre that says, "Daniel—jump!"
Student C:	We're not saying we want to do nice, clean, happy things. We're talking about how do we deal with those kinds of things that are too much to handle.
DN:	Perhaps you should welcome "things that are too much to handle." Perhaps "too much" is just what you should be ready for. If you stepped on a tack, a violent "ouch" would erupt. Wouldn't it be wonderful if you could dance with a response as innocent and immediate as that "ouch"? By the very nature of improvisation, if you are open, sensitive and responsive, it is possible to experience a raw emotion, whether it be joyous, triumphant or devastating.
Student C:	OK, you experience the emotion. You can experience an emotion of sadness without getting up and crying onstage. I think that crosses a thin line.
DN:	How do you feel about actors who cry onstage? The ironic footnote to all of this is that for most actors, being able to weep real tears in rehearsal, onstage or on camera is an ultimate—an unequivocal proof of their talent.
Student C:	They cry as the character.
Student E:	Being in character gives the actors a distance.
DN:	Is it allowable for dancers to cry in character? All of this is what actors experience, what opera singers experience. Guitar players experience it. Why not dancers?
Student A:	Well, we haven't experienced it yet. We have not experienced that control.
DN:	What do you mean by "control?"
Student A:	We don't have the handle on it to be able to deal with it, to preserve the distance of ourselves, so the rage just doesn't go berserk.
DN:	Berserk? You can't hurt yourself. Your partner can't hurt you. That's unthinkable. You would never improvise hitting your head against the wall. You know the size of your space. You never slam into a wall. You don't barge into other bodies. You know where you are. Of course there's control. You're never in danger of going crazy, but you are in danger of walking away from

the most precious experience open to an artist—a genuine emotion, albeit a very strong one. If you're going to improvise, you have to be reaady to get into the experience, the shocking experience of a very strong emotion: ecstatic, hilarious or terrible, whatever.

Student A: And what I am saying is that we're not used to dealing with those emotions. We just aren't.

DN: I agree. Dancers usually aren't. They tend to be addicted to control, and most of you slam the door against that wild forest which is not out there someplace but inside you, whether you perceive it or play the game of not looking. How's about looking? Are you willing to risk it? That is what I am asking you.

Student C: I would like to do it again and again. For me, if I don't return to what I started yesterday, what I touched yesterday, I will feel that I barely touched the tip of something and left what was the real challenge for me. I found that when I went home yesterday, I thought about what happened to me and did not want to go on to the next problem because I wanted to take what happened to me yesterday and get back into it, to take it further.

DN: I am finally hearing what you are saying. You're just not used to it—to be dancing and experience an emotion of such depth. I hope I am bringing you something that you have not done before. It is a way of improvising like no other.

   Once you say "OK, I will walk into this arena and accept the ground rules," you should be ready. You say you are not used to it? I'd be surprised if you were. Now we have two questions: One, are you willing to try it? And two, do you think that if something is found that happens time and time again, that gets deeper and more subtle and still provokes a very strong emotion, do you think it is a suitable or an unsuitable thing to be performed in public? Remember, you mentioned this matter of tears in front of an audience.

Student C: Daniel, if we are going to be dealing with this kind of thing, we need help in walking through it, or do you want us to go outside of the group and work it out?

DN: That's one way, but remember, I always leave time after you've all finished an improvisation to review in your own mind what happened and whether there was something to be remembered, understood and perhaps returned to at a later time. I also add the option and time to look back with your partner at what happened between you. Finally, we all meet after the EGAS to ask questions and discuss what happened. At any one of these steps, you may get the very best kind of help and understanding you can ever find: from yourself. Talk to yourself and there, there should be no barriers. You can bring up anything in your mind and no one can criticize you for what you are thinking. With your partner, inevitably there will be some barriers, even with a close friend. In the larger group session, the inhibitions understandably multiply. One inhibition I would like you to respect. The specific character and task you created is for you to know and we to sense from what you dance, never from what you tell us. We should never know your image, not the name of the person you were thinking of or any of the details. Our shared talk should be about ways, methods and procedures that help or inhibit the flow of the work, exactly as we are doing this moment.

Student A: But should I leave this place feeling torn up, or should we talk about it here, or should I go seek help from somebody else?

DN: If you are torn up, you have several choices, and only you can decide the one for you. You can say, "I will return to this tomorrow and do the same thing again." You can talk to a friend. You can rent a studio and do it all by yourself. You could put it all into your personal journal and try to get a grip on it by thinking it through as you write about it. Or, you can forget about it. But to lay out before all of us the specifics of what upset you as a subject of discussion would be to remake our purpose. From a group dedicated to realizing the artistic potentiality of dance improvisation, we would become a gathering practicing therapy and I would have to be what I am not—a skilled and practicing psychologist. If you want to talk to me outside the class about it, I would be honored by your trust. That I could handle. [I am not sure I like my answer. A participant is upset. Does he.she raise the matter in class? Are personal matters appropriate for class discussion? Are we talking about a matter of taste or decent compassion for a troubled person? I can understand a dance company coping with this but a class poses problems and I am without a clear answer.]

Student B: I don't think she is saying the specific, I think she is asking how we are going to deal with it in the context of this class if at all.

DN: We're doing that right now, talking about it. That is the first step. The question was asked, "What do you do when you are rocked with a genuine feeling of rage, or a genuine uncontrollable cry? What do you do with emotions that rock you?" I say if you choose not to walk away from it, not to forget it or not to make believe it didn't happen, you have a golden opportunity. In the pit of that moment of despair or rage or whatever, reach out for the most wonderful movements for it. Search for the metaphor that grasps it like Michelangelo's stones clasp the twisted figures. Let flower the best dance that you ever did in your life. That is one way and that way is the reason we are here.

Student A: That sounds wonderful and easy to say but I was very thrown and so I couldn't let it flower. Instead I went home to bed.

DN: You do what you have to do. Either you walk away from the emotional hit or, because you are an artist, a dance artist, you, then and there, let it fertilize the moment and the movements. You have before you, difficult though it may be, the rarest experience: to be able to dance and to know that what is taking place is so, that you did not make it up, that it is there, that something is going on, something that exists in you as surely as you have a heart, lungs and legs. It is there in you and thus exists in the world, as much as this floor under us and that you are creating and moving off something that *is*.

In the days of the sixties, we had a word that was beaten to hell, *authentic,* and much as I am leery of using that word because so many phonies used it as a cover for inauthentic experiences, I can unequivocally say among some of you in this class yesterday there was an authentic experience. If you come to grips with it, it is a fuse for dancing and dancing about something that *is*, which is a lot better than so much dance that is about things that are not, things that are synthetic, things that are cute, things that are vulgar, things that are seductive, things that are copied. You are dealing with something that is, something that is there.

The task, and I will not say it is easy, nor should you expect it to be easy, is to find ways of letting it emerge, to let it go out into dance. Let the river flow into dance, into the plains of dancing. Instead of just crying, why shouldn't the tears, as well as the laughter, flow into dance? And, if you can't do it today, you can remember it for some day down the line when you can and want to deal with it.

Student A: I think I would like to know how to get into that place and still keep the strength of that emotion.

Student B: I think she is asking what I asked yesterday, about how to translate those raw emotions into movement.

DN: The moment you are flooded by a powerful emotion seek the movement metaphor that will contain it.

Student C: You talked to us about the movement metaphor but we really didn't get into how to find it.

DN: I do it all the time. That is how I make my dances. That's how I make my living. But, I cannot do this for you. I cannot show you how to go from here to there, from your emotion to the right metaphor. Your emotion needs your metaphor. Only you can sense the poem of what is surging through you. You have got to make the move and you may mutter to yourself, "That's not it," and fish for another, but "No, I don't like that." You keep going in the improvisation until you say, "Ah, this begins to make some kind of sense," and plow forward and through to an expression of what it is you are doing and feeling.

How you are going to do that is what I hope you will find here. It can be done for you but it shouldn't. What is the answer for me is not the answer for you. Are you game to take that responsibility and pursue it?

Student A: Yesterday, it somehow felt wrong to start dancing. It felt like this character just would not release.

DN: Every character has a dance. There is a dance for everyone. That yellow line has a dance that belongs to it and the cream line has a different dance. The brown wood has a dance to it. Your fingernail has a dance to it. Everything has a dance to it, just as there is a chemistry to everything; there is a physics to everything; there is a poem to everything; there is a song to everything. Everything has weight, everything has energy, and everything has a dance and most especially a character who cannot release. Martha Graham did a violent piece called *American Provincial* about people who could not release. Your character who would not release has a dance and quite probably a violent dance.

Student C: I may be wrong in saying this, but I think breaking into that raw emotion, most of us broke down because we broke out of character, but if we did it over and over again, we could get an emotional distance from ourselves and from the character.

DN: Like Polonius hiding behind the screen is a thought, an unspoken belief, I would love to skewer. Throughout the theatre, most art, and certainly dance, there is a conviction that though the appearance of passion is a desirable and for many a necessary component of art, it must not be *felt* by the performer, only *shown*. There is a school of aesthetic theory that claims it is distancing from the object that makes art. Marcel Duchamp signs a wine bottle rack and offers it up for display in a gallery or museum and it will no longer be used as a rack for wine bottles because now it is an object of art. Those bottles are now permanently distanced from wine. At the opposite pole from this sophistication, the mime of the classic ballet dancer gives all the outward signs of a deep, if not melodramatic emotion while deliberately presenting a carefully controlled attractive pose. Genuine feeling would be messy, self-indulgent and *difficult to control.*

It is precisely that one word, *control,* that contains the crux of what we are talking about and the loss of control that troubled some of you so much. Both in the making of dance and its performance, many opt for control as opposed to abandon and emotion. It is OK to bring high energy to the act of performance—to give a fiery display—as long as the emotion displayed is not felt. The fear is of feeling deeply and a consequent loss of control and thus loss of the art. It would become the *real thing,* which is not the art thing.

The curse of this thinking is its illusion of purity. The reality of art is a mess, a constant oscillation of deliberate and conscious control and a reckless immersion in the maelstrom of the moment when all the pieces—self, object, music, the air—become an indivisible one. The immersion is present in all fields of life and those to whom it happens have an entry to joy, even if some immersions are tragic or painful. Dancers need two legs: control and letting go.

To weep is to see and to understand. It only demands the courage not to turn away but to keep looking and come to grips with the pain and shape it for the rest of us to get a glimmer of another's insides and the courage to look within ourselves.

Student C: I can accept what you just said but of whom are we talking? Us? Me? Or the character I broke away from? *I* was weeping, not the character, and that's what felt wrong and why I couldn't continue.

DN: What happened to you is what happens to every performer in every performance. At the center of your concentration was X, your character. On the periphery were a multitude of things that were not directly related to X or what X was doing. There is no way that you or any dancer, singer or actor can completely exclude from your awareness that multitude of things: a slippery spot in the floor, the sight of palm fronds whipped by a strong wind just outside the studio window [this was in Hawaii], a shot of pain from a stone bruise in your left metatarsal, an unexpected memory of a door being slammed shut in your face. Why is it so surprising or shocking or unwelcome when what the character is caught up in calls up a bruised chunk out of your own life? How else can you understand anybody or anything unless you too have been living, suffering and exulting?

The art of concentration onstage, or anywhere in life, is not to expect a pure and uninterrupted focus on one thing but the discipline to accept and use every distraction, every irrelevancy, to turn back to the central focus of the performance. This includes every unexpected impingement from your own past. Everything is and can be related to everything.

A question for you. If in the middle of that improvisation when you were being X, your attention was diverted by palm fronds outside your studio windows being violently agitated by the wind, could you make any connection with that and what X was doing and thinking?

Student C: [A very long pause on the tape.] Yes, there is a connection. The wind and the palm fronds do speak for X.

DN: And if you as you, wept, did your personal tears have anything to do with X? I am going to guess that what happened was that the distance between you and X collapsed and the imagined life of X became a living life. There's a lovely word out of biology: *symbiotic*. It means that two organisms are living off each other. When you stopped, you blocked the kind of symbiotic action that gives great performances their power. If you ever allow the truth of the character and the wisdom, truth and pain of your own life to embrace, anyone witnessing you do this will be privileged. They come to the theatre seeking just that and you gave it to them.

Student C: OK, I'll take what I ran into yesterday and pursue it.

DN: Is there anybody else? Come on, talk.

Student F: How do you feel about working with things that happen to yourself?

DN: There isn't any part of the world that isn't a valid focus, so why not you?

Student G: I know, but the problems we have been working seem to be directed away from us.

DN: There is no reason why you cannot deal with yourself specifically, to become yourself ready to do a certain task. You don't have to become somebody else.

Student G: I thought I was following your rules.

DN: Good point. I may have been in error in how I phrased the setup. In a Hub Meditation there is no reason why you cannot become your X, your character. You are as legitimate an artistic object as anything else in the world. Some of the best things Van Gogh ever did were self-portraits.

Student F: What do you do when the images you're using are not productive?

DN: You work on an image, a dance, and one day you see that you are not getting anywhere and you drop it, but did you really plow into it? Did you really try it this way? that way? and the other way? It's easy to say "Oh, this is nothing but a plain old oak chair," but did you take the moment to notice the subtle and well-conceived design! It's plain, but the curves of the back and the seat are not only graceful but recognize the complexity of the human body. There is the intricacy of all those parts: legs, braces, back struts and seat all fitting together and so sturdy. The varnish is worn through here. A long and honorable use. Who sat in it? Look at the classic beauty of the oak grain: a history of many winters and summers. Tip it over. Oh! It's filthy. Three wads of dried gum. Who did that? Look at all the mangled screw heads! An inexperienced carpenter! You could take it apart, make sawdust out of it, or burn it. There's a crack. Wood is so vulnerable in the tropics. What kind of people need chairs? Many don't or won't. Look at you. You're all seated about on the floor. You can write six or seven hundred pages about this chair. Your image may never deliver. But while you are working on it, make sure you tip it all around before you drop it. Anything else before we proceed?

Afterword: What I failed to recognize at the time is that the act of weeping is too disorderly for dancers to cope with *while dancing*. Any number of emotions can flood a dancer dancing and still be contained, but to weep is to go out of physical control: the body shakes; the breath is expelled, quickened and intensified; the face goes into an involuntary grimace of grief; and tears spill down the face. Actors love to cry and those who cannot, when the script calls for it, secretly feel that they are less talented than those who can do it on demand. Dancers are horrified when they are out of control. This group, however, spoke of *weeping* and *rage*, using them almost interchangeably. Rage too can push a dancing dancer to the outer limits of physical control. So, their uneasiness did have a point.

Honesty requires that I be clear about the text of this discussion. It is extensively edited because recorded conversations are drenched in repetitions, syntactical horrors, vague formulations, mumbled speech, competing voices, speakers too far from the microphones and the rambling nature of many minds searching for meaning in an important and disturbing experience. I have tried to make out of that moving mess a coherent text that flows with a modicum of clarity. In the editing process, I tried to the best of my biased ability to express the thoughts of the students without being completely self-serving. Undoubtedly, if the dancers could really recall and recount that session, the text would be quite different. If need be, let them write their own book. I would look forward to that!

Appendix C.
Hello Farewell Hello

HELLO FAREWELL HELLO

Conceived and Directed by

Daniel Nagrin

Music: (Musicians' names here. They varied.)[1]

THE SEQUENCE

The Inarticulates

Pygmalion and Galatea

The Articulates

Hello to Now

Hello Farewell Hello is an evening length
work without intermission, whose dance
and music live within a designed structure
containing choreographed elements which
flow into improvisation.

The Scenario

Ideally, the work is performed in the round, and that is how it will be described here. The audience is seated in a circle around an area at least thirty-five feet in diameter. There is an entrance at each quadrant of the circle. We performed it with three men and three women.

---

1. There were always two musicians, playing instruments of radically different textures: a piano and an accordion, later a cello and a saxophone. I can imagine a male and female vocalist or a vocalist and a percussionist (a subtle one). See pp. 123–24 above.

The Inarticulates

HFH.1 House lights fade out and in the dark the dancers enter, walking from all parts of the space as a faint glow of cool, speckled light comes up. They are talking so quietly that the words are not audible. From work done previously in rehearsal, each dancer has unearthed, out of her.his past or imagination, one who was loved but to whom that love was never spoken. The whispering/mumbling is a poem about this person lost in the past. The dancers' meditative walks carry them in and out of the dance area, at times behind the audience. In time, each comes to a stop somewhere in the outer portion of the dance floor. Pausing, the dancers, each in her/his own time, speak aloud and clearly for the first time what was never spoken, three times in three different directions. Their utterances may overlap. The third and last utterance is toward the center.

HFH.1a *Processional.* The speckled light on the audience fades out and grows a bit brighter on the dancers. The silence that follows cues the music. (Our processional music had a blues base in twelve sections, each for twelve slow gliding strides.) The dancers cross the space twelve times, each in their own world. Every cross is a poem to a different part of the beloved, a poem that describes, evokes or becomes that body part. We had the same sequence for all: first the hair and then the eyes, the mouth, the neck, the chest/bosom, the shoulders, the elbows, the belly/voice, the pelvis, the thighs/knees, the feet and finally the totality, the beloved, entire. The form of the twelve crosses take its cue from Circles (4.1). Each cross uses that particular part of the body as the focus of the movement—as the pen of the poem. On the last beat of the last cross, the dancers pause to become the beloved—to become a statue of the beloved.

HFH.1b *Museum.* As the last chord of the processional music fades, all ease away from the "statue" configuration into a casual stance and begin a strolling about. For the first time they become aware of each other. A few dancers exit, leaving four or five looking each other over. "Which one of these could be my love?" In looking, each is careful not to be caught looking. The musicians, though silent during this interval are as active as the dancers, looking and asking the same question.

Sooner or later, each dancer pauses near, but not in front of, the one they have "found" and freezes into a "statue" of themselves and how they feel toward that person. What follows is a fantasy game we are never allowed to play in a museum. "Do not touch the statues!" In Museum, one by one the dancers "unfreeze" and become free to touch and/or manipulate the one who has captured his.her interest. He.she can, in metaphoric motion, express the tenderest or the most outrageous feelings for the "statue." Actions can involve dancing before the statue and/or manipulating it like a puppet. No one is around to see! The music can support or tease the dancer, follow or contradict the action. When this expression is completed, the dancer again becomes a "statue" focused on and near, but not in front of, the one who caught their interest. When the last dancer finishes there is silence.

HFH.1c   *Wind II (6.13).* Now is the time to do Wind II. Odds are it will not be as neat as the original version. Though all are looking at the person who interests them, more than one may be attending to the same person. The dancers continue through the five stages of Wind II, starting with stage one, the "spare gesture," and so on to the end. All the motions are in the context of seeking a loved one. In the stillness that follows the last moments of stage five, all slip into a "casual" body tone, that is, "all stop dancing" and turn to confront who has been "pursuing" them—if there was such a one. A choice will be made: "Which will I go to?" "Who will I go off with?" Or, "Will I go off alone?" What transpires here is left to the impulses of the moment. The dancers leave, together or alone.

Through all of Wind II, each of the musicians has focused on the dancer who interested them the most in Museum. When Wind II starts, they will follow the identical ground rules that govern the dancers through all the five stages, including a shift of attention from the one person to all the dancers in stage three and to one dancer in stages four and five. In the silence, the lights dim to dark as the dancers exit.

HFH. 2   ***Pygmalion and Galatea II***

As the lights come up six dancers are revealed moving in two opposing circles of three. Each passing provokes an embrace and possibly a leaving. Each encounter provokes a response of submission or domination—all for the sake of love. In time, the pairing becomes "permanent." The musicians, also, transfer their attention from one dancer to another until a strong connection is made with one. The encounters are tentative and exploratory. Every passing involves a profound or swift scrutiny of the other. The exchange can range from no-contact curiosity or even hostility to an intense erotic embrace—whatever emerges out of the mutual examination. One may desire an embrace and the other reject it. In time all choose someone to "bond" with.

The action of the musicians is no different than that of the dancers. In the "encounters," they weave in and out of the music of each other, each in their own character, a Pygmalion searching for a Galatea and vice versa. In this scenario, either musician might guess the choice of the other but not really know.

As the couples form, they face each other to contemplate: "Am I the dominant one or the submissive one? If I am to be Pygmalion, what can I do with the one I love to shape him.her to my ideal lover?" The Galatea figure's meditation: "What is it that I am and want to do for my Pygmalion?"

When the meditation produces a clear vision of what each wishes to do, they reach arms to the other. When both reach, Pygmalion performs an embrace that shapes Galatea toward his.her ideal and ends in a freeze. Galatea slips out of that and steps back to observe the embracing "statue" of

Pygmalion and then bends and embraces her.him hinting at what she.he is offering to Pygmalion, ending that in a freeze out of which Pygmalion slips. And now Pygmalion, actively takes the role of sculptor shaping Galatea, who now becomes a passive statue of Pygmalion's desire. A general configuration is created and then parts of the body are put into repetitive motion. When satisfied that it is complete, Pygmalion steps back to assume a complementary moving statue expressing her.his role. The moving statue of Galatea dances an acceptance of what he.she believes is wanted. The two may or may not be in harmony. There is harmony if Galatea clearly senses what is expected of him.her. If not, Pygmalion, in dance, attempts to guide Galatea "correctly." Through all this, Galatea has been passive. At some point Galatea, using what has been given him.her begins to modulate toward what it is that he.she wants so much to give and do for Pygmalion. Pygmalion will only accept what Pygmalion postulates as the perfect Galatea. Galatea insists on being what Galatea has to give. It is conceivable that the two will be in harmony. If that occurs, when both are aware of this success, they join in a statue of that vision. If, as is more probable, there is disharmony, the duet continues until both are convinced of a failure, and they freeze in a hostile stand-off. When all three couples have finished and becomes statues of what happened to them, the music must stop also.

(We decided in advance who was who and who joined whom. Thus every Pygmalion had a Galatea. This version of *Hello Farewell Hello* is looser than the original. What if two Pygmalions decide to pair? Or two Galateas? Recall that after the mutual meditation is completed by signaling with outstretched arms, Pygmalion steps forward to embrace the passive Galatea. If both make this move, one will have to pretend to be passive—until it becomes unbearable—which should make for a dynamic duet. If both remain passive, one will have to take up the burden of being the manipulator. Contradictions in character make for the most interesting people on stage——and in life.)

How do the musicians do what the dancers have done—musically? Two ways: (1) By agreeing to identify with one pair of the dancers, each supporting, cajoling or mocking one of the pair with their music. (2) By focusing upon each other and ignoring the dancers. In a mutual meditation, they choose a role of a Pygmalion or a Galatea and then in music play out that relationship. How is this done? If something is strongly experienced in the mind-heart of a dancer, it can be danced. If something is strongly experienced in the mind-heart of a musician it can be sung, beaten out on drums, played on the piano or stroked on the strings of the cello. How does the river of sound pouring out of a clarinet embrace the voice of a bass baritone? I do not know. I am not a musician. It is the musician's problem. That the way exists, I am certain. It is not the obvious or commom method of music-making but it is and has been there since the very beginning of music-making. Of that, I am also certain.

HFH.2a   *The Picadors' Walk.* Each of the Pygmalion and Galatea couples ends in a freeze confronting each other, harmonious or hostile. When the last couple finishes, all begin a clockwise walk, never losing the eyes of the other. The walks spiral out to the perimeter and then in until each couple is almost breathing in the other's face. There may be a confrontational pause or they may continue without a pause to spiral out away from each other until they reach the perimeter again and exit one by one until only two are left, a Pygmalion and a related Galatea. They stop again and confront each other across the space. Sooner or later one relents the separation and takes a fierce step toward the other who abruptly turns away and leaves.

HFH.2b   *Ariadne's Dance.* The one left freezes like the deserted Ariadne (she saved Theseus from the Minotaru's deadly labyrinth, but he deserted her on the island of Naxos). What is wanted here is a dance of death and rebirth. What we did: The Ariadne figure stood there, a statue full of longing, and bit by bit, particle by particle, decayed and crumbled to the floor; but some part resisted, and bit by bit and particle by particle, life was regained until the figure was erect. There was actually strength—a new strength, not seen before. This phoenix-figure covered the space to an exit, but not the exit taken by the one who turned away. This was done in silence. The lights dim to a low level.

HFH.3   ### The Articulates or, Make a Phrase

There are sounds of party music, laughter and talking. Six dancers enter, couples leaning, clinging and dancing—popular, contemporary and even outrageous couple and group dancing. They all gather, still dancing in one tight area, center stage. One minute of this and one by one, predetermined couples peel away, still dancing to find a private space to continue together. No couplings are the same as in Pygmalion and Galatea. (We decided in advance who would be with whom.)

The music peters out as the couples leave the center area. In the silence, the couples pause to face and contemplate each other asking themselves, "What moves, what motions, what energies will bring this dear person to a sweet release, to a climactic burst of joy?"

The body is at ease during this meditation. When the dancer finds a strong sense of what will be needed she.he will allow that feeling to infuse the body and hold that position until the partner similarly moves from a waiting body to an involved body. The first person to signal ready begins by making a short phrase of movement. The second person learns it. The phrase is a gesture doing something for, to or about the partner: a movement metaphor for caressing, teasing, delighting, humoring, playing with, protecting, enfolding, embracing, exciting the partner—any one or all of these. The teaching is limited to imitation and abjures speech. When the "teacher" is satisfied, there is a nod, and now both do the phrase together and the partner adds a phrase to it according to his.her understanding and feeling for the other. This is learned by the first mover who then adds to the two phrases a third one after getting the nod of approval and thus, a chain of phrases is spun out first from one and then added to by the other. When does it stop? When it is finished. The dancers will know. It will feel finished.

Of course, all along, we have been talking about loving and being loved. In direction and teaching, I often avoid the word because it is a treachery, seducing dancers, actors, singers, and just plain human beings to "make like love" rather than doing all the little specific things that lovers do, the things that truly create the ineffable aura of what we so glibly call up as "love." There is no soggier trap in the world than *trying to feel love*—onstage—or in life. It is a slough of generalizations, pretense, banalities that are a picture of love, but are not love. Chafing another's aching, cold feet with bare hands, praise for a small victory, forgetting to breathe while lost in the bottomless depth of eyes, not stirring an aching arm for fear of waking the other are all doings that sweeten the air and sometime later on, one might say with surprise, "I felt love." While doing this dance, forget "love" and do lovely things to, for and with your partner—specific metaphors for specific acts to make your partner experience a burst of joy.

One technical point: when this dance is first done, in the studio, all the learning should be done mirror style. While facing the partner, to copy the raising of the right arm, raise the left. When there is an ease in mastering the entire structure and the work is oriented toward developing a performance version, shift to actual imitation: the raising of the right arm is now matched by raising a right arm. The reasoning? It just looks more exciting and more interesting to see two people facing each other, doing the same motion and moving in opposite directions.

When both dancers sense that the entire linkage of phrases is completed, they run through it twice, without stopping. Then they separate, each with the identical task, the task that faces all dancers once they have learned an extended piece of dance: to do the movement as given and *make it their own seamless statement—all of it.* "Seamless," because in Make a Phrase, each dancer is dealing with some moves out of her.his body and some from the partner. Put plainly, this is a rehearsal to be able to perform with style, conviction and integrity the entire flow of moves, not just to be able to get through it. The first partner to finish can stand or sit close to the rehearsing partner until he.she gives a signal of readiness.

When the second is finished rehearsing, they face each other and dance in unison the entire chain of moves twice without interruption. That done, without pause, they enter into what can best be called a "movement row," since it is so close to what musicians call a "tone row." In the early 1900s, Arnold Schönberg developed a structural method for composing music in which all the twelve notes of the scale were used in whatever order a composer chose, and for the entire length of the music, "that order is sacrosanct. . . . Thus, any given pattern of . . . twelve different pitches can appear . . . in four forms: forward, backward, upside down, and upside down backward."[2] In Make a Phrase, there is only one direction, forward, but with many possible variations. The sequence of the chain of moves as evolved by the partners is inviolable but each move can be done at any tempo, at any dynamic, in any part of the space, at any level—in the air or on the floor—it can be turned, it can be repeated any number of times and finally it can be "trilled," that is, a pair of neighboring phrases can be repeated any number of times. Only two variations are not permitted: the original order cannot be altered and no new moves may be brought into the sequence. For *Hello Farewell Hello*, dancers and musicians leave "backward, upside down, and upside down backward" to the avant-garde composers. Even they are deserting those esoteric ploys.

Obviously, within the framework of the movement row, there is a tremendous amount of freedom. With all this freedom, on what basis do the dancers make their choices? Two factors alone determine everything: (1) the internal intention, and in *Hello Farewell Hello* that is to bring the partner "to a climactic burst of joy"; (2) what the partner is doing and how the partner is responding. When the partners succeed in giving each other that elusive "burst of joy," they leave their space and together go to rest before the musicians. Make a Phrase is finished when the third couple comes to sit with the others.

What are the musicians doing through all of this? There are four ways that the musicians can do Make a Phrase: The best and most sophisticated way would be to ignore the dancers from the very beginning and perform the same process as the dancers musically and in terms of their own internal imagery. They finish in their own time, which might be before or after the dancers. How do the two musicians relate to each other? Whoever starts first establishes tonal center for whatever follows.

An easier way would be if they agreed on one couple and on which of the two each would focus. It is worth repeating here that "following" what the dancer is doing is only one of ten thousand ways the musician can relate to the dancer's actions. A musician, relating to a dancer, can ridicule, support, challenge, mock, see into, attack, embrace or even imitate. Whatever is strongly felt while observing the dancer is the material for making music. A third way would be for each musician to choose to relate to any one of the six dancers, who may or may not be partners. A fourth way could occur accidentally or intentionally. Both pick the same person as a focus. This I would love to hear, done deliberately with musicians fluent in the Workgroup ways. The odds are, each would relate in a radically different way to the one person they are both observing. This last way might be the best way to give unity to the music that emerges. We did not do *Hello Farewell Hello* enough times nor work with the same musicians long enough to make the many experiments

2. Eric Salzman, *Twentieth Century Music* (New York: Prentice-Hall, 1974), p. 113.

that would be necessary before one could come to even a tentative conclusion.

The amazing and wonderful thing about dancers and musicians sharing an intention is how, in time, they can reach a state for which they have been working and know that Make a Phrase is over, that they have mutually succeeded in giving joy and receiving joy. In *Hello Farewell Hello* we are dealing with a dance of loving by articulate people. They are dancers who are writing love poems with their bodies.

(Note: There are an infinite number of other intentions that can drive Make a Phrase, and in fact, in the ensuing years, I have introduced it to many groups, with no reference to *Hello Farewell Hello*).

To recap, after all of these asides: Make a Phrase ends with the three couples finished and seated on the floor before the musicians.

HFH. 4   *Hello to Now*

Musician I, improvising alone, finds an eight-count rhythm that is likely to get everyone moving. Upon finding the rhythm, she.he signals Musician II who, using the rhythm just found, seeks out a tune that joins in happily with that rhythm. When both musicians are satisfied, they give the nod to each other and to the dancers, who now rise to their feet to begin improvising to find an eight-count phrase to the music. All the dancers can join in. All seek to choreograph the danciest, *repeating* eight-count phrase. As soon as a dancer can do the phrase just created twice through fluently and with security, he.she leaves the floor.

When the last dancer is finished, the music stops and all the others come back on to the floor. The musicians now launch into their newly found rhythm and tune. The dancer who finished last teaches her.his phrase to all, and when satisfied that all have learned it, claps to signal the next dancer. Any one of the dancers who feels that his.her phrase will flow well out of what has just been learned lets out, "Next!" and dances twice what has just been learned and without a pause demonstrates and teaches his.her phrase. When satisfied that the phrase has been learned and linked to the first phrase, he.she signals and a third dancer takes over the teaching of a new phrase, always starting with doing the phrase just learned, twice. It spices things up if each "teacher" changes direction from the previous phrase. When the eighth "teacher" claps hands signaling "Learned!" the music stops and without music all "walk" through the entire eight phrases, each done twice with low energy focused only on remembering the sequence.

This done, the musicians whip into a musical introduction and all the dancers go full out to do the entire dance of eight phrases, each danced twice. Without a musical break, the dancers stroll toward the musicians and sit to listen as the musicians take over for an improvisation equivalent to sixteen times eight counts and finishing in a way that contains a clear musical cue for the dancers to begin what will be two more repeats of the entire dance.

The first run is a raucous, high energy version, yipping permitted, followed by a final repeat. This last time is a gradual easing off into a subdued and elegant version with a gradual dancing exit, in any order, through any and all exits.

The End

Some Final Notes on *Hello Farewell Hello*

First, consider the matter of who decides the pairing. Is this to be left to impulses of the moment, meaning that from performance to performance they will vary, or should they be predetermined? At the time we did *Hello Farewell Hello*, we had a fine group of dancers, all good improvisors but uneven in their shared experience. Three had been there from the very beginning and five were comparatively new. A talented five, but with too short a history in the scope of our work to risk couplings that might dry up. At the time, it never even entered my mind to leave these choices to the dancers. In the studio, during the early stages of experiment, I left the dancers free to choose, all the while noting which were the undynamic relationships and which were vital. Coming closer to public performance, I would carefully cast almost all pairings, and the company accepted these choices without caviling. I believe my choices produced exciting interactions. In an ideal improvisation company, by which I mean a group that has worked together for several years, this would not be necessary or even desirable. Impulses and matings of the moment would lend the vitality and surprises that life constantly serves up. My preference is to leave it to the moment and the dancers. Very risky, unless all the dancers have had a solid chunk of time working with each other, considerable experience improvising in this mode and are *very good at it.*

A related and complex question faced us and anyone who might do *Hello Farewell Hello.* In Pygmalion and Galatea and in The Articulates, are the lovers to be only heterosexual or should fantasy, imagination and chance allow for heterosexual and homosexual love? Most of the Workgroup company opted for chance. Actually, there were brief same-sex couplings in some of the first few traveling encounters of Pygmalion and Galatea but I arranged that the final Pygmalion and Galatea figures represented a heterosexual interaction. Note: the Pygmalions were not all male and the Galateas were not all female.

The reasoning of the company was that if we were going to do people, that's the way it is, some this way and some that way. I felt that an extended homosexual Pygmalion and Galatea encounter would appear to be what the piece was about and probably what audiences would remember most. Not only was this 1973 but everything about us—-our style, our casting, our aesthetics, our performance ethic—-was swimming against the stream of the post-modern style that dominated at that time. What I felt we needed most was for people to see how we were working, to see the unique way that we found movement and how we related to each other. Whatever we did looked as if it were really happening. Introducing an extended homosexual duet would have pushed aside what we were really about.

If one were to make a concordance to this history of the Workgroup, the phrase, "each other," would probably appear more than any other. That was the key to our work. By and large, we did everything by consensus. This was one of the few times when I exercised my role as artistic director against the majority of the company. Who was right? Who the hell knows? It is still a problem that anyone doing the work today would have to face. I have no advice to give except to say that if I were directing *Hello Farewell Hello* today, I would let the couplings fall where they may.

Sequential Index of EGAS

Sequential Index

Alphabetical Index of EGAS

Alphabetical Index

Subject Index

The name of each EGAS and the numbers of the pages where it is described appear in **boldface** type.

Subject Index

Subject Index

Subject Index

Subject Index

Spinning (11.1), 172
Ssuma Chhien, 101–02
Stackhouse, Sara, 124
Stanford University, jazz workshop at, 143, 145
Stanislavski technique of acting, 38
Steamboat Springs, 4
Steinberg, Richard, 46, 79, 183
Steps, a video dance, 106, 121
Stillness (1.1), 5, 151, 174
Studio work for groups new to the work, 174
Sufis, 172
SUNY at Brockport, 131, 138
SUNY at Buffalo, 186
Swarthmore College, 124
Syncopation, 147–48

Take a Walk in Your Own World (9.12), 139, 174
Tamiris, Helen, 4–5, 31*n*6, 61, 143, 159, 162, 193
Tandem Solo (1.8), 9–10, 174
Taoism, 20
Taos, vacation and notes, 47–48
Teachings of Don Juan, The (Castenada), 72
Technical requirements for performance, 178
Technicians of the Sacred, 94*n*10
Tell a Dream (3.8), 24–26, 40, 174
Tell a Poem (3.9), 26
Ten Rungs, The, 57
Theodore, Lee, 145
These Are Perilous Times (4.5), 44–45, 174
Tight Trio, The (5.8), 58
True Repetition (6.3), 72, 172
Tsuai, Yung Yung, 68, 79
TV, 162, 163*n*1
Twentieth Century Music (Salzman), 211*n*2

Ungar, Robert, 101, 107
University of Maryland at College Park, 29–32
University of Minnesota Workshop at Grand Rapids, 15–17
University of Oregon, jazz workshop at, 143
University of Texas Workshop in Austin, 17–29, 137
Use Your Head (3.7), 23

Vasulk, Woody, 45
Verdon, Gwen, 144
Video, 45, 163
Vietnam, 102

Weidman, Charles, 193
Welk, Lois, 124
What Are You Hearing? (8.4), 118, 174
Whatever Happens Happens (4.3), 41, 174
What Happened? (7.1), 101, 173
What is male?/What is female?, 82, 89–92, 137. *See also* Appendix B
Who or What is Alive in the Music? (10.5), 149
Why do You Dance? (5.14), 65, 174
Widman, Annelise, 10
Wind I (5.10), 60, 104, 107
Wind II (6.13), 92–94, 174, 175, 207
Workgroup: beginning of, ix–x; philosophy of, x; invitation to workshop, 33

Yoga Mirror, The (3.3), 19, 35, 39, 40, 174
Your Familiar (8.3), 118, 174
Your Secret Totem Animal (8.2), 117–18, 174

Zimet, Paul, 40, 59, 60–61, 121
Zukov, William 183